Cinnabaris
Series of Oriental Studies – IV

Cardamom and Class
A Limbu Village and its Extensions in East Nepal

CARDAMOM AND CLASS
A Limbu Village and its Extensions in East Nepal

IAN CARLOS FITZPATRICK

With a preface by Professor David N. Gellner

Vajra Publications
www.vajrabooks.com.np; www.vajrabookshop.com

Published by
Vajra Publications
Jyatha, Thamel, P.O. Box 21779, Kathmandu, Nepal
Tel.: 977-1-4220562, Fax: 977-1-4246536
e-mail: bidur_la@mos.com.np
www.vajrabooks.com.np; www.vajrabookshop.com

Distributor
Vajra Book Shop
Kathmandu, Nepal

All photographs by Ian Fitzpatrick

ISBN 978-9937-506-66-3

Printed in Nepal

Acknowledgements

As with any project that stretches itself across multiple continents and over numerous years, I have accumulated a long list of unpayable debts to a large number of people, communities, institutions and places, some of whom I may have unintentionally omitted.

Since I originally intended to carry out research in Sikkim, I would like to thank Barun Mukhopadhyay of the Indian Statistical Institute in Calcutta for his support in the earliest stages of this project, and also Dr. Anna Balikci-Denjongpa and the Namgyal Institute of Tibetology in Gangtok for their offer of local affiliation and their help with finding contacts and potential fieldsites in Sikkim.

It was in Sikkim that I first met Dr. Mark Turin and Dr. Sara Shneiderman, who were happy to share their knowledge of the Himalayan area as well as contacts in Nepal, and continued to be immensely hospitable and supportive throughout my fieldwork in both Gangtok and Kathmandu. It was thanks to them that I met Sushila Buju in Kathmandu, who as both a friend and talented teacher helped me to rapidly improve my knowledge of the Nepali language. Towards the end of my stay in Sikkim, I exchanged a number of long emails with Professor Martin Gaenszle who was instrumental in pointing me towards the Limbu in east Nepal. I am grateful to him for his "spontaneous suggestion" and to Dr. Mélanie Vandenhelsken and Dr. Grégoire Schlemmer who, together, helped to strengthen my decision to move from Sikkim to east Nepal.

I am deeply grateful to Dr. Mrigendra Karki for the practical and logistical help he provided in Kathmandu as well as for sharing his time and thoughts with me over meals and walks. With his help, together with that of Prof. Nirmal Man Tuladhar, the Centre for International Relations and the Centre for Nepal and Asian Studies at Tribhuvan University in Kathmandu, I was able to affiliate as a foreign researcher and successfully apply for a research visa. My thanks to Dr. Keshab Man Shakya who shared his knowledge of Nepal and provided me with a large list of contacts which eventually led me to the Kirat Yakhtum Chumlung. With the help of the organization's chairperson Arjun Limbu, general secretary Yograj Limbu, and Deoman Limbu, who contacted representatives of local branches of the organization in east Nepal as well as friends and family, I was able to plan a first exploration of the area and eventually find the village of Mamangkhe.

In Kathmandu, Bikram Thapa of the Summit Treks travel agency was always able to find ways of getting me onto a bus or plane to or from Kathmandu at the last minute, despite the uncertainties of travel (*band cha ki chaina?*) during my fieldwork period. I was also fortunate enough to know Jessamine Dana and Roz Evans in Kathmandu, who offered me a place to stay when I first moved to Kathmandu, and provided both emotional and intellectual support whenever I returned from the field for breaks. The house belonged to Jagat and Susmita Basnet, who frequently invited me for wonderful meals, conversations, and events, and were generous, caring and thoughtful friends.

Additional thanks also to Bidur Dangol at Vajra Publications and Raj Bhai Maharjan at Dongol Printers for helping with the preparation of this book.

While not strictly part of this project, prior to my fieldwork in Nepal, I was able to attend a research methods training course in Bolivia with funding provided by the US National Science Foundation and a Marie Curie Fellowship. The course was organized by a group of anthropologists who make up the Tsimane Amazonian Panel Study (TAPS) and I am particularly grateful to Professor Ricardo Godoy, Dr. Viki Reyes-Garcia and Professor William Leonard for their inspiring and rigorous approach to fieldwork and anthropological investigation. In particular, the course provided me with an invaluable introduction to survey design as well as the experience of carrying out the survey, analyzing the data and preparing the consequent written material.

Above all, I feel an immense debt of gratitude to the people of Mamangkhe. Their astonishing generosity, humour, patience, curiosity, and liveliness kept me going despite the physical remoteness of the village, and psychological difficulty of living so far from the familiar. Many thanks to Tika Ram who helped me to learn Limbu, and spent so much time with me working in fields and forests, and discussing the differences between life in Europe and Nepal over millet beer. Thanks also to Sirijana for her infectious laugh, Phul Bahadur for his stories of fighting in the Second World War, and Singh Bahadur and his family for their kindness. During the first year of fieldwork, I lived with Ran Hang, Chitra, Kamala, Nirmala, and Sukhlal, to whom I am endlessly grateful for helping me gain my bearings and quickly become comfortable living in the village. I became close to a large number of people who lived in the cluster of houses by the main road in Ward 4 including Sirini, Indra Bahadur, Bir Bahadur, Dhan Adrisya, Dhane, Buddha Raj, Surya, and their extended families, and I am most thankful to all of them for their immediate acceptance of me and their constant kindness. For the second year of fieldwork, I moved to a neighbouring house and would like to express my gratitude to Chandraman, Buddha Maya, Garje, Dhan Bikram, Aitaman, and Tika Maya for letting me live and share so much of their day-to-day life.

Beyond Ward 4, I developed friendships with a large number of people in the village. Many thanks to Dil Kumari for teaching me the secrets of *khɛsuŋ*-making, inspiring me with her tremendous energy and enthusiasm, and making me laugh so hard. Thanks also to Dipak, my first close friend in the village, and the first person to understand what on earth I was doing there. I am grateful to Indra Bahadur, Lakshmi, Nabin, and the rest of the family for trading stories, gifts, and adventures, and for making me my Nepali clothes, as well as to Tej Bahadur, Gaj Bahadur, Deo Kumar and Siva, and Ganga Prasad and his family.

I also feel indebted to the countless people outside the village—whether relatives of villagers in Mamangkhe or strangers—who at various times offered me water and shelter during my travels in Taplejung and Jhapa.

In Oxford, I am indebted to COMPAS for providing me with office space, to Dr. Nick Van Hear for making it possible for me to work in COMPAS and for his friendship and encouragement, and to my fellow cellar-dwellers Alan Gamlen, Cetta Mainwaring, Hayley Lofink, and Karin Heissler, for creating a unique work environment of mutual support, laughter and many shared late nights of word processing. I also want to thank my confirmation assessors Dr. Robert Parkin and Dr. Charles Ramble who provided thorough and constructive suggestions on portions of my thesis, and to my co-supervisor Dr. Laura Rival for her continuous support, and insightful and stimulating comments throughout the project. Thanks also to Mark Stanford for many inspiring discussions about theory and methods in the social sciences, to Sandra Smith for her help with the maps, and to Ben Margolis and Sophie North for being such wonderful and supportive friends.

I would also like to acknowledge and thank those responsible for the financial support that made my research and writing possible, including, the PhD studentship from the Economic and Social Research Council and a travel grant from the ICOMOS INTACH UK trust fund.

Thanks, of course, to my family, Michael, Ana, Daniel, and Molly, who in different ways contributed to my fascination with travelling, learning languages, and living in unusual places. They have constantly encouraged me to pursue my interests and supported me throughout my studies.

Finally, a special note of thanks to my principal supervisor, Professor David Gellner, who spent countless hours reading through my long email reports from the field and always did everything he could to advise, support, encourage and inspire me from the early days of proposal writing through to the final stages of thesis writing. I cannot imagine a more supportive, generous and patient supervisor.

Table of Contents

Chapter 4: Cardamom   131

Conclusions 271

List of Tables

List of Figures

Maps

Figure 1: Map showing location of Mamangkhe VDC and Khewang village in Taplejung District, the settlements of Medibung, Tharpu and Gopetar in Panchthar District, and the town of Phidim in Panchthar District.

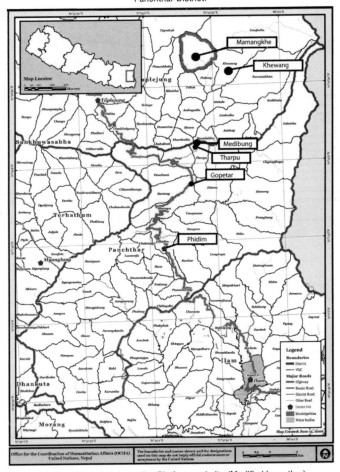

Source: UN Nepal Information Platform website (Modified by author)

Figure 2: Map showing location of the settlements of Happenchowk, Aitabare, Hadiya, and Budhabare and the town of Birtamod in Jhapa District.

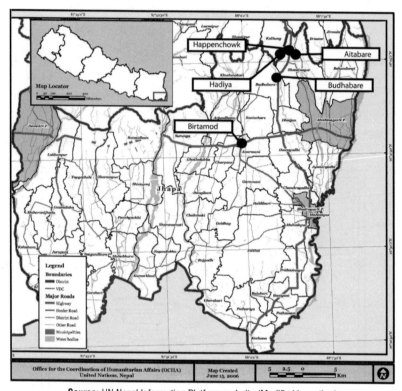

Source: UN Nepal Information Platform website (Modified by author)

Figure 3: Map with Mamangkhe village in detail showing location of all wards.

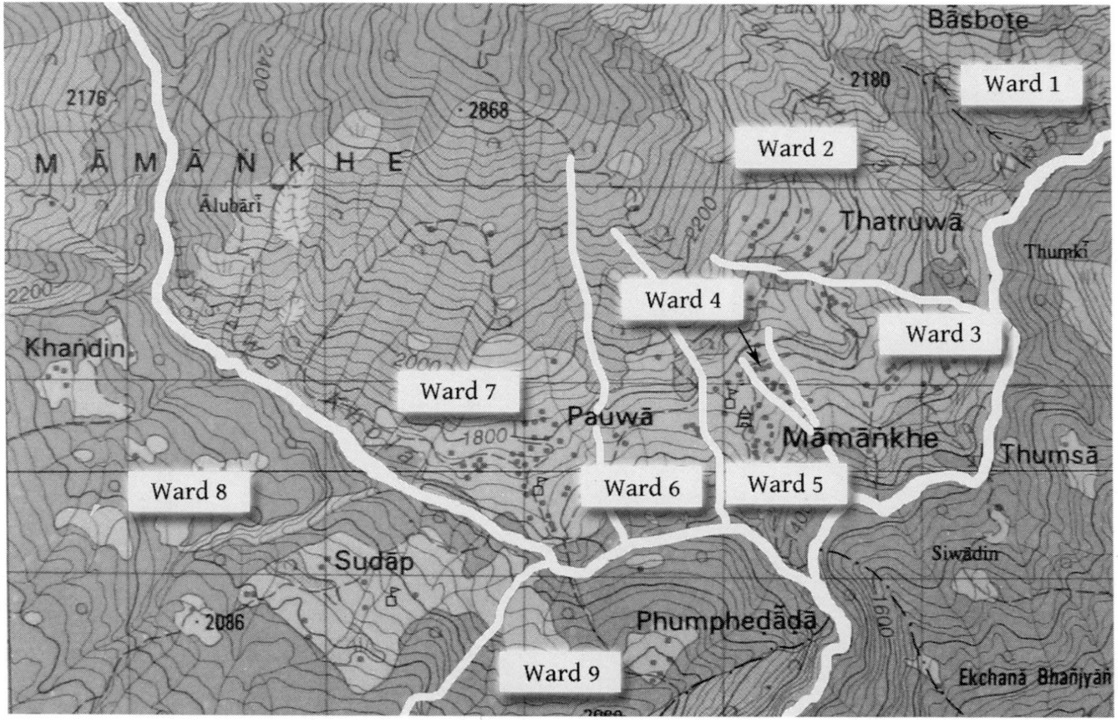

Source: Finnish Meteorological Institute and the Government of Nepal, Survey Department (modified by author with help from Sandra Smith)

Preface

Class, as a topic of academic study, has become increasingly unfashionable in the academy. This is perhaps surprising in the study of Nepal, where Marxist-inspired ideologies dominate both political parties and the universities. Older works, such as Seddon, Blaikie, and Cameron's *Peasants and Workers in Nepal* (Seddon et al. 1979) tried to study class formation, but where are their modern successors?

When anthropologists have tackled class, it is, paradoxically, class as status group, class as defined by consumption patterns. In the Nepalese context, the leading and much-cited work in this genre is Mark Liechty's *Suitably Modern: Making Middle-Class Culture in a New Consumer Society* (Liechty 2003). This is a fine and, in the Nepalese context, pathbreaking work, but it does not broach the question of the *production* of middle-class identity in schools, offices, factories, and other workplaces. Nor does it ask the classic questions about ownership, wealth, and land that underlie the emergence of class.

It is therefore particularly welcome that a young anthropologist should tackle the emergence of class in a rural setting using the quantitative survey methods necessary for any economic anthropology, but also participant observation and close-up, hands-on fieldwork (both literal and metaphorical). Ian Fitzpatrick was also accomplished in both local languages (Nepali and Limbu). The Limbus are lucky to have attracted an ethnographer with such linguistic skills.

Cardamom is one of the few cash crops that, if a peasant works hard and has a reasonable run of luck, can lead to serious accumulation of wealth in a relatively small number of years. Ian Fitzpatrick has therefore been able to reconstruct the recent history of class formation in the village of Mamangkhe, the out-migration that this has led to, the paradoxical process by which a once multi-caste settlement has become 'the most traditional Limbu village', and the ways in which migration, cardamom production, and debt interact and produce class differentiation. This detailed and important ethnography is a worthy successor to the classic works on the Limbus of Lionel Caplan and Philippe Sagant and a significant addition to the corpus of ethnographic works on Nepal as a whole.

Professor David N. Gellner
Oxford, September 2011

Introduction

There is a considerable degree of continuity between the Nepal that emerged from the Gorkha conquest in the late 1700s and the Nepal of today. The economy continues to be largely subsistence-based and 86% of the population located in rural areas (CBS 2007). Yet Nepal has been affected by its rapid incorporation into a global economy through a number of processes, including: the increased dependence on a national and international market economy which has penetrated even the remotest corners of the country; a large increase in both population and land under cultivation; an increased proportion of the working population of Nepal becoming involved in foreign labour migration; and the transformation of cultural values through a set of economic and social conditions associated with wealth, prosperity, 'modernity' and urban Nepal. These processes have provided many villages and households across Nepal with a means (and desire) to change their economic and social conditions. The integration of rural Nepal with an urban-based market economy has provided subsistence farmers with the opportunity of supplementing their income with market-oriented production of food and goods. Such production and trading of goods has, of course, taken place for hundreds of years, but the recent penetration of the market has facilitated the distribution of products and linked more directly than ever before the fate of the remote rural village with that of the global market.

This dependence on the global market, for both goods and labour opportunities, has made rural households considerably more vulnerable to the fluctuations of the global economy. It has also had a profound impact on the nature of villages and households in rural Nepal which have become far more spatially dispersed—as households and individuals become more mobile and migrate to urban areas—as well as economically differentiated, with some households benefiting from involvement in these global market processes, while others are "left behind". Although these processes of social and economic change may have accelerated in recent times, villages have in fact been undergoing more subtle processes of transformation for hundreds of years. It is perhaps one of the results of a discipline which was for so long dominated by an overwhelming focus on culture that few anthropologists have carried out detailed studies of how social and economic systems change (Cameron 1996, Guneratne 1996, Humphrey 1985, Mikesell 1988, Prindle 1983, Schrader 1988).

This book focuses on the history of economic differentiation within a village in north-east Nepal. It does this by describing the changes in productive processes which have taken place over the last two hundred years and the impact these changes have had on the distribution of resources throughout the village. It shows how the history of subsistence production is marked by the migration of non-Limbu populations to the village and how these were able to take control of a large amount of Limbu-owned land. It focuses particularly on how the introduction of cardamom production changed the distribution of wealth across the village by giving a large proportion of households access to a high-value cash crop. More recently, international labour migration has opened yet another pathway to economic and social opportunities. The overlapping of these three productive processes has benefited many households, and encouraged the development of a dispersed village as households and individuals relocate to peri-urban settlements in the plains of south-east Nepal. Despite the increased economic opportunities made available by the global market for cardamom and labour, there remains a certain proportion of households who own little or no land, are increasingly burdened by debts, and struggle to subsist.

The book therefore attempts to answer a number of specific questions related to the emergence of economic differentiation, the role that changes in production—particularly the development of cardamom cultivation—have played in this, and the socioeconomic impact of international labour migration. Broadly, these questions are as follows:

1. What is the relationship between changes in production and changes in the distribution of wealth within the village?

2.   How has a village in north-east Nepal become increasingly integrated with the national and international market economy and what have been the repercussions of this process?

By examining the history of economic differentiation in a village in east Nepal, this study makes a contribution to anthropological studies of socioeconomic change. The study shows how, as a result of both its own particular internal dynamic and increasing involvement with national and global processes, even a remote village in east Nepal contains a degree of economic heterogeneity usually associated with urban areas. The book also makes a contribution to studies of migration by detailing the process by which villagers become migrants, the socioeconomic impact of migration on the village, and the relationship between cardamom production, international migration, the emergence of a dispersed village, and economic differentiation. Finally this book offers a contemporary ethnographic portrayal of Limbu economic, social and cultural life in a village in east Nepal.

Chapter 1
Theoretical Context

This book examines the relationship between cardamom production and the formation of economic and social stratification, or class, in a predominately Limbu village in north-east Nepal. It shows that while a caste-based study may be useful when looking at the history of villages in east Nepal prior to the recent penetration of markets and the cash-based economy, a class-based approach is fundamental for understanding the contemporary process of social and economic differentiation of ethnic groups and households within villages.

It is therefore critical of anthropological studies that have sidelined the analytically useful concept of class and the study of inequality within villages. They have tended to do this by focusing either on inter-ethnic relations and dynamics (e.g. Caplan 1970, Levine 1987, Mumford 1989), or by studying single ethnic groups and marginalizing intra-ethnic economic differentiation. To some extent, this absence is explained by the fact that rural areas of Nepal have only recently begun to be integrated into the national and international economy. Factors such as increased labour migration and the remittance economy associated with this, the improvement of rural infrastructures connecting rural areas to urban centres, the tourist industry and, in many parts of Nepal, the development of cash crop production systems, have all contributed to the social and economic transformation of rural Nepal. They have also all contributed to growing inequality across the country (Blaikie et al. 1980). These recent developments have yet to be fully reflected in ethnographic studies of Nepal.

While there has been a large amount of ethnographic research on villages and communities in Nepal since the 1950s, few of these studies have been long-term diachronic studies or re-studies of social and economic change (Blaikie et al. 2002). Macfarlane (1976, 2001) recently provided a glimpse of what such a study might show by describing changes which had taken place over a thirty year period in the village he first visited in 1969. In his landmark study of a Gurung village in central Nepal, Macfarlane (1976) predicted that the population growth rate at the time would cause an ecological disaster and "growing unemployment, inequality, landlessness, malnutrition, soil erosion and other effects... [would be] likely to accelerate rapidly" (Macfarlane 1976: 312). Returning to the village thirty years later he published a short article describing some of the changes he observed and trying to explain why the expected ecological disaster had not happened (Macfarlane 2001). There are many similarities between the descriptions of these changes in the village of Thak, and current conditions in Mamangkhe, the village that this book is based on. The first of the changes that Macfarlane notes is dietary (2001: 107), such as the easy availability, for those with cash, of iodine salt, oil, sugar and rice, among other market goods. These were goods that, even as recently as 40 years ago, villagers in Mamangkhe had to walk for several days to purchase, often carrying heavy loads of village products for barter. Others that Macfarlane mentions are the falling value of land (ibid.: 108) and the increased cost of living.[1] Villagers in Mamangkhe who can afford to buy land prefer to invest their money in land outside the village, and several villagers have been unable to sell their land for years. He also notes that "almost every family is heavily indebted" (ibid.), a situation very similar to that found in many villages in east Nepal (Caplan 1970, 1972; Sagant 1983). Broadly, he finds that "while the ecological situation is stable, the economic position of the village has declined greatly and real poverty is emerging" (Macfarlane 2001: 109-110). Importantly, he also mentions how village cultural and social traditions, such as co-operative labour, and shamanic and musical traditions have almost all ceased to be practised in the village, though they are being revived in towns.

While many of the economic and social changes in Thak match, to a large extent, the historical changes mentioned by villagers in Mamangkhe as well as current conditions observed during fieldwork, there are a number of important differences. The first is that the

---

1 Macfarlane (2001: 108) presents (somewhat anecdotal) evidence of this: "The wage for ploughing in the fields in 1969 was 10 rupees for a day's work. The cost of a chicken was 8 rupees. Now [2000] the wages are about 50 rupees and the cost of a chicken is 400 rupees or more".

situation of "real poverty" that Macfarlane briefly describes, with dramatic statements such as "people are actually poorer now than they were then [in 1969]" and "the people may be starting to starve", is nothing like the economic situation in Mamangkhe village, where many families either grow enough food to feed themselves or make enough money to buy it. The second major difference is that in Mamangkhe, cultural and social traditions such as co-operative labour, shamanic rituals and healing ceremonies, as well as cultural performances with music and dance, are common occurrences. Macfarlane's comment that "after several thousand years of maintaining a cultural tradition,[2] the old ways have largely been wiped out" (2001: 109) is supported by Seddon's remark that "this, alas, has happened not only in Thak, but across rural Nepal, and indeed across the developing and developed world" (Seddon 2001: 122). Yet my research in Mamangkhe shows that certain aspects of Limbu culture, such as Limbu language use, ritual performance and the activities of shamans, show considerable resistance to change or, at least, resistance to being "wiped out".

Although much broader in scope and less anthropological than Macfarlane's study in Thak, the work of Blaikie, Cameron and Seddon (1980, 2002) provides an insight into social and economic change in western Nepal over a similar time period. A rapidly growing population combined with a lack of investment in infrastructure, industry and agriculture, leads them to describe Nepal as a country in crisis:

> The country is now in a period of crisis, a crisis whose major components, over the next decade, will include serious over-population relative to employment opportunities, ecological collapse in the densely populated and highly vulnerable hill areas...and the elimination of certain important 'natural' resources...These will be associated with an increasing inability to pay for imported commodities, with growing food shortages, and consequently with the development of widespread unrest in both rural and urban areas (Blaikie et al. 1980: 13-14).

---

2   This is an unverifiable claim and one could be critical of Macfarlane's apocalyptic vision of sudden change among the Gurung by pointing out that no one knows what sorts of changes were going on "several thousand years ago" and whether the Gurung then, if indeed they even existed, were the same as the Gurung today.

Following a restudy (or re-survey) carried out in 1997-98, they conclude that although their most dire predictions did not materialize, many of their structural predictions were borne out, including: no significant development of commercialized agriculture; the appropriation of poor peasants' land by "an expansive class of capitalist farmers"; and, perhaps surprisingly (and somewhat in contrast to the experience of east Nepal), no "rapid economic differentiation leading to more individualistic accumulation" (Blaikie et al. 2002: 1267). Although their conclusions are likely generalizable to large parts of rural Nepal, they are based on a sample of households (677 in 1974-75 and 155 in 1997-98) in western Nepal, which has a different history to east Nepal.

The history of east Nepal, which was one of the last areas of Nepal to be conquered by the Gorkha army in the late 18th and early 19th centuries and, in particular, the history of the economic relationship between Limbu communities and the Kingdom of Nepal, helps to explain some of the economic and social differences between east Nepal and other parts of the country. With regard to land, the most important source of wealth in Nepal, communal authority superseded the authority of the state through the recognition by the state of *kipat* tenure among the Limbu of east Nepal. With kipat tenure, individuals had rights to land by virtue of being members of a particular social unit. This system thus "deprived the government of resources in the form of both land and revenue... [and] prevented the government from establishing effective administrative control over the whole of its territory" (Regmi 1976: 92). Some degree of economic and cultural autonomy may have given east Nepal a slight advantage over other parts of the country that were more heavily administered and taxed. While the long-lasting partial autonomy of the Limbu from the Nepali state may explain some of the economic and cultural differences between Limbu villages and villages in other parts of Nepal, this autonomy was definitively abolished after the official ending of kipat with the Land Reform Act of 1964.

It was around this time that a villager in Mamangkhe successfully introduced cardamom cultivation from Sikkim as a cash crop. Cardamom cultivation, for those who have any uncultivated forest or marginal land available, provides a means to earn potentially large amounts of money with relatively little labour or investment. While kipat tenure and a history of resistance towards the Nepali state may have helped the Limbu maintain their cultural traditions, migrating non-Limbu settlers, particularly high-caste Hindus, were able to appropriate kipat land within Limbu communities. In the case of Mamangkhe, many became wealthy enough within a few generations to migrate to settlements in the southern plains between 1960 and 1980. It was cardamom cultivation and, to some extent, earlier cardamom-related labour-migration to Sikkim that enabled, and still enables, a section of Limbu society in the village to become wealthy enough to migrate from the village in a kind of "second wave". Fundamentally though, it is only a *section* of society that has been able to do this, just as it was only a *section* of the high-caste Hindus who had been able to become wealthy and leave the village earlier.

For Caplan (1970, 2000), who studied the history of Limbu and high-caste Hindu relations in a village in east Nepal, kipat had been able to divide the community between the Limbus, whose "sense of self" was very much tied to kipat and their claim to the past, and the "newcomers" or recent settlers. In Caplan's view "Kipat provided a means of belonging to a place and a distinctive community...Conversion of the land to raikar severed that connection and transformed the land into what it had never been before—a commodity" (Caplan 2000: 211). In contrast to Caplan, this book shows how kipat land, to some extent, had always been treated as a commodity. High-caste Hindus, who first settled in Mamangkhe as early as 1789, were able to rent land, and eventually buy land, which they either still own today or have recently sold. It was in fact by treating kipat land as a commodity that high-caste Hindus were able to become so wealthy. More fundamentally though, this study is critical of the dichotomy that Caplan makes between the Limbu and the Bahun-Chhetri, as he fails to show that although the two groups—that is Limbu and Bahun-Chhetri—may be culturally homogeneous, they are internally economically heterogeneous: there are both poor and wealthy Limbu just as there are poor and wealthy Bahun-Chhetri households (Dahal 1996). In Caplan's study *Land and Social Change in East Nepal* he mentions a "small class of affluent Limbus" three times (Caplan 1970: 113, 170, 207), but always in reference to Limbus associated with the Gurkhas.

Whether there was more economic differentiation within the Limbu than Caplan seems to show is impossible to say. This book emphasizes that while Caplan's *caste*-based study of economic and social change is useful for the study of historical relations—that is from the period of pre-Gorkha conquest through to the formal abolition of kipat in 1964—a *class*-based study is essential to understand the more recent differentiation and stratification of society in contemporary Mamangkhe and throughout Nepal. More specifically, this book contributes to the study of rural-class formation in Nepal, by examining how households and individuals in rural Nepal accumulate capital and redefine themselves socially and economically through the purchase of property, migration, and the adoption of different social and cultural practices. This study of rural-class formation is grounded by theories derived from anthropological political economy.

Anthropological political economy

The emergence of "political economy" during the late 18th century is associated with the work of Steuart—"What economy is in a family, political economy is in a State" (Steuart 1770: 2)—Smith (1977[1776]), Ricardo and Mill (1862[1848]). The original object of political economy was the study of the means by which human society creates wealth through the production and distribution of goods. Where political economy examined the means by which labour and systems of exchange produced the "wealth of nations," neo-classical economics examined markets, prices, and elaborated models of individual behaviour in accordance with rational choice theory. A specifically anthropological political economy stemmed largely from the work of Marx, although political economy in anthropology can be seen as a heterogeneous collection of theoretical and methodological approaches, some Marxist and some not.

During the 1970s the term "political economy" in anthropology came to be associated with critiques of structural anthropology, the relationship between anthropology and (neo) colonialism, and the frequently ahistorical perspective of the discipline. This was tied to the general radicalization of universities during the Vietnam War, the growth of the Teach-in movement in the United States (Wolf 1999[1969]: xvii), the emergence of radical groups such as the Anthropologists for Radical Political Action in 1971, and the establishment and circulation of new journals. The term officially came of age in 1978 with a special issue on political economy in the journal *American Ethnologist*, and a number of anthropologists (Gutkind and Wallerstein 1976, Magubane

1979, O'Brien 1979, Schneider and Schneider 1976) made central use of the concept in their publications. The term "political economy" in anthropology was strongly influenced by a number of theories which had emerged in the years before and continued to influence discussions well into the 1980s. Dependency (Frank 1967) and world systems theory (Wallerstein 1974) as well as the theory of modes of production (Foster-Carter 1978, Rey 1973) were fundamental to the development of a specifically anthropological political economy which had absorbed elements of Marxist economic theory and its critical approach to capitalism.

In contrast to the structural Marxism of the 1970s, which was largely ahistorical and concerned with a sociological analysis of social organization (ideology) and reproduction (material relations), political economy shifted both geographical scales, to include large-scale political and economic systems, and temporal scales, to include the history of the impact of external forces on communities (Ortner 1984: 141). In Ortner's assessment of political economy, there are primarily three aspects of the approach which she considers positive: (1) the willingness, *contra* cultural ecologists "to incorporate cultural or symbolic issues into their inquiries; (2) the emphasis on regional processes; and (3) the commitment to an historical anthropology" (ibid.: 142). On the negative side she considers political economy to be "too economic, too strictly materialist" (ibid.) and accuses its capitalism-centered approach of ignoring the structure and history of societies on the periphery of the world system.

This is in fact a problem that anthropologists have grappled with for decades: the theoretical and methodological tension between global and local processes, large-scale social theories and small-scale ethnographic detail, structure (economic determinism) and agency (the freedom of individuals). Marcus and Fischer (1986) suggest that "the dilemma in anthropology between a literature weak on culture, but strong on political-economy analysis, and one strong on cultural analysis, but weak on political economy is primarily a problem of representation or textual construction" (1986: 86). The dilemma though is not simply resolved through the process of writing itself, but originates in the choice of theoretical and methodological stance. While examining the penetration and impact of capitalism on communities, a political economy perspective sees a unity between structure and agency, between determinative social and economic pressures and the activities of human subjects.

Roseberry's (1988) survey of anthropological political economy outlines the rich variety of approaches to show that political economy is both about "the juggernaut of capitalism" and "real people doing real things" (Ortner 1984: 144). He begins with an overview of the early work of four Marxist-informed (North American) cultural anthropologists: Wolf, Mintz, Leacock and Nash (Roseberry 1988: 163). Wolf and Mintz elaborated on Steward's cultural ecology to develop a "cultural history" approach which examined anthropological subjects through both local and world history (Roseberry 1988: 172). Leacock's (1954) work concerned the origins of inequality and the effects of colonialism on particular groups of people (Roseberry 1988: 164). Nash took a more ethnographic approach to political economy, focusing, as Leacock, on feminist issues, and examining the social and cultural responses to capitalism among tin miners in Bolivia (Nash 1993 [1979]).

Roseberry then discusses the influence of the work of world-system, dependency, and mode-of-production theorists. Broadly speaking these approaches studied the impact of historical, political and economic processes—such as the slave trade, international markets and capitalist development—on human populations (Roseberry 1988: 169). These analyses often "slipped into a kind of functionalist reasoning" and "the emphasis on structural determination was often too strongly determinative, leaving too little room for the consequent activity of anthropological subjects" (ibid.: 170). In contrast to this, Marxist-influenced studies of class, peasantry, politics and resistance to capitalism made human activity the centre of their analysis (Ong 1987, Stoler 1985). These studies were criticized for paying "too little attention to the structures of power that shape and constrain resistance" (Roseberry 1988: 171).

Again the problem continues to be that of integrating cultural and ethnographic content with structural context. In Roseberry's view "what requires stressing is the unity of structure and agency, the activity of human subjects in structured contexts that are themselves the products of past activity but, as structured products, exert determinative pressures and set limits upon future activity" (1988: 171-172). Roseberry considers that Wolf's (1982) work *Europe and the People without History* provides an important example of a more "unified" political economy. The focus of this historical and anthropological study is to show that societies cannot be considered bounded, isolated and unchanging. He shows how over the last five centuries they have been fundamentally shaped and transformed by the international capitalist system (Asad 1987: 594). Asad rightly points out that although Wolf considers the history of world capitalism to be that of European colonialism interwoven with the histories of societies in Asia, Africa and the Americas, it is still an unequal history: "in the formation and growth of industrial capitalism the main story has been written by Europe, and later also by those who have adopted Europe's historical project as their own" (Asad 1987: 604).

Despite being described as a "unified" political economy approach, the work of Wolf invariably places the theoretical emphasis on the impact of external forces on particular societies. Contrary to this approach, ethnographic historical anthropologists focus on the "internal development dynamics" of societies to show the way external forces are internally mediated (Ortner 1989: 16-17). Ortner describes these two approaches as contradictory: "political economists accuse the ethnographic historians of "culturology" of a form of idealism or mentalism that does not recognize the impact of the real world, while the ethnographic historians accuse the political economists of ethnocentrically projecting their notions of agency and social action into other times and places" (ibid.). In *High Religion* (1989), a cultural and historical study of the Sherpa, Ortner aims to "de-victimize" the Sherpas by describing "the ways in which people are *always* reinterpreting their situation, acting on it in their own terms, and making the most they can out of it" (1989: 100) to make their own history. More specifically, she depicts Sherpa society as made up of "big people", "small people", and "little big people", each of which developed different cultural and economic strategies in reaction to the pressures from both outside (the Nepali state) and inside forces.

In her study, "big people" are the wealthy and influential members of the Sherpa community who make their money from trade, renting land to tenants, and earning interest on loans. "Small people" emerged as the descendents of brothers who received the smallest inheritances and were burdened by the taxation system and the increased parcellization of land. The "little big people" are the monks and nuns, caught somewhere between the big people and the small people. As traders, entrepreneurs, and tax collectors (*pembu*), big people received economic protection from the state. As their wealth increased, economic and social differentiation was exacerbated, resulting in the decline of their political legitimacy. Small people were able to circumvent the difficulties created by tax extraction and land shortages by migrating to Darjeeling which offered opportunities for wage-work and petty enterprise. Migration to Darjeeling provided small people with a source of both wealth and self-empowerment which helped them to hold their own vis-à-vis the big people. Locally, the cultivation of potato, introduced around the mid-1800s, increased the total food crop production of the small people which allowed the wages earned in Darjeeling to be used more as a surplus than for purchasing food (Ortner 1989: 158-159). This surplus was used by small people to participate in the monastery foundings, and to purchase land and "reverse the slide to smallness set in motion by parcellization" (1989: 165).

In *High Religion*, Ortner offers an example of another way of navigating the path between larger and smaller-scale processes, between the impact of exogenous processes on local populations and their internal resistance and contribution to them. Despite her dichotomy of political economy and ethnographic history, Ortner's use of what she calls a *theory of practice*—"a theory of the relationship between the structures of society and culture on the one hand, and the nature of human action on the other" (Ortner 1989: 11)—appears, in fact, to bridge both theoretical positions by offering a detailed (historical and ethnographic) anthropological political economy of the way the Sherpa were both shaped by the State and other external forces, and in turn shaped their own society and history.

In short, anthropological political economy provides a rich set of approaches and concerns which can be linked together in a variety of ways in its "attempt to place anthropological subjects at the intersections of local and global histories" (Roseberry 1988: 179). This book is an attempt to place anthropological subjects at this "intersection" by focusing on a number of historical, social and economic processes in a village in north-east Nepal. It makes use of anthropological political economy by focusing on two related concepts which have been examined in the work of historians and anthropologists influenced by Marxist analyses of the development of capitalism in Europe and elsewhere: (1) modes of production; and (2) social and economic differentiation or class formation.

Modes of production

The concept of *modes of production* became an important theoretical concern for Marxist anthropologists in the 1960s and 1970s. In Marx's own formulation, the *mode of production* refers to the combination of *productive forces*—the labour, tools and natural resources—and the *relations of production*—the socially organized relationship between humans in the sphere of production. For Marx "the mode of production of material life conditions the social, political and intellectual life process in general. It is not the consciousness of men that determines their being, but, on the contrary, their social being that determines their consciousness" (Marx 1970 [1859]: 181). The limitation of Marx's own writings on the mode of production concept was that they were mostly engaged with European capitalist production, and dealt only cursorily with pre-capitalist or non-European modes of production. This led anthropologists, and other scholars, to develop elaborations of the basic concept, usually simply a new set of typologies, such that they would still be relevant for the analysis of non-western societies.

Sahlins (1972) introduced the term *domestic mode of production*, to emphasize that production was above all else a domestic activity managed and carried out at the household level. Meillassoux (1972) pointed to the co-existence of various modes of production: "recognition of various economic formations comes generally from the observation of different 'ways of living', such as hunting, cultivating, cattle herding, etc. ...Economic formations can be, and usually are, a combination of several modes of production, one being dominant, i.e. governing the basic relations of the society at large" (1972: 98). Following Godelier's (1978) discussion on the Asiatic mode of production, Coquery-Vidrovitch (1978) developed the concept of a specifically African mode of production.

Throughout the 1970s, anthropological studies became increasingly mired in debates over appropriate interpretations and uses of the concept of modes of production, with most of the focus on defining typologies and categories. These discussions cast a shadow over the usefulness of *modes of production* as a model for analyzing both how humans organize themselves in relation to the environment, and the dynamics of change that result from this. As Wolf put it "the utility of the concept [of modes of production] does not lie in classification but in its capacity to underline the strategic relationships involved in the deployment of social labor by organized human pluralities" (Wolf 1982: 76). In the preface to the second edition of his book, Wolf (1997[1982]) describes how he still considers the idea of *modes of production* "analytically useful":

> Its emphasis on how a society mobilizes social labor draws attention at one and the same time to the human relations to the natural environment, the social relations of humans to humans, the institutional structures of state and society that guide these relations, and the idea through which these relationships are conveyed (ibid.: xi).

In his study of the interrelationship between European capitalism and non-European societies, Wolf makes use of the concept of modes of production to focus on the underlying political-economic relationships between different societies: "The use of the concept enables us, above all, to inquire into what happens in the encounters of differently constituted systems of interaction—societies—predicated upon different modes of production" (Wolf 1982: 77). Despite his broad conceptualization of the concept as laid out above, Wolf still outlines a three-tier typology of modes: (1) capitalist, which he argues provides the key to understanding the others; (2) tributary (corresponding to Marx's feudal and Asiatic modes); and (3) kin-ordered, which emphasizes the social relations and kinship involved in labour processes.

Wolf's approach, which focuses on the relationship between different societies and their respective modes of production, is effective as long as it remains with larger-scale political economic processes and deals only briefly with ethnographic details. Smaller-scale village-level studies can be influenced by Wolf's enthusiasm for the concept of modes of production, but have to integrate a variety of approaches to make sense of the particularity of the research site.

This book focuses not so much on categorizing modes of production, determining the relationship between them, examining whether multiple modes can co-exist or what the relationship is between modes of production and other Marxist concepts such as the *economic base* and *social formations*. The concept of *modes of production* and the debates surrounding the proper definition and use of the concept have been useful in highlighting the centrality of the process of production for understanding broader economic and historical patterns. It is specifically to avoid getting embroiled in these debates that the use of the term *modes of production* is avoided and the broader concept of *productive processes* brought to the centre of the analysis.

While accepting Godelier's definition of production as "the totality of the operations aimed at procuring for a society its material means of existence" (Godelier 1978: 60),[3] the study of such a "totality" in a society that is interconnected with other societies (with their own "totality") is an impossible task. For this reason, in the context of this book, a limited number of what are considered to be the most significant productive processes were separated out from this "totality" and their relationship with other political-economic and historical processes analysed. The first of these productive processes, common to all households throughout the village, is subsistence agriculture: the domestic production of crops and animals to feed the household. The second productive process is cardamom cultivation. In contrast to the first, the products of which circulate within the village, cardamom cultivation is market-oriented or cash-crop production and the products—dried cardamom pods—circulate both inside and outside the village. Finally, the third productive process is wage labour with a particular focus on international labour-migration. This is considered to be a productive process in the sense that it is through labour migration, and the wages that result from this, that families are able to procure or supplement their material means of existence. Since each of these processes has its own history, the focus on this tripartite mode of production necessarily emphasizes the dynamics of change both within the processes themselves and their relationship to other elements in the wider economy and society.

In the study of these interwoven productive processes, both the particularities of the village and individuals' experiences (their life histories), and longer-term structural transformations of the village become part of the analysis. It is by examining the history of the village through the productive process in particular that the concept of economic and social differentiation emerges. This process of

---

3   He continues "so defined, the concept of production opens out on to all possible forms of operation of this kind, those that are characteristic of economies of food-gathering, hunting and fishing, in which a territory is 'occupied' and the resources needed are 'found' there, and also those that are characteristic of agricultural and industrial economies, in which what is needed is 'produced' by 'transforming' nature" (Godelier 1978: 60-61).

differentiation, or nascent rural class formation, is a direct result of changing productive processes which, for a variety of reasons, certain households have been able to take advantage of more successfully than others. This has led to a situation in the contemporary village where wealth (in any number of forms: e.g. ownership of land, total cardamom production, value of surplus food production) is unevenly distributed between households in the village. A Marxist-influenced political economy framework, with its concern with the role of production, classes and the state in the generation of wealth (Wolf 1982: 19-20), is particularly suited to the analysis of economic and social differentiation in the village. Economic differentiation, also described as 'nascent rural class formation' above, is the second concept which this book makes use of in its broader theoretical framework.

Class formation

> Fine-grained analyses of class formation in the modern world have not reached the necessary degree of ethnographic specificity, but there is nowhere else for anthropology to go unless it is to become sloppy (or even good) economic history, or a monotonous recitation of the by now all too obvious fact of the importance of the world system. (Smith 1984: 491)

The concept of class formation is above all related to the concept of "class", a synonym of both "economic differentiation" and "stratification". Whereas the latter terms refer to the (usually arbitrary) division of society into strata related to any kind of social or economic difference, the term "class", used in a variety of ways by scholars in different disciplines, emphasizes the structural commonalities between groups of people sharing a similar position within a social hierarchy. The advantage of using the term "class" over either "economic differentiation" or "stratification" is the way this term leads the analysis towards an understanding of the social relations of production. Classes are not "just any "empty places" in social structure which can be ordered in a hierarchical fashion" nor are they "divisional units within systems of social stratification" (Wright and Perrone 1977: 33). Classes become constituted through groups of people's relationship to production and are therefore rooted in the productive process. This Marxist view of class is summarized by Lenin:

Classes are large groups of people differing from each other by the place they occupy in a historically determined system of social production, by their relation (in most cases fixed and formulated by law) to the means of production, by their role in the social organization of labour, and consequently by the dimensions of the share of social wealth of which they dispose and the mode of acquiring it. Classes are groups of people one of which can appropriate the labour of another owing to the different places they occupy in a definite system of social economy. (Lenin 1971: 486)

Since classes are "historically determined", and since societies everywhere have different histories, it seems reasonable to accept Smith's claim that "it is impossible to come up with any universally valid criteria of what establishes class relationships in all societies" (Smith 1979: 142). Furthermore, Smith adds that "since class has to do with access to valued resources, so many other elements in the social formation [Lenin's "social economy"] may be brought into play—such as the ideology of kinship, or the use of physical might (power)—that it would be misleading to restrict class analysis to an examination solely of the forces and relations of production" (ibid. 142-3). This analysis, which allows for elements outside the bounds of what Smith considers the purely economic, seems to hint at the influence of Weber on the analysis of class.

A Weberian analysis of class is one which sees class as "life chances" determined by economic (market) relations. Although class as a concept played a relatively minor role in Weber's sociological studies, his work is often referred to both in critiques of Marx's writings on class, and recent (e.g. neo-Marxist) attempts at reformulating Marx's theories of class (Burris 1987, Wright 2005). Weber's concept of class is succinctly presented in a section of *Economy and Society* which outlines the differences between class, status and party (Weber 1978: 927):

In our terminology, "classes" are not communities; they merely represent possible, and frequent, bases for social action. We may speak of a 'class' when (1) a number of people have in common a specific causal component of their life chances, insofar as (2) this component is represented exclusively by economic interests in the possession of goods and opportunities for income, and (3) is represented under the conditions of the commodity or labor markets. This is "class situation".

In this short passage, Weber emphasizes that classes are above all determined by economic conditions and market interaction. The other elements which condition the distribution of power in society are "status", which may influence class position but is not solely determined by it, and "party", which is defined through political ideology and activity.

Marx and Weber both coincide in their understanding that the ownership of economic assets used in market exchanges affects "life chances". For Marx, though, unequal access to economic resources leads not only to differing "life chances", but also to the exploitation of one group by another. Exploitation emerges when the labour effort of one group (the surplus labour: all labour which is more than what is needed for the labourers to reproduce themselves) is appropriated by another group. The concept of exploitation is central to Marx's understanding of class and, more broadly, capitalism as an economic system, for two main reasons. The first is that for Marx, exploitation is the main reason for the ongoing conflict between what he conceives as two main classes in a capitalist system, the workers and the capitalists. The second is that exploitation is the way that capitalists are able to generate a profit from their invested capital. They do this by appropriating the surplus value from workers in a variety of ways. This appropriation (surplus extraction) applies both to workers in industrialized countries and to rural farmers in developing countries.

Many of these mechanisms of surplus extraction are outlined by Deere and De Janvry (1979) and apply just as well to rural Nepal, which is dominated by subsistence production, as they do to Peru, the focus of their analysis. Whether the appropriation of surplus value is done through taxation, direct appropriation (such as through sharecropping arrangements), or more indirectly, such as through usury with high interest rates, the mechanisms all benefit certain households who are able to maintain their economic advantage over other households. In the case of the research site in east Nepal, the most common forms of appropriation are related to: sharecropping, "extraction via the terms of trade" (buying commodities in the village at unfavorable prices from the producers), and usury. The authors mention four other forms of surplus extraction or appropriation: rent in labour services (*corvée*); extraction of surplus value, which applies to capitalist relations of production; rent in cash, or complete rental of land such that the risks of production "are shifted completely from the landowner to the peasant producers"; and finally taxation, in the form of land taxes, market taxes, export taxes, income taxes, and so forth (Deere and De Janvry 1979: 607-8).[4] These processes of surplus extraction will be analysed throughout the book and form an important part the discussion on class formation.

As with the literature on *modes of production*, there continues to be a wide-ranging, and somewhat unproductive debate between scholars in different disciplines about the most accurate ways of defining and using the concept of class. While neo-Marxists attempt to synthesize Marxist and Weberian approaches by pointing out the similarities between them, Weberians continue to criticize the Marxists for ignoring non-economic and non-class forms of domination such as religious and ethnic conflicts, and gender and sexual oppression (Giddens 1981, Parkin 1979).

There are also Marxist anthropologists that have tried to expand the notion of class to include non-economic notions of stratification such as the way economic differentiation among peasants leads to polarization at a political level (Momba 1989). Examining the historical process of rural class formation in the Southern Province of Zambia, Momba shows that while cash crop production has resulted in wide economic differences between villagers, rich and poor cultivators are still members of the same class—the peasantry (Momba 1989: 357). Class differentiation has expressed itself through the increased political involvement of richer peasants who have taken on leadership roles, rather than through the transformation of richer peasants into capitalists. Other scholars have also emphasized that shared interests among the peasantry means that peasants should be considered members of the same class (Shivji 1973, Williams 1976). The debate on what constitutes a class and the process of class formation has occupied anthropologists even longer than the concept of *modes of production* described above.

---

4 Taxes on cardamom production do exist in the village, but these are borne by merchants and traders who mostly live and work outside the village and in any case resort to "extraction via the terms of trade" by buying cardamom at prices that are always substantially lower than the going rate in the market towns to the south of the village.

Many anthropologists have largely avoided the more theoretical aspects of the debate by using *class* as a synonym for economic (income, wealth, land ownership) and/or occupational stratification. This notion of class is useful for describing the economic stratification of society at any given time, but lacks a processual and historical perspective which is so fundamental to the broader concept of *class formation*.[5]

A processual perspective would allow for the analysis of how both the placement of people within classes and the classes themselves change over time. With regard to this book therefore, there are two primary points to be made which in turn affect the conceptualization of class and class formation. First of all, economic differences, measured any number of ways—with income, land ownership, total production of cardamom, or household surplus production of food—have existed in the past and continue to exist in the village today. In other words, any of these economic variables can be applied to understand where households are to be placed within an economic hierarchy. There is a second crucial point to be made though. Not only do these differences— or inequalities—exist, but there are processes at work which allow villagers both to actively increase these differences (in relation to other villagers), or challenge and reduce them. It is here that a number of threads of theory which have been elaborated upon in the previous sections can be drawn together.

The simple differentiation of people or households into classes based on a combination of economic indicators is not enough if we are to grapple with the broader questions posed by an anthropological political economy framework. This descriptive categorization of classes must be paired with an historical, ethnographic and economic analysis of how these economic differences emerge in the first place (class formation), and the means by which certain villagers have been able to exacerbate these differences.

---

5   Wolf submits that it was this processual (Marxist) understanding of class which may have led to social scientists rejecting the concept altogether: "It is likely that it was precisely the conception of political economy as a structure of classes that led the nascent social sciences to turn against the concept of class. If social, economic, and political relations were seen to involve a division into antagonistic classes, endowed by the structure of the political economy itself with opposing interests and capabilities, then the pursuit of order would indeed by haunted forever by the specter of discord" (Wolf 1982: 20)

This approach to class formation has parallels with the ways villagers understand and talk about economic differentiation. When discussing the economic conditions of any household, villagers use the dichotomy of rich (*dhani*) and poor (*garīb*)—occasionally qualified with the word "very" (*dherai*). Together with this simple categorization, villagers frequently provide some background detail to support their statements. This background is often related to a productive process and, as a result, to the ongoing process of economic differentiation: "his father was in the army"; "he harvested 800 kg of cardamom this year"; "he made a lot of money abroad"; and "they have no money because their father had debts and had to sell their land". The categorization of economic difference within the village—using the terms *dhani* and *garīb*—is always paired with an understanding of the means by which households have become rich, or the reasons for their poverty. The "local categories" and the analysis of these categories by villagers therefore match the theoretical aims of using the concept of class formation. That is: to describe the economic differences within the village, and to provide insight into the ways in which these differences are perpetuated and changed.

With regard to the first aim, this book makes use of a number of variables to describe economic differences. Among these the leading variable is *household surplus*.[6] As a proxy for income, this variable depicts both the marked differences between high-surplus and high-deficit producing households, and the wide distribution of data across the village. The absence of any strongly polarized economic data related to income and wealth leads the analysis away from a dichotomous class framework, as presented for example by Ortner (1989) with her categories of "big people" and "small people".

Instead, recognizing that any variable will result in a different economic hierarchy and that all variables show a wide distribution across the village, this book focuses on the process of class formation rather than on the categorization of classes *per se*. This is because it is this process of class formation which is leading to the increasing

---

6 This is calculated by adding the total value of cereal (maize, millet and rice) and cardamom production in 2007 and subtracting from this the total cost of household rice consumption per year. A *per capita* figure can then be calculated by dividing the figure for *household surplus* by the number of household members residing in the house at the time of the survey.

economic and social polarization of society. It is this process which may eventually result in the formation of far more distinctly separated classes than are currently found in the village.

Class in South Asian anthropology

Since the 1960s, a considerable number of studies have explored the subject of class in South Asia. The majority of these studies have focused on India, where the subject of class has often been paired with that of caste. By and large these different concepts—class and caste, as well as power—were viewed as sharing many similarities in the ways that they produced and maintained structural and social hierarchies within and between societies.

The work of Srinivas (1952, 1955, 1968) was important for elaborating the notion that caste systems were not static or fixed systems but fluid and continuously changing: "the caste system is far from a rigid system in which the position of each component caste is fixed for all time. Movement has always been possible..." (1955: 30). The concept of *Sanskritization*, which he first introduced in his study of the social and religious life of the Coorgs of South India (1952), refers to the process by which members of lower castes adopt elements of a "Brahmanic way of life" in order to rise higher in the caste hierarchy. Rosser (1966), in his study of social mobility in the Newar caste system, shows how Sanskritization takes place when, for example, a Jyapu (traditionally a farmer caste) tries to become a Shrestha (a merchant caste). He outlines four stages in the "process of caste transformation": first, they change their surname; second they change their religious behaviour away from Buddhism and towards Hinduism; third they will change social circles, joining Shrestha associations and interest groups; and finally they try to marry their sons to Shrestha women (1966: 94-98).[7]

Sanskritization, which Srinivas uses very specifically to refer to members of a low caste who adopt the cultural norms and values of high-caste Brahmins, is only one of the ways by which stratified groups

---

7   Quigley (1996) argues that Rosser mistakes a process of caste mobility for a process of caste fragmentation. Jyapus do not and indeed cannot become Shresthas. Instead "much the more common patterns for upwardly mobile aspirants is to form marriage circles and exclusive *Guthis* [form of voluntary association] among themselves" (ibid.: 83).

negotiate and challenge their position within a social hierarchy. For Rosser, caste mobility, although expressed through social and cultural changes, is intimately tied to political and economic factors and as such, reference to these is crucial for a fuller understanding: "the rise of the Rana despotism, the incidence of economic change and increased occupational diversification, the status inconsistencies of wealthy and influential Jyapus or of increasingly impoverished Gubhaju priests... Without a full recognition of the basic significance of these factors, Newar caste behaviour is unintelligible" (Rosser 1966: 137). In short, while he hardly mentions class in his study, it is clear that besides Sanskritization, many of the social strategies employed by Newars, as well as the underlying causes of mobility, can be traced to economic factors—many of which may be considered as class-related.

While caste continued to be a central concern for many anthropologists working in India throughout the 1960s (Dumont 1970, Fürer-Haimendorf 1966, Srinivas 1962), a number of anthropologists specifically examined the underlying economic and political causes of mobility within castes, framing this mobility in much more explicitly "class-related" terms than earlier scholars of caste. Béteille (1965) was one of the first anthropologists to study both caste *and* class—within a single village located in Tanjore District of South India—and to examine the differences and relationship between them. Recognizing that caste, class and power are all socially stratified within societies, he shows that although there is a large degree of overlap between caste and class in the village, the class system has increasingly become independent of the caste system. He divides classes according to both the type of ownership and control of production, and the kind of involvement in the process of production such that sharecroppers and agricultural labourers belong to different classes (Béteille 1965: 187). He considers castes to be status groups and defines them in terms of their "style of life" (ibid.: 188). This results in the proliferation of castes (as status groups) with only relatively few social classes.

According to Béteille, in the past, the class system was subsumed by the caste system, and economic activities were patterned along caste lines. Over the last 50 years, processes such as westernization, urbanization, increased geographical mobility, and the penetration of a market-based economy, have all contributed to the opening up of the local economic system as the village is increasingly drawn into larger economic—and non-caste based—processes. He concludes that "the processes of economic change and political modernisation have led the productive system and the organization of power to acquire an increasing degree of autonomy [from the caste system]" (ibid: 225).

A similar process of social change is described by Bailey (1957) in his study of a highland village in Orissa. Whereas originally the *warrior* caste was dominant—they owned the land, managed political affairs, and were positioned high up on the ritual hierarchy of caste (1957: 9)— the gradual penetration of the market economy, which provided non-warrior castes with alternative sources of income to those derived from agriculture, reduced the monopoly over resources of the warrior caste. Traditionally, members of non-warrior castes would have depended on the warrior caste—by maintaining a ritual and economic relationship with them—for their share of the resources. Non-warrior caste members were able to earn money outside the village and use it to purchase land which had belonged to *warriors*. Warrior caste members had begun to partition land for inheritance partly because smaller plots were more manageable for households who couldn't afford to hire additional labour but largely because of population pressure as the total village population continued to grow. Land was sold by warrior households who were unable to survive and needed capital, and was bought by non-warrior caste villagers who had access to capital from sources other than cultivation. Where the *warriors* had owned all the land within the village in 1885, they owned only 28% of it by 1953. Similarly to Béteille's study, what Bailey was examining in the village of Bisipara, while never mentioned explicitly, could be described as the transition from caste to class-based relations, or at least as the relative increase in importance of class against caste-based relations. He concludes that: "in the village the hierarchy of caste-groups is no longer a complete reflection of economic realities, nor an adequate means of ordering political relations" (Bailey 1957: 275).

Kapadia's study of gender, caste, and class in rural South India focuses particularly on the lower-castes and the impact of economic mobility on gender and caste relations. Contrary to Srinivas, Kapadia points out that much of what Srinivas would consider caste mobility is actually an attempt by groups to change their class status:

> The imitation of the Chettiar lifestyle by the upwardly mobile lower castes probably cannot, according to Srinivas's own criteria, be

considered true . This is because, in a context of continued and strong anti-Brahmin feeling, this lower-caste adoption of upper-caste norms is, instead, an attempt to appropriate a prestigious cultural style that enhances their change in class status. They do not seek to make a claim to higher caste status...Brahminization now has more to do with class mobility that with the legitimation of a higher caste status. (Kapadia 1995: 11)

Lower castes are more interested in becoming "urbanized" and "modernized" than "Brahminized"; more interested in changing their class than their caste ranking (ibid.: 47). In relation to kinship, Kapadia describes how the impact of economic mobility on these "urbanized" lower castes has been to create a class-based (economic) division between "marriageable" and "unmarriageable" kin within each endogamous caste group: "it is 'urban' norms and the new non-kin marriage patterns that are viewed as 'nagarikam' (sophisticated, civilized behaviour)" (ibid.: 67) In other words, class-based social relations are developing within castes as a result of economic differentiation.

While primarily economic factors affect caste-based social relations, status considerations still play an important role. The example Kapadia draws on for this relates to the untouchable Pallars, who are considered "polluted" by other castes in the village. She describes how the landless Muthurajahs have been able to earn money in non-agricultural activities and improve their status, yet the Pallars, who are also landless, have remained impoverished. The reasons for this are economic but strongly related to caste and the continued belief in untouchability. It is because they are untouchable that the Pallars "lack the social standing and the social connections that would encourage others to lend them capital" (ibid.: 197).

Thus far, this section has briefly explored the work of a number of anthropologists who have either directly or indirectly used the concept of class to understand processes of social change resulting from economic changes. The importance given to class as the principal factor causing or resulting from economic changes varies from one analysis to another. Where some scholars (e.g. Béteille) consider class to have superseded or delegitimized caste to some extent, and to be functioning independently of it (class outside caste), others (e.g. Kapadia) consider class to have done little more than rearranged caste hierarchies and strengthened economic and gender inequalities (class within caste). In the final part of this section one of the few contemporary works on class in Nepal will be examined.

Unlike the works discussed above, Liechty's (2003) study of middle class culture in Kathmandu focuses entirely on consumption, with very little discussion of caste, ethnicity, or politics—important topics in other ethnographies of Nepal. The three sections in the book, other than the introduction and conclusion, deal with class and consumerism, media consumption, and youth culture. The concept framing the whole analysis is *class*, and in particular, following from the works of Gewertz and Errington (1999) and Sloane (1999), the emergence of a middle class:

> Over the past few decades in Kathmandu, an almost entirely new 'intermediate' social 'stratum' has emerged in the social gap between historically polarized national elites and urban commoners. In the process, members of this middle class have had to construct entirely new forms of cultural practice (Liechty 2003: 7).

Liechty uses a decidedly Weberian conceptualization of the middle classes by considering them primarily as consumers of goods in the market place rather than as owners of the means of production or as sellers of labour. He justifies this emphasis on consumption by describing it as "one of the key cultural dynamics of middle-class life" (ibid.: 30). Similarly to Béteille, he argues that whereas caste played an important role in determining the socioeconomic rank of a person in the past, in contemporary Nepal "caste is becoming less and less likely to guarantee (whether by privilege or exclusion) a person's social standing" (ibid.: 56). Liechty brings this down to the "city's new cash and market-oriented economy [which] demands that people pioneer new forms of cultural practice, identification and privilege" (ibid.).

While Liechty's focus on consumption has the advantage of providing an ethnographically rich analysis of previously little-studied cultural domains such as fashion and cinema, it offers very little insight into the 'production' and 'reproduction' side of middle class formation and consolidation. Middle class identity is produced and reproduced in multiple environments; not just through the act of consumption. The educational system, tourist industry, hospital and office environments, among others, all contribute important influences to the "process of cultural formation that is underway in the lives and practises of middle-class people in Kathmandu" (ibid.: 249). In his conclusion Liechty explains that "class is not a 'thing' but rather a practice or project" and that "we need to move beyond the passive, objectifying, immobilizing question 'what is class?' to the active, processual question 'what does class as cultural practice do?'" (ibid.: 265).

Yet the focus on what class *does* rather than what class *is* does not necessarily lead the analysis directly, or at least solely, towards practises of consumption. Although it may be true that the middle class tries to distinguish itself from the "provincial vulgarity of the urban poor," while trying to define a "modern-but-still-Nepali lifestyle of moral and material restraint distinct from excess" (ibid.: 61), members of this middle class are nonetheless involved in some way in the process of production. It is their specific involvement in production which provides them with surplus cash and time, both fundamental to the process of consumption. As Gellner (2004) points out, although the middle class may be contributing to the suburban sprawl depicted in a photograph (Liechty 2003: 6), "any close examination of how the buildings in question are used would quickly show that many are rented out room by room to the new working class: migrants from the hills who have nowhere else to go" (Gellner 2004: 102). In other words, what the middle class does—its cultural practice—is tied directly to both the working class and the process of production. It is not enough to analyse consumption independently of production and imagine to be describing the fullness of class-based cultural practice, when both are intimately tied to each other.

Conclusion

This overview of a number of anthropological studies of caste and class in India and Nepal shows how the concept of class has increasingly replaced—or at least supplemented[8]—the concept of caste in the analysis

---

8   Pandian (2002) argues that the upper castes in India (he refers largely to Brahmins) have increasingly avoided talking of caste by "transcoding caste and caste relations into something else" (2002: 6) in order to downplay the continued relevance of the concept. A result of this is that "what gets encoded...as Indian culture is what is culture to the Brahmins/upper castes" (ibid: 9). Pandian's main point is that caste still matters and it is Brahmins who have "neutralized the caste factor in the garb of modernity with a view to deny the Dalits their rightful place in the public spheres and politics"

of social hierarchy and stratification. While the centrality of the concept of class, and the way that it is used in each analysis varies, these studies all consider it fundamental for understanding the ways that social and economic hierarchies (or inequalities) are created and continue to be maintained. Similarly to the work of Béteille and Bailey, this book shows how the increasing penetration of a market-based economy, as well as the active engagement with these markets by villagers, has redrawn the parameters of wealth and inequality at the local level. Unlike the work of Liechty, this book focuses largely on production rather than consumption, as it is through involvement in a number of productive processes that certain villagers have begun to form a sort of incipient rural middle class.

(Rohini 2002: 3076). While agreeing with Pandian that caste still matters— "At the national level, only a person blinded by ideology can fail to see the play of the caste factor" (ibid: 3077)—Rohini disagrees with Pandian that "to preserve their culture the subaltern has to be one step outside the fold of modernity" (ibid.) as this would be advocating a form a caste seclusion. Without getting too caught up in these debates (Gavaskar 2002, Natraj 2003), suffice it to say that the contention of this chapter has not been to claim caste no longer exists or has no value as a concept, rather that class has increasingly become an important concept for studying social hierarchy and economic differentiation.

Chapter 2
Historical Context

Kirānti history

The Nepalese chronicles (*vaṃśāvalī* in Sanskrit and Nepali), which have entries starting in the 11th century, describe how the Kirāntis were the first dynasty to have ruled ancient Nepal, i.e. the Kathmandu valley, for more than 1,000 years. They were driven out by the ancestors of the Licchavi, the earliest dynasty for which archaeological evidence and inscriptions are available (Lévi 1985: 78-85). Beyond a few traditions which refer to various kings and religious practises taking place during this long historical period, there is very little substantial evidence known about this "Kirānti period" of the Kathmandu valley. The modern Nepali term Kirānti or Kirānt is related to the much older Sanskrit term Kirāta which first occurs in the Atharvaveda, the last of the four vedas. The term Kirāta appears in other Vedas and ancient texts, as well as the Purānas and the Rāmāyana, and the Kirāta are usually portrayed as wild people living in forested mountain areas (Lévi 1905: 74-78). A number of ancient Greek sources—historians, merchants and geographers—refer to the Kirāta as Cirrhadae or Cirrhadeae. Throughout these scattered references, the Kirāta are usually described as hunter-gatherers who live in forested mountainous areas on the fringes of civilized India (Chatterji 1951: 17-19).

This notion of living on the edge of civilization is encapsulated in Slusser's (1982) etymological analysis of the term Kirāta, with *kira* meaning "edge" and *at* meaning "to roam" (Slusser 1982: 9). The historian G.P. Singh considers the term to be connected with the medicinal plant *Cireta* (*Swertia chirata*) which was collected by Kirāta mountain-dwellers for the Aryans in the plains (Singh 1990: 96). The Kirāta scholar Iman Singh Chemjong (2003) proposes, with no hesitation, that the term Kirat is a "corrupt form of Kiriat, Kiryat or Kirjath which means a fort or town in Moabite language of the Mediterranean region." (Chemjong 2003: 2) According to Chemjong, the ancestors of the "Kereti tribe" were expelled from Babylon and led a nomadic life, spreading east and north-east, eventually migrating to the Himalayan area. Whether the Kirāta originated in Babylon, in Kashmir (Rönnow 1936), or had always lived on the northern and north-eastern periphery of the Indian civilisation, a conceptual separation has to be made between the Kirāta historical epoch, and the ethnic groups that self-identify as Kirānti in Nepal today. Shafer (1954) connects the Kirāta mentioned in the Mahābhārata with the Rai and Limbu ethnic groups who designate themselves as Kirānti (Shafer 1954: 124-125).

One of the earliest uses of the term Kirānti to refer to specific ethnic groups was in the *Account of the Kingdom of Nepal* by the missionary Giuseppe da Rovato. Visiting Kathmandu at the time of conquest by Prithvi Narayan Shah around 1770, he reported that an independent nation, called the Ciratas, existed only five to six days journey east of the Kathmandu valley (da Rovato 1790: 307-322). The British emissary Colonel Kirkpatrick visiting Nepal in 1793, made a possible mention of the Kirānti in his own *Account* in a list of the "principal vernacular languages of the country" in which he included "The Kurraute", as well as the "Limbooa" (Limbu) (Kirkpatrick 1986[1811]: 220). While it is hard to trace continuity from the very early history of Nepal, that of the Kirānti dynasties in the Kathmandu valley, to the various ethnic groups who consider themselves Kirānti in contemporary Nepal (Rai, Limbu, Yakkha and Sunuwar), it is clear from most accounts that the term Kirant refers to both an ethnolinguistic unit and geographical area. George van Driem suggests that commonalities between Tibeto-Burman languages point to a genetic unit he calls MahaKirānti "which includes the Kirānti languages [Rai and Limbu] in the strict sense and the Newaric languages Barām and the Thangmi" (van Driem 2001: 599). He concludes that the Kirāntis mentioned in the earliest chronicles may have been more directly related linguistically to the Newar ethnic group than the linguistic forebears of the modern Kirānti peoples of eastern Nepal (ibid: 599-600).

Francis Buchanan Hamilton, who also published an *Account of the Kingdom of Nepal* (1819) eight years after Kirkpatrick, mentions the Kirat as an ethnic group living to the east of Kathmandu: "East from the territory called Nepal Proper, the mountains were chiefly occupied by a tribe called Kirat, or Kichak" (Hamilton 1819: 7). Hamilton describes how although the Kirat "in remote times, seem to have made extensive conquests in the plains of Kamrup and Matsya, now constituting the districts of Ranggapur and Dinajpur" they were nevertheless "subject to Rajput princes". He continues: "The Kirats formed the principal strength of these Rajput chiefs, their hereditary chief held the second office in the state, (Chautariya), and the Rajputs, who were united with them, did not presume to act as masters, to invade their lands, or to violate their customs" (Hamilton 1819: 7-8). In other words, Kirānti groups had entered a pact with the Rajput princes such that in exchange for gaining an important position in the office (*cautariyā* is a principal officer of the state), and presumably contributing militarily as in a typical feudal society, the Kirānti groups gained important political, geographical and cultural autonomy from the Rajputs. The key point to be brought out of Hamilton's historical description was the autonomy of the Kirānti groups. There would continue to be a complex political and cultural relationship between the indigenous populations of east Nepal and both the migrant non-indigenous populations and the expanding Kingdom of Nepal. This will be explored in more detail below.

What is interesting about Hamilton's *Account* is the inconsistent and confusing classificatory relation within the category of Kirānti and between Kirānti and non-Kirānti groups, such as the Limbu and Lepcha. This is, as Gaenszle rightly points out (Gaenszle 2000: 9), typical of much of the early literature on ethnic groups in east Nepal. In one section of his *Account* Hamilton describes the Limbu as a group within the Kirants: "Among the kirats was settled a tribe called Limbu, the manners of which were very nearly the same, and, indeed, the tribes intermarry" (Hamilton 1819: 54). In another section, talking about the populations in the western parts of "Chayenpur" (presumably Chainpur of Sankhuwasabha district) he refers to the Limbu as a population separate from the Kirant: "The most numerous tribe is Kirat, next Limbu, then Magar...then Khas and Rajputs" (Hamilton 1819: 160). Gaenszle writes that in an account by Campbell (1840) "the ethnonym "Limboo" is a generic term including also the "Kerautis" (=Kirati), "Eakas" (=Yakha) and "Rais" (Campbell 1840: 595). To complicate things further, Campbell's "Note on the Limboo" divides the "Limboo tribes" into two:

the "Hung" (probably from the term *hang* meaning king in Limbu) and the Rai, counting 28 Rai clans within the Limboo tribe (Campbell 1840: 599), when clearly the Limbu were a separate ethnic group altogether.

The British civil servant Brian Hodgson, who first arrived in Nepal in 1820, also appears somewhat confused by the relationship between the term Kirant and the names for the various groups that inhabit east Nepal. In a note originally published in 1847, he writes about the Kirántis as a group both united by their history and divided by tribes: "Adverting to the high recorded antiquity of the terms Kirát or Kiránt and Kirát or Kiránti, as applied respectively to the country and people even to this hour, it is remarkable that the Kirántis themselves do not readily admit the genuineness or propriety of those terms...and seem to have none at all for their country...The Kirántis, always ignorant of letters, have been now for a long time depressed and subdued; and huddled as they now are into comparatively narrow limits, they are yet divided among themselves into numerous tribes and sects, speaking dialects so diverse as not to be mutually intelligible" (Hodgson 2001[1880]: 398). If nothing else, what united these tribes was their geographical distribution across east Nepal.

Hodgson was in fact one of the first to report the relationship between ethnic groups and the geographical divisions of eastern Nepal. The entire region east of the Kathmandu Valley, was divided into "Wallo" or "Hither Kiránt", "Mánjh" or "Middle Kiránt", and "Pallo" or "Further Kiránt" (Hodgson 2001[1880]: 398). This tripartite division of the Kiránt region was related to the distance of each region from Khas country, which extended from Kumaon in the west to Nuvakot in the east, and was not how the Kiránti groups themselves perceived the land to be divided (Burghart 1984: 107). It was Pallo, or Further Kiránt, which comprises most of what are today Nepal's Kosi and Mechi zones and the nine districts within them. Hodgson called this "Limbuán", the territorial area traditionally associated with the Limbu ethnic group, which lies between the Arun River and the Singalila ridge which marks the current Nepal-Sikkim border and the Mechi River to the south of that. The other two subdivisions of the Kiránt territory, Middle and Hither Kiránt, were part of what Hodgson called "Khwombuán", which extended from the Sunkosi to the Arun River. Hodgson's term Khwombáun or Khambuván as it is known today, may have originated from the Kiránti kingdom of Khambu conquered by the Gorkhalis in

1831 VS (1774-75). This kingdom of Khambu may have provided the term for the region which became known as Khambuvān, a region which straddled both Hither and Middle Kirant and lay just west of Limbuvān. While the latter is more obviously tied to the Limbu ethnic group, Khambuvān was increasingly considered the territory of what became collectively known as the Rai.[9]

In the years since the People's Movement (*jan āndolan*) of 1990, the term Khambuvān has been used more and more frequently by Rai groups in reference to their traditional territory and indigenous rights. Other ethnic groups, such as the Tamang with "Tamangsaling" and the Tharu with "Tharuhat", have also begun to call for political divisions to be made along ethnic lines, but many of these territories have little basis in historical facts. While some of the indigenous populations outside the Kathmandu valley were put under strong pressure to assimilate the language, culture and religious beliefs of the ruling class during the late 18th century onwards, the Limbu population and the territory of Limbuvān, which lay further to the east, took a lot longer to subjugate and control.

History of Limbuwan

The history of Limbuwan is very much tied to the history of the modern state of Nepal. Prithvi Narayan Shah (1723-75) is considered the father of Nepal and although he was responsible for extending his kingdom's rule and creating the momentum towards a unified country, the boundaries of Nepal as they are today were only set down much later with the Treaty of Sugauli in 1816. In 1743, Prithvi Narayan Shah (PNS) became the king of Gorkha, a small kingdom in modern-day Gorkha district about 50 miles northwest of Kathmandu. At this time, the Kirānti people were organized as independent kingdoms scattered across east Nepal.

According to Pradhan's (1991) history of the Gorkha conquest, the Kirānti peoples, or "Kirats", although enjoying complete political autonomy were under the nominal suzerainty of rulers in the Sena dynasty which controlled the area between the Kali Gandaki River and

---

9   The term *rāi*, meaning lord or headman, was originally a title applied by Hindu rulers to semi-autonomous tribal groups in east Nepal. The term *khambu* has seen increasing use more recently.

Nepal valley to the east.[10] Beyond the adoption of Hindu names and certain notions of purity, Hinduization of the Kirats was not strong (Pradhan 1991: 82). Pradhan mentions that a history of the Limbu, published in Nepali, details a supposed agreement made between the Sena ruler and the Kirat: "The agreement stipulates that the dewan [Magistrate or minister of state] would be the person elected by ten provincial (tribal) chiefs of the Kirats for a tenure of five years" (Pradhan 1991: 82). Pradhan also describes how a system of revenue collection by Kirat officers called Subbas who served under the dewān was already in place at the time of the Gorkha conquest.

At the time of PNS's accession to the throne, the various kingdoms of Nepal such as the Malla dynasty in the Kathmandu valley, the Khasa and Sena, had experienced a decline in their power and increasing territorial fragmentation (Pradhan 1991: 89). According to Pradhan "these states were inhabited by different tribes and groups who had no definite consciousness of their shared achievements in the past nor any unity of faith or language" (ibid). PNS took advantage of this situation by quickly making alliances with neighbouring principalities.[11] He formally began the Gorkha conquest by capturing Nuwakot to the east of Gorkha in 1744, an important point along trade routes between Tibet and the Kathmandu valley, which was known as the Nepal valley at the time. A long period of war began, with Nuwakot as the new capital and centre of operations, and the Gorkhalis extending their control of many parts of Nepal by moving east as far as the Kirats and south as far as British (East India Company)-controlled India. Having surrounded the main urban areas of the Kathmandu Valley and basically blocked trade in and out of the valley, Kirtipur was the first to fall in 1766. Kathmandu and Patan were taken in 1768, Bhaktapur in 1769, and PNS became the king of the Nepal Valley in 1770, having moved his capital from Nuwakot to Kathmandu (Stiller 1973: 123-131).

Only after PNS died in 1775 did the Gorkhali army make the first substantial forays into east Nepal with the Battle of Chainpur in 1776

---

10 This seems rather strange as the Kiranti territory lay to the east of the Nepal Valley and this was controlled at the time by the Malla dynasty.

11 An example of this would be PNS marrying a woman from Makwanpur, which was at the time ruled by the Sena dynasty, a principality which controlled important trade routes between the plains and the Kathmandu Valley.

during the 3-year reign of Pratap Shah. The pressure to control the fertile Tarai in the east had increased with Bhutan invading Nepal (1770) and Kosh Bihar (1772) and the British getting closer to Morang (Pradhan 1991: 109). It was only under Rana Bahadur Shah, who ruled between 1777 and 1799, that the Gorkhali army began to successfully consolidate its control of east Nepal and the Kirānti populations. The history of this success could be divided into two phases, with the first being the Gorkha conquest of Hither (*wallo*) and Middle (*majh*) Kirant, and the second being the conquest of Further Kirant, or Limbuwan. According to Pradhan (1991), the greater part of Majh Kirant was under Gorkhali control by 1773 (1991: 117). This relatively quick victory by the Gorkhalis over such a large population and area could, in part, be explained by the absence of a united opposition among the Kirānti who were divided internally. Other reasons for this success were the support that the Gorkhalis found from the high-caste Hindu populations that had migrated to the area from western Nepal, and the fact that although the Sena armies had firearms, the Kirats were "chiefly armed with swords and bows" (Pradhan 1991: 117). According to Pradhan, the Kirants in newly controlled Hither and Middle Kirant were forced to support the Gorkhalis: "The Kirats, who had accepted the Gorkha rule, had been asked "to do away with other chiefs" and were told that the terms offered to them "did not apply to the nine lakh [900,000] Kirats of the other side" (Pradhan 1991: 122), that is, the Kirants in Limbuwan. Only after the control and pacification of Hither and Middle Kirant did the Gorkhalis focus attention on controlling the Limbu populations in Further Kirant.

Throughout the early 18th century, the Limbu alternated their allegiance between Sikkim and Nepal (ie. the Kathmandu Valley). Risley (1894) suggests that political tensions within Sikkim had led the King to demand too much from the Limbu who switched their allegiance to Nepal: "Throughout this commotion the Raja harried and distressed his Limbu subjects so much by calling them out unnecessarily to fight and again to build forts and walls, that in despair they threw off their allegiance and joined Nepal, so thus Sikhim (*sic*) began to lose the Limbuana country" (Risley 1894: 15). Just before the Gorkha conquest of east Nepal, the Limbu had therefore allied themselves to the Newar kingdoms of the Kathmandu valley, and as the Gorkhali army advanced into the east, it was able to recruit Limbu populations into their army:

"Limbus were first recruited in the Gorkhali army as early as the Battle of Cainpur, and in 1776 many Limbus fought on the Gorkhali side against their own people" (van Driem 2001: 604).[12] Victory in the Battle of Cainpur against the Sikkimese king, led the Gorkhalis to increase their control of east Nepal, but due to strong Limbu resistence, and the continued presence of the Sikkimese forces, it was only in 1786 that the annexation of Further Kirant was complete, and the war in Limbuwan ended.

Land in east Nepal

Despite partial control of Limbuwan from about 1782 and more substantial control from 1786, political, cultural and economic resistance continued in various forms through to the fall of the Rana regime in 1951, and elements of this resistance could be said to exist still today. The Gorkhalis' expansionist ambitions were finally halted with the Gorkha war (1814-1818) between Nepal and the British East Indian Company which ended with concessions by the Gorkhali government and the Treaty of Sugauli outlining the new borders. Throughout the Gorkha conquest of east Nepal, the two principal motivating factors for the war had been to control trade routes between Tibet and India, and to control land in the fertile Tarai area (Pradhan 1991: 157). The desire to control land was in turn perpetuated by a policy of providing land grants, as well as other economic privileges, to high-caste Hindus who had assisted the Gorkhali army, as well as to military personnel, government employees and higher-ranking members of the royal court (Pradhan 1991: 112).

These land grants, given under different conditions and tenancy agreements, were all part of the governments *raikar* land tenure system. *Raikar* refers to land which ultimately belongs to the state and from which the state collects tax. Secondary forms of land tenure developed from the *raikar* system, the most important of which were known as

---

12 Pradhan (1991) points out that although the recruitment of Kirants permitted the expansion of the Gorkhali army "it is doubtful whether the Limbus were recruited in the regular army. Documents are vague regarding this, but apparently the Limbus rebelled later when attempts were made to conscript them. Moreover the policy laid down by Prithivinarayan was to recruit only the Khasas, Thakurs, Magars and Gurungs" (Pradhan 1991: 130).

birtā and *jāgir*. *Birtā* land grants were given conditionally to individuals within the nobility, upper castes or religious groups and were usually tax free. *Jāgir* were land grants given as remuneration to government employees and functionaries who would be known as *jāgirdārs*.[13] The development of the *jāgir* system was strongly influenced by the absence of a monetized economy and the feudal principles of landownership and social privilege. With the creation of a class of land owners, the *jāgirdārs*, "all that the government was required to do...was to prepare land records and, later, lists of tax assessments, leaving the more difficult task of collection and utilization to the Jagirdar" (Regmi 1965: 6). Ownership of *jāgir* land entitled the *jāgirdār* to collect money (taxes and fines) and non-agricultural produce (fish, forest resources). With the *jāgir* and *birtā* systems, the new government was able to do three things simultaneously: use a non-monetary means of compensating employees; promote the reclamation and cultivation of underused land and wasteland; and encourage a particular section of society, the upper-caste Hindus in particular, to migrate and settle in east Nepal.

Kipat

While land tenure and land ownership in most of Nepal was organized around the *raikar* system, specifically under either the *jāgir*, *birtā*, or *guthi* systems, land in Limbuwan was organized under a separate system which came to be known as kipat. Whereas with *raikar* land, ultimate authority over land rested with the government, under kipat, land was held communally and individuals had rights and access to it by virtue of being members of an indigenous ethnic group with traditional rights of residence (Regmi 1965: 82). Unlike *raikar* land, kipat land could not be sold or given over to non-community members (Regmi 1978: 535), and waste land and uncleared forest as well as cultivated land was all considered kipat by the Limbu.

Regmi (1965) described how the term kipat was in use in parts of western Nepal before the conquest of eastern Nepal began in the 1770s (Regmi 1965: 83-84). Prithvi Narayan Shah apparently never used the term in any of his orders or letters, and it was only during the reign of Ran Bahadur Shah that it was first used. Chemjong translates the term

---

13 According to Regmi (1965: 20), 93.5% of all *jāgir* was given to people who served in the Gorkhali army.

kippo:t in Limbu as "a kind of revenue-free, freehold ancestral land (of Limbus)" (Chemjong 2002: 57). The term *taŋsiŋ-khɔksiŋ* in the dictionary also refers to "first ownership of land" and "first inhabited land; main land; original land" (Chemjong 2002: 167), but there is no indication that these concepts directly refer to the term kipat.

Despite the inherent inalienability of kipat land from Limbu communities, and despite encroachment on kipat land being prohibited, settlement in Limbuvān was nevertheless encouraged. Before the Gorkha war, east Nepal had been controlled either by the Sen Kings or Sikkim and both had encouraged settlement into Further Kirant by assigning land as *jāgir* and *birtā*. Gorkha rulers, and later the Rana dynasty, continued with this practice until the overthrow of the Rana regime in 1951. Overall, in 1952 around 4% of all the land in Nepal was under the kipat system (van Driem 2001: 608), and in 1965 Regmi noted that "only approximately one third of the cultivated land in Pallo-kirat is estimated to be under Kipat tenure" (Regmi 1965: 85), in other words some two thirds of inalienable kipat land had been sold, taken or somehow appropriated by non-Limbu populations over the years since the Gorkha conquest.[14]

Other non-Limbu populations in east Nepal, particularly those in Middle Kirant or *mājh* Kirant, lost most of their kipat lands much earlier than the Limbu in Further Kirant, with a series of legal incursions on kipat rights which forced kipat to be converted to the governmental *raikar* system. By 1910, the government had confirmed the abolition of kipat in *mājh* Kirant (Regmi 1965: 90).[15] Despite this, the kipat system in Limbuwan survived through the fall of the Rana regime and was only finally abolished with the government's land reforms of 1964, though

---

14 This is not to say that prior to the Gorkha conquest all the land in Limbuwan had been kipat, since as mentioned, there is some evidence that *jāgir* and *birtā* land grants had been made under the Sena rulers. Certainly, though, the majority of the land must have been under Limbu control. Whether the land ownership system prior to the Gorkha conquest was identical to the later kipat system is difficult to know.

15 Forbes (1999) writes about a Yamphu-Rai community by the Arun River which still had the kipat system in place until the cadastral survey of 1994. This community lies within the boundaries of Further Kirant, where the kipat system continued until very recently. According to van Driem (2001: 602), the western boundary of Further Kirant runs along the Arun River and includes the Mewahang area to the west of the Arun, but the administrative borders were reshuffled in 1963-64 AD (ibid.).

formal registration of previously held kipat as *raikar* took place as late as the 1990s in some parts of Limbuwan.

The government appears to have been anything but consistent in its approach to kipat and the immigration of non-Limbu communities into Limbuwan. While obviously aiming to placate the rebellious Limbu, it nevertheless clearly encouraged non-Limbu groups to settle in Limbuwan and cultivate land. Regmi shows how prior to 1883, there was no specific restriction on the rights of Limbu communities to give away their kipat land, and land thus alienated was registered as *birtā* by non-Limbu buyers (Regmi 1965: 97). In 1883 it was specifically mentioned that kipat land could not be alienated, and in 1903 "orders were issued to permit the alienation of Kipat waste or *pakho* lands to non-Limbu settlers, on condition that they reclaimed or converted them into paddy fields...[this] was therefore intended to encourage resettlement" (ibid.: 98). Additionally, taxation and the control of trade were less severely implemented in Further Kirant than in the other Kirants which resulted in the relative prosperity of Limbuwan in particular and may have been an incentive for non-Limbu populations, largely Hindu, to settle in the area. Another incentive, according to Regmi, was provided by the Limbu population themselves. There was both an abundance of cultivable land and an acute shortage of labour and the Limbu needed labour, capital and agricultural knowledge for the development of cultivable land (Regmi 1965: 97, Jones 1976: 65). The extensive land grants made by the Limbu eventually led to conflicts between them and the Hindu populations when land was no longer in abundant supply, and the government ultimately sided with the Hindu populations.

One method for both placating Limbu communities and encouraging migration was to incorporate the traditional political structure of Limbu communities into the state administrative structure. Limbu chieftains, traditionally important members of sub-clans and patrilineages, were granted the title of *subbā* and, similarly to the *jāgirdārs*, collected taxes from both the Limbu, who lived on kipat plots related to their lineages and sub-clans, and Hindu immigrants who had settled on kipat land. The *subbā* were also able to mediate local disputes, fine and punish villagers within their area of control (Jones 1976: 65). As a result of this system, the Hindu immigrants were initially politically subordinate to the Limbu chiefs. When the government allowed land to be alienated, that is converted from kipat to privately owned *raikar*, Hindu populations were not only able to have more secure access to land, but were paying their taxes directly to the government and not to the *subbā* or *thari* (the head of a clan or *thar*) as they were known. Resentment increased among the *subbā* and, in 1901, the government responded by outlawing the alienation of kipat land.

Despite this measure, the political and economic power of the Limbu irreversibly declined and the Hindu population became economically dominant. Caplan (1967) suggests that with restricted access to land, and the economic benefits of being *subbā* diminished, "Limbu leaders, like the majority of their lineage kinsmen, found it impossible to maintain their level of consumption and meet minimal social obligations" (Caplan 1967: 110). As a result, the Limbu turned to the Hindus for financial assistance in the form of loans which would be given in exchange for temporary possession of kipat land as usufructuary mortgage, until the Hindu creditor was repaid in full, with access to kipat land covering the interest on the loan. Increased debts led to increased amounts of kipat land being mortgaged, which in turn led to increased debts. In an effort to escape the circle of debt, many Limbu were led to sell their land and title deeds forcing kipat land to be converted to *raikar*. While the 1901 government ruling banning the alienation of kipat land may have stopped outright conversion of kipat to *raikar*, it did not stop kipat land being mortgaged. As few Limbu were ever able to pay back the mortgage principal, this land was effectively taken from them. Additionally, a system known as *bāḍ*, where further money was borrowed from the original creditor by threatening to repay the mortgage and sell it to another buyer for more money, led to yet further indebtedness among the Limbu (Jones 1976: 66). Ultimately, this all led to many Limbu becoming landless and obliged to work on other people's land as sharecroppers, find wage labour as agricultural workers, government employees, or Gurkha soldiers, or migrate elsewhere.

Although the land reforms of 1964 meant that all kipat landholders, or *kipaṭiya*, had to register their land in the land reform offices and pay taxes to the government on their fields, it was only when land was surveyed by the government that it was finally converted to *raikar* and kipat was abolished throughout Nepal. Throughout the period of the lead-up to formal abolition of kipat as a result of the cadastral survey, access to the kipat system of land tenure had meant that despite economic problems, the Limbu still "owned" their kipat land—whether it was mortgaged or not. As Caplan wrote in 1967 "the kipat system of land tenure, by guaranteeing Limbu rights in perpetuity, keeps ajar the portal of economic change" (Caplan 1967: 112). For Caplan, the survival of kipat as a system was very much tied to the survival of Limbu cultural and political identity (Caplan 1970: 195).

The research carried out for this book in the remote village of Mamangkhe, where kipat was formally abolished in 1985, brought to light at least three important points. First, the kipat system was compromised from the very first decades of the immigration of high-caste Hindu groups, which began as far back as the late 18th century. In this regard I agree with Campbell's assessment that the "uniqueness of *kipat* status has been overworked" particularly when portrayed as the exception to a state project that aimed to construct national identity "by severing links between ethnic identity and local place" (2003: 95-96): kipat seems to have been as much controlled by the politics of wealth as any other land-tenure system of the time. Second, in the specific case of Mamangkhe, and certainly in other villages with a similar economic history, it was cardamom cultivation more than anything else[16] which kept ajar the "portal of economic change" and not the kipat land tenure system. Finally, the recent growth in ethnic awareness and associated interest in Limbu history, culture and language among the Limbu, as well as the revival of notions of a Limbu state—the Limbuwan of old—and Limbu political movements, all show that despite the elimination of the traditional kipat system of land tenure, the Limbu have perhaps never lost sight of their reputation as a fearless, rebellious and independent ethnic group.

---

16 By cardamom cultivation I refer to both the initial phase of migrant labour to Sikkim to work in cardamom plantations, and the more recent introduction of cardamom in the village. Most recently of course international labour migration has provided the most significant opportunity for increasing economic wealth, as will be seen in more detail in Chapter 5. Participation in the Gurkha, Nepal or India army was never as extensive in Mamangkhe as it appears to have been in other Limbu villages (Sagant 1996: 278-312).

The Limbu

Most of the Limbu population of Nepal lives within the nine districts of east Nepal which made up the traditional Limbu territory of Limbuvān.[17] According to the last Nepal Census (2001), the Limbu population in Nepal was 359,379, with a total of 308,037 (86%) living within the nine districts of Limbuvān. Although there was probably a time, before the 1800s, when the Limbu were the majority ethnic group in east Nepal, in Limbuwan they account for less than 10% of the total population of the nine districts, with the highest proportions of Limbu in Taplejung, Panchthar, and Tehrathum districts: 42%, 40% and 35%, respectively. The Census of India (2001) reports that 37,265 people speak the Limbu language, most of whom probably live in Sikkim, with some smaller populations in Assam, and Bhutan. Current estimates indicate a total population of around 400,000 Limbu in the Himalayan area.

The Limbu call themselves *Yakthuŋba*, generally using the term "Limbu" when speaking in Nepali, and sometimes using the term *subbā*, originally the name of an administrator and authority figure chosen to represent a village or lineage within the village (in the same way that the term *rāi* had been applied elsewhere). They refer to their language, the largest of all the Kirānti languages, as *Yakthuŋ paːn*. There is no agreement as to the origin of the term Limbu. G. van Driem (2001: 665) suggests that the name may derive from the word *Liʔmbi*, meaning "those on the other side of the mountain range", preserved in Rai from the now-extinct Dumi language. Several villagers in Mamangkhe explained that the term Limbu derives from two Limbu terms: *Li* meaning "bow", as in the word *toŋli* meaning bow and arrow; and *mbu* derived from the verb *apma* meaning to shoot (*abu* meaning "he shoots"). In other words, *Li-mbu* means, "he shoots a bow". According to Chemjong (2003[1967]) the term *Yakthuŋba* means "stronger people than Yakha Kirat people" (2003: 54), probably derived from Yakha, another Kirānti ethnic group in east Nepal, and *Thumma*, the verb "to be strong" in Limbu.

Chemjong's (ibid.) history of the Limbu describes how before the Limbu arrived, there were eight feudal chiefs who ruled over east Nepal.

---

17 These nine districts are: Taplejung, Panchthar, Ilam and Jhapa, all in the Mechi Zone of far east Nepal; and Sankhuwasabha, Terhathum, Sunsari, Dhankuta and Morang, all in the Kosi Zone (with Bhojpur district not included) east of the Arun River.

He describes a number of ethnic groups including the Lapcha (Lepcha), and Bodo Kirat. According to Chemjong, the Limbu are related to the Shan-Mokwan people who migrated from North Burma, via Assam, and settled in east Nepal having gained permission from the eight feudal chiefs (2003: 47-49). Eventually they revolted against these chiefs and, after winning, fixed the borders of their new territory with a "northern boundary in Tibet; the southern boundary in the Indian plain at Jalal Garh near Purnea; the eastern boundary at river Teesta and the western boundary at river Dudkoshi" (2003: 51). They decided to name this new territory Limbuwan and divided it into ten kingdoms to be ruled by the descendants of the "Ten Leaders of Shan-Mokwan people" (ibid.: 52). The kingdom which would have included the village where this research project was carried out was Yangwarok (ibid.: 53), which villagers called Yangrup, and the king Thindolung Khokya Hang "built his fort at Hastapur and ruled Mabo, Thebe, Loksom, Seling, Tamling, Saling, Kambang and other tribes" (ibid.). Mabo is the dominant Limbu clan in Mamangkhe, and most of the others are common clan names in the area east of Taplejung bazaar up to the Kabeli River, traditionally known as the Yangrup kingdom. Chemjong therefore proposes a somewhat confused history of origin for the Limbu which combines the ancient Kirant migration from the west, with the Shan Mokwan, the ascendants of the Limbu, migrating from the east.

There are no clear and consistent accounts of the historical origin of the Limbu, and many ethnographers have dealt with this problem by simply not addressing it in detail. Jones and Jones (1976) for example, wrote that the ten kingdoms of Limbuan "correspond to the legendary founding of Limbuan by ten brothers who are believed to have migrated from Tibet and India" (Jones and Jones 1976: 8) without citing sources, and Caplan (1967, 1970) simply never deals with the early historical period. Subba (1995) offers the theory that the Limbu descended from three groups of "Kiratas": the Lhasagotra who migrated from the north; Kasigotra who migrated from the south and southeast; and the Khambonba-Lungbongba who were indigenous to the area (Subba 1995: 21). He then writes that the original ten brothers may have been residents of Benares at one time and crossed Nepal into Tibet, and five of the ten returned and settled in Limbuvān (ibid.). The origin history of the village, although not consistent across informants, tells a slightly different story to those mentioned above. While the specific details varied, they all referred to Lhasa in Tibet as the origin of all Limbu and none of them made any connection with the ancient Kirats who ruled the Kathmandu valley, though they were aware of the history.

The origin history for the Limbu as told to me by several informants[18] runs roughly like this: There were three brothers who all lived in Lhasa, Tibet. The eldest brother, *jeṭha*, was called Khapeng Hang, but he was lost in Lhasa and never travelled. The second brother, *māila*, was called Tokle Hang, and he travelled to Assam by crossing the Tista River. The third son, *kānchā*, was called Murek Hang, his other name was Lhasa Gotre, and he was the forefather of the Limbu. It was ten brothers, the descendants of Tokle Hang, who defeated the Lepcha who were living in the area and ruled over Limbuwan in separate kingdoms.

These kingdoms are still mentioned by Limbu today to differentiate between different groups. The Limbu of the Mewa and Maiwa areas are considered marginally different from the Limbu of Yangrup, but despite these administrative districts existing right up to the early 1950s, the differences between them are not particularly marked. Generally speaking there is a tremendous amount of cultural and linguistic homogeneity across the whole Limbu population and although there are considered to be four main dialects of Limbu, all of which are classified as Kirānti languages within the Tibeto-Burman language family,[19] the difference between them is not as stark as that between many of the Rai languages. The four dialects of Limbu are Phedāppe, Chathare, Pānchthare and Tamarkhole (or Taplejunge). Pānchthare is the dialect that is being used to promote the language in written form as well as in various forms of media as developed by, for example, the *Kirat Yakthung Chumlung* (Limbu Cultural Association). Tamarkhole is the dialect spoken in the north of Limbuvān and therefore includes the area where this research was conducted. It also includes the valleys of the Mewa and Maiwa rivers where several previous anthropological studies were conducted (Sagant 1996, Michailovsky 2002).

The legal code Muluki Ain of 1854 classified the Limbu as "Enslavable Alcohol-Drinker" (Höfer 1979: 141) situating them below the "Non-

---

18 In particular, Tika, Phul Bahadur, Deoman (Gavisa), and Gaj Bahadur.

19 van Driem (2001: 663-64) classifies Limbu as a Greater Eastern Kiranti language together with Yamphu and Lohorung and in opposition to other Rai languages in the Eastern Kiranti language group, as well as in opposition to Central and Western Kiranti languages.

enslavable Alcohol-Drinker" groups such as Gurung and Lepcha, but above impure and untouchable castes. A later version of the Muluki Ain (1863) reclassified the Limbu as "Non-enslavable Alcohol-Drinker" who could serve in the army (Höfer 1979: 182). More recently, the Nepal Federation of Indigenous Nationalities (NEFIN) and National Foundation for Development of Indigenous Nationalities (NFDIN) have reclassified Janajati[20] groups into four geographical areas (mountain, hill, inner Tarai, and Tarai) and five socioeconomic types (endangered, highly marginalized, marginalized, disadvantaged, and advantaged). The Limbu, who are geographically associated with the 'hill' area, are classed—together with the Gurung, Magar, Rai and other groups—as disadvantaged.

The Mabo(haŋ) clan

Probably the most important distinction between Limbu groups is the clan. There are more than 270 clans, including sub-clans (Subba 1995: 26), with different clans following different food taboos. Subba, quoting Angbohang (1978), writes of sixteen major groups of Limbus, including the Mabohaŋ, Thegim, and Shreng. There are, according to this, 26 subgroups of Mabohaŋ, 11 of whom do not eat buffalo meat. Whether the Mabohaŋ mentioned here are the same as the Mabohang of Mamangkhe is hard to say. Certainly the Mabohang, who call themselves Mabo for short (removing the suffix *hang* or *haŋ* meaning king), are very clearly made up of only 7 sub-clans and all of them eat buffalo meat.

These 7 sub-clans are as follows: Lejenji, Sabara, Hedungba (Mangle), Para, Lungdoyu, Mangar, Lekokwa (Tumbangbe). Each of these have a story associated with their name. The Sabara's ancestor, for example, was said to have looked like a monkey (*sɔba* in Limbu). Marriage is generally not allowed if both individuals are from the same sub-clan. Marriage between sub-clans is allowed only if no marriages between the same two sub-clans have taken place in the last seven generations by either the mother or father's ancestors, though in practice only three to five generations are commonly known and traced back. Members of the same sub-clan will not eat salt, known as *nun*

---

20 The term *janajāti*, meaning 'ethnic community', came into usage in the 1990s to represent ethnic minority groups which did not include Hindu castes of the Tarai.

barnu, for up to 4 days around the period of a relative's funeral. There are many variations to this food taboo, with stricter families fasting for at least one day, some families including a taboo on eating chillies, and some not drinking millet beer since salt and chillies are used in the preparation of *marcha* or *khɛsuŋ* (L.) (yeast cakes) used to ferment the beer.

Information gathered during the baseline survey of the village indicated that there are multiple terms for the same sub-clan name, and that some villagers consider the Hedungba and Mangle or Mangar[21] to be close brothers, that is, close enough not to marry and not to eat salt during the funerals of relatives from either sub-clan. It is thought that up to 58 years ago, the Hedungba and Mangar were of the same sub-clan and that, following the death of Bhagi Dhoj around 1951, the Hedungba did not respect the no-salt rule. This caused a split in the lineage. Since that date, Mangar and Hedungba Mabos have intermarried. At a recent meeting of ex-Subbās and villagers interested in historical matters, held in the village in February 2008, it was decided that since Mangar and Hedungba were actually still brothers, marriage between them should not be permitted and the no-salt rule at funerals needed to be respected across the sub-clan divide. It was suggested that both sub-clans should be called Mangle, though this proposition did not appear to have been widely taken up in the months that followed the meeting.

It is said in the village that the Mabohaŋ came from Tapethok to the north west of Mamangkhe. Originally there were five brothers and the eldest stayed up in Tapethok while the four youngest brothers migrated to the Kabeli River area. As the Mabo split into sub-clans, the Lungdoyu, considered the oldest of the sub-clans, moved to Tharpu, the Hedungba moved to Thechambu, and the Mangar moved to Mamangkhe. The Mangar-Mabo, at least so they claim, are the oldest Limbu inhabitants of Mamangkhe. As the oldest inhabitants of Mamangkhe, much of my genealogical research focused on them.

---

21 There is still considerable confusion and inconsistency in the village about whether the correct term for one sub-clan is *Mangar* or *Mangle*. Some individuals were even insisting that the term should be dropped altogether and only *Hedungba* be used. Generally I prefer to use the term Mangar as this was the most widely used term in Ward 4 where I was based and hence the term I heard most often.

Besides occasional jokes about the origin of clan names, there was little evidence of any inter-clan or sub-clan conflict among the Limbu in the village. There is some rivalry between wards in the village, and wards tend to be dominated by one or another sub-clan group. Yet this is nothing compared to the conflict between higher status Char Jat and historically subservient Sora Jat in Gurung society as described by Messerschmidt (1976).

The Mangar-Mabo

There was only one Mangar Mabo villager who could name his patrilineal ancestors back 13 generations to the ancestor considered to be the first Mangar, having split as a sub-clan from the main Mabo clan. This genealogy starts with Mɛnkho and ends with Phul Bahadur, who was already a great-grandfather in 2007. The names of the ancestors are:

Mɛnkho, Kham sepa, Meandoŋ, Mangme, Sulbimba, Oyamphuŋ, Pakhan Tigɛ, Kemba, Kum Saili, HaŋSiŋle, Chamba Siŋ, Narayan Siŋ, Sattra Haŋ and Phul Bahadur.

Although Mɛnkho is considered the first Mangar Mabo, the split between the Mangar Mabo and the Hedungba or Mangle Mabo began two generations before Mɛnkho. There was said to be a Limbu called Iwa Haŋ who had come from Tibet, and he had two sons: Higɛ', the eldest, who had a son called Hedungba; and Kɛwa, the youngest son of Iwa Haŋ, who had a son called Mɛnkho. There is a story about the origin of the term "Mangar" for the Limbu sub-clan. The story goes that Mɛnkho's father was actually a Magar—pronounced Mangar in Nepali—who had travelled to the far east of Nepal from his own village in the west and had slept with a Limbu woman. The great-grandson of Mɛnkho was called Mangme to refer to his Magar origins, and it is from there that the sub-clan name "Mangar" was derived. In recent years there has been a revived interest in Limbu history with an attempt made by a group of Lungdoyu-Mabo from different villages to produce a comprehensive genealogical chart for the sub-clan which goes back 10 generations from the oldest living Lungdoyu, although there were apparently a number of mistakes with this chart. The Mangar-Mabo have also put together their genealogical chart but have yet to print it out. A prominent village shaman, a Mangar Mabo, is studying the Limbu script with the intention of eventually writing out what he knows of Limbu oral history and mythology, known as *mundhum* (L.). This interest in Limbu history and the renewed interest in the Limbu script, as witnessed by the introduction of Limbu language classes in the local school, parallels the general rise in ethnic awareness and activism throughout Nepal over the last decade, though most noticeably during and after the last years of the Maoist "People's War".

The Limbu today

The fact that such debates as: should members of two sub-clans be allowed to marry, should the no-salt eating rule be respected during funerals, or should the Mangar-Mabo actually call themselves Mangle-Mabo, are still held in the village, indicates the importance that Limbu cultural categories still have today. Beyond the Limbu though, restrictions on marriage, food and ritual taboos, and the associated caste-based notions of clean and unclean or impure groups within communities, still exist throughout Nepal. The lower-caste groups in Nepal, such as the tailors and blacksmiths who live in Mamangkhe village, are considered by most of the Limbu, as well as the upper-caste Hindu population, to be ritually unclean, *pāni na chalne jāt*. Food and water cooked or served by them is not accepted by either the Limbu or Brahmin and Chhetri groups. They are never invited into houses and sit on benches on the veranda outside the doorways to houses they visit. The exceptions to this are a small number of Limbu supporters of the Maoist movement and a small number of shopkeepers who allow any customers into their house to consume food and drinks. In total, approximately six Limbu households allowed lower-caste villagers into their houses and started doing so in 2002. For an outsider, these seemed to be behavioural habits, more than anything else, which would take a specific conscious effort to change. In the few cases where families had adopted the unusual position of ignoring caste-based rules of purity, it seemed to have been either a result of financial incentive or ideological conviction.

A different form of ideological conviction can, in part, be said to have encouraged the survival of one of the most important elements of Limbu cultural life: the Limbu language. The widespread use of the Limbu language is a significant feature of Mamangkhe village. The village has a reputation for being a particularly "Limbu" village in comparison with other villages along the Kabeli River valley and villages closer to Taplejung bazaar. Villagers often commented with pride that Limbu was one of the few languages in Nepal with its own script. The Limbu script used today was revived in the early 1970s by the Limbu scholar Iman Singh Chemjong (Imānsiṃha Cemjoṅ). This was a slightly elaborated version of a script originally invented in the early 18th century by a monk living in Sikkim called Sirijaṅgā, who was also known as the "Lama of Yangrup", since he originally came from Tellok village half a day's walk down river from Mamangkhe. Books written using this Kirānti script featured both indigenous Limbu deities and myths, and those of the Buddhist doctrine. It is said that as a result of the success of the new script and the growth of Limbus' sense of ethnic identity, Sirijaṅgā was considered a threat to the aristocracy and murdered for the King by monks. Limbu books were destroyed both in Sikkim and later in Nepal by the Rānā regime and it was only because B. H. Hodgson and R. K. Sprigg managed to salvage a small number of books in the 1950s and take them to London, that the script was saved and reintroduced years later. The only other available work on the original Limbu script was that of A. Campbell who in 1855 had published a copy of the script (Campbell 1855).

Since the "People's Movement" of 1990, there has been a growth of Limbu language popular writings, magazines and school books using both Devanāgarī and the Limbu script. G. van Driem (2001) notes that 38 primary schools in Limbuvān teach Limbu language for grades 1 and 2, though this must have increased in the last few years since school books are now available through to grade 5. Mamangkhe is the only village in the whole of the Kabeli River valley that has a compulsory Limbu language course in its schools (books published in Bhaktapur, Nepal). In Sikkim, where the Limbu script has been in use since the 1970s, secondary school level courses are available and there is a continuous exchange of teaching and reading materials between Sikkim, Darjeeling and Nepal. The increased use of the Limbu script in printed media (Shneiderman and Turin 2006: 57, van Driem 2001: 676) and the interest in teaching the Limbu language are both part of the wider politicisation of ethnicity and ethnic activism since the 1990s (Gellner et al. 1997). This politicisation is not in fact a new phenomenon when one remembers the continual resistance shown by the Limbu against the expanding Gorkha kingdom from the 18th right through to the mid 20th century.

Certainly much of the more explicit political activism of the Limbu seems to have faded during the years after the formal abolition of Limbu traditional land tenure and the Land Reform Act of 1964. Although there was opposition to land reform, for many families the possibility of being freed from debt or being allowed officially to lay claim to tracts of land was an advantage. The last political act before this had been the uprising against the Rana regime by the Limbu between 1950 and 1951. According to Whelpton, although the Newar also felt strong resentment towards Rana rule and against the British and Parbatiyas, "it was among the Limbus of the eastern hills that ethnic particularism was strongest. Plans for a declaration of independence in 1950/1 were never fully implemented but there was violence against Brahmans, some of whom had to take temporary refuge in the Tarai" (Whelpton 2005: 162). According to Whelpton, it was newer Limbu leaders and not the traditional Limbu headmen, the *subbas*, who stood in local elections during the setting up of the new Panchayat system in 1962, and as a result it was these same leaders who finally gave in to the Land Reform Acts and the abolition of kipat. While the *subbas* continued to be important symbols of the Limbu tradition, they had lost much political authority. To put it more bluntly "the old vehicle of Limbu ethnic assertiveness had lost its effectiveness, and the Limbus were slow to organize newer ones" (Whelpton 2005: 180). The "People's Movement" of 1990, which forced the King to lift the ban on political parties, allowed far greater ethnic activism to take place than there had been even before the 1950s. Levels of education had increased throughout Nepal and this, combined with the legalisation of political parties, allowed groups to demand greater recognition of their language, culture, economic and political needs (ibid.: 178-9).

Before 1990, there was only one Limbu periodical, called *Pāruhāṅg* (van Driem 2001: 676). In 1989, the Kirat Yakthung Chumlung (KYC), a national Limbu cultural organization, was established and in 1990 it was registered with the government. Also in 1990, the Nepal Federation of Indigenous Nationalities (NEFIN) was established (although it was originally known as the Nepal Federation of Nationalities or NEFEN) with the support of various smaller ethnic organizations such as the KYC. The KYC now publish a Limbu monthly known as *Taːnchoːppa*, as well as a number of literary magazines, booklets, and, together with the more recently established Limbu Language Development Association

(LiLDA) more substantial works of non-fiction, fiction and poetry. In 2007, the KYC completed the construction of a large new office building in Kathmandu which contains a large conference hall, offices, classrooms, and a library. Although not strictly a political organization, one of the eleven objectives of the KYC is to "undertake activities for the achievement of Limbuwan autonomy under the federal system to ensure country's national integrity and sovereignty" (KYC website). Political movements have also gained strength since the 1990s, some of which were extremely active in the run-up to the Constituent Assembly elections in 2008 and continue to be active since the elections.

The *Limbuwan Mukti Morcha* (Limbuwan Liberation Front) was the first political party to call for the formation of an autonomous Limbuwan region in east Nepal, but it was not allowed to run in the 1990 general elections. After the Maoist "People's War" ended in November 2006, the Federal Limbuwan State Council (FLSC) became increasingly active organizing strikes and blockades in east Nepal during the lead up to the elections, uniting with other political parties in 2007 to demand, among other things, a Federal Democratic Nepal with ethnically based autonomous states. The FLSC, together with other autonomy movements such as the Tamangsaling Autonomous State Council and the United Tharu National Front, formed the umbrella organization Federal National Democratic Forum, which was registered in January 2008, just in time for the April 2008 elections where they won 2 of the 601 seats in the Constituent Assembly. Since the elections, various political factions have continued to call for the creation of an autonomous Limbu state. Most recently, the Limbuwan Autonomous Concerned Forum stated it had joined the *Limbuwan Mukti Morcha* (which is affiliated to the Maoist Communist Party of Nepal).

While the activities of the political movements calling for an autonomous Limbu state are mainly concentrated in the southern districts of Jhapa, Morang and Sunsari, the impact of their strikes and the disruption of transport and access to the northern districts have a significant effect on communities everywhere. At the village level, although there is considerable variation of opinion about the activities of these groups, there is a widespread sense of both distrust of the government and the need for autonomous economic change. The former is most noticeable in the general lack of discussion and interest in governmental politics, with the exception of the month leading up to the elections in April 2008, and conversations about whether there is a strike or blockade, a *bandh*, going on or not. The sense of a need for economic change results partly from the experiences of Limbu villagers who have been abroad and returned with enough savings to reduce their debts, purchase land and property, and provide private education for their children. In large part this sense is based on the historical experience of Parbatiya settlers who migrated to the village and within a few generations had raised enough capital to migrate to urban centres in the south. While the call for an autonomous Limbuwan state is raised by ethnic activists in the new political space created by the "People's Movement" and the Maoist insurgency, politics generally remains far from everyday life in the village.

The Limbu of today, at least those in the village, seem to be repeating the pattern of economic success and migration that numerous Parbatiya settlers so successfully carried out. With the recent introduction of cardamom as a cash-crop, and the increased availability of market goods, economic patterns of production and consumption have changed dramatically. Despite this, certain elements of Limbu culture, such as language use and ritual practises, are as resilient as ever. This book is therefore a study of both change, particularly economic change partly caused and supported by cardamom production, and a study of resilience. In the sections above on Limbu history, I have emphasized the element of resistance for which the Limbu became renowned. Historically, resistance was largely a political act carried out by the Limbu against the Gorkha Kingdom and Hindu settlers. Since the formal abolition of *kipat*, the absorption of many of the political concerns of the Limbu by national parties such as the Maoists, and the assimilation of the Limbu into economic modes of production much like everyone else, cultural resistance has become a means by which Limbu villagers can continue to emphasize their autonomy from a state still dominated by a high-caste Hindu minority.[22]

Recent ethnography

In the nineteenth century, reports (with some ethnographic detail) on the Kirānti in east Nepal were generally limited to the works of Hamilton

---

22 According to the Nepal Census (2001), the Chhetri and Brahmin populations combined were 29% of the total population.

(1819), Campbell (1840), and Hodgson (2001[1880], 1858). These were followed by two categories of publication: works on non-Limbu Kirānti groups which mention the Limbu; and works on Nepali ethnic groups in general, and particularly ethnic groups associated with the "Gurkha" soldiers of the British Army, which include the Limbu. The first category includes work on the Khambus (Bell 1903) and Jimdār Rāi (Barnouw 1955). Barnouw even notes that "no ethnologist has yet done field work among the Rais and Limbus in Nepal itself, although a few writers have briefly described some of their customs" (Barnouw 1955: 15). The second category includes the work of Adam (1936), who briefly describes "tribal organization" and the "institutions of Nepalese civil law", but only mentions the Limbu twice: once in reference to the number of clans they have (he suggests 62, although clearly there are many more), and later, in reference to food taboos, when he mentions that some Limbu do not eat the flesh of a certain bird. A little more detail is provided in accounts of the Gurkha soldiers containing descriptions of Kirānti groups. Vansittart's book *The Gurkhas* (Vansittart 1906[1890]) was the first of this kind, and was followed by Northey and Morris' own *The Gurkhas* (1928) which includes a complete chapter on the Limbu (1928: 213-37). Both authors later published their own *Gurkha* books (Morris 1933; Northey 1937). There is only one work from this period which focuses entirely on the Limbu (Biswas 1934/35: 481-82) but it provides little more than a cursory glance at the ethnic group.

With the formal end of the Rana regime in 1951, it became easier for foreign researchers to travel and work in Nepal. In the 1950s, Christoph von Fürer-Haimendorf was one of the first foreign anthropologists to be allowed into Nepal, and although he initially focused on the Sherpa (Fürer-Haimendorf 1964), he travelled through much of the country, often accompanied by the Nepali anthropologist Dor Bahadur Bista. Bista's (1972) overview of Nepali ethnic groups in his *People of Nepal* was originally published in 1967 and includes a fairly detailed chapter on the Limbu. This was one of the first ethnographic accounts of the Limbu and although it was not based on long-term fieldwork, it provides a useful overview of Limbu society and culture.

In the 1960s, anthropologists first began carrying out fieldwork based on long-term research in Nepal. The focus of research shifted from the broader and less detailed studies of Nepali ethnic groups in general, or the Kirānti in particular, to village-based studies of particular ethnic groups among the Kirānti such as the Limbu and various Rāi groups. One of the first ethnographic studies of the Limbu was carried out by Lionel Caplan between 1964 and 1965 in a settlement close to Ilam bazaar in east Nepal. Caplan (1967, 1970, 1972, 1990, 1991) studied the process by which Limbu-owned kipat gradually became converted to privately owned land by high-caste Hindus who had migrated to the area. His study is extremely critical of high-caste Hindus who are portrayed as economically exploiting the Limbu, appropriating their land, and causing the erosion of traditional kipat land rights. His study was critiqued by Dahal (1996), in a short article, which raises a number of methodological problems: first, he accuses Caplan of incorrectly generalizing the behaviour of all Brahmins from an extrapolation based on his study of two Brahmin brothers; and second, Caplan is accused of simplifying social relations to a high-caste Hindu versus Limbu dichotomy, when in fact high-caste Hindus were also taking land from other Hindu villagers.

Despite this, Caplan's work is still considered a landmark piece of anthropological research in the way it is able to combine a detailed, village-level study of economic and social relations together with the larger history of land ownership in Nepal, all at a time when kipat was about to be formally abolished by the state. A similar study to Caplan's was carried out by Upreti (1975).

The most comprehensive study of the Limbu was carried out by Philippe Sagant who worked between 1966 and 1971 in the Mewa Valley in Taplejung district, east Nepal. Focusing particularly on ritual, history, political organization, technology and to some extent economics, he published a large number of articles in French, a number of which were eventually translated and published in his book *The Dozing Shaman* (1996). The ethnographic detail and variety of subjects he focused on is remarkable (Sagant 1969 a,b; 1970, 1973, 1976 a,b,c,d; 1978 a,b; 1980, 1981, 1982, 1983, 1985, 1987). One subject that Sagant did not deal in depth with was the ongoing economic transformation of Limbu society as a result of increased market integration, migration, and new economic opportunities. These are concerns which have become increasingly important in Nepal since the 1960s and 1970s when Caplan and Sagant carried out their fieldwork.

The only other ethnographic study conducted among the Limbu was that of R.L. Jones and S.K. Jones who carried out fieldwork in

Tehrathum between 1967 and 1969 (Jones R.L. 1973, 1974, 1976a, 1976b; Jones and Jones 1976). Their focus was on the institution of marriage, domestic organization, and the role of women in Limbu society. With the exception of one article (Jones 1976a), their work emphasizes the stability of Limbu society and pays little attention to the broader economic and political dynamics of change discussed in the work of Caplan and Sagant. A number of other ethnographic studies based on less systematic and shorter fieldwork, yet valuable nonetheless, include: Chaitanya Subba's (1995) overview of Limbu culture and religion, which often reads more like a list than description; and Tanka Bahadur Subba's (1999) comparative study of three Kirata communities, which includes the village of Tangnam in Panchthar district, east Nepal.

Aside from the ethnographic studies mentioned above, a large amount of research has been conducted on the Limbu language, perhaps more than on any other aspect of Limbu society and culture. This research began with the work of scholars such as Kirkpatrick (1811), Campbell (1855), Hodgson (1858) and Senior (1977[1908]), who were the first to list Limbu words in their original and with English equivalents. Konow (1909: 283-304) was one of the first scholars to provide a grammar of Limbu, followed by Sprigg (1959) who attempted to classify Limbu verbs. The most comprehensive study of the Limbu language was carried out by the scholar Iman Singh Chemjong's (2002), who published the first tri-lingual dictionary in 1962. The first linguistic anthropologist to work on the Limbu language was Michailovsky (1986, 1993, 1999, 2002) who worked on the Tamarkhole dialect in Taplejung between 1977 and 1978. Weidert was the first to work on the Panthare dialect of Limbu, publishing a collaborative grammar of Limbu (Weidert and Subba 1985). George van Driem (1987, 1997, 1999), who carried out research on the Phedāppe dialect as spoken in a village in Tehrathum district between 1984 and 1985, published *A Grammar of Limbu* (1987). Around this time, the fourth dialect of Chathare Limbu was being studied by the native speaker Tumbahang (1986) with the completion of a descriptive grammar in 2007 (Tumbahang 2007).

This overview of most of the recent ethnography on the Limbu shows that although linguistic research has been carried out continuously since the mid 20th century, social and cultural anthropology on the Limbu has suffered from a considerable gap to date since the work of Caplan, Sagant and the two Jones in the 1960s and 1970s. In addition to this 30-year research gap, no work has been conducted on the Limbu in eastern Taplejung. This particular research project was undertaken with the hope of contributing a contemporary perspective on the Limbu of the somewhat lesser-known area of east Taplejung, an area known in the past as Yangrup. It shares many of the concerns that Caplan (1970) raised in his study of Limbu-Brahmin relations but provides more perspective on the economic and social history of a village, focusing in particular on the transformative effect of the recently introduced cardamom plant. By focusing on a more remote Limbu village, it was, *a priori*, assumed that conditions would be diverse from the areas studies by Caplan and, in particular, that kipat would have lasted much longer. However, as it transpired, economic relations between the Limbu and high-caste Hindus were very similar in both the village Caplan studied and the one selected for my research (Mamangkhe). Additionally, the variable of cardamom cultivation, which was absent in Ilam during the 1960s, made the research site ideally suited for studying economic change.

Conclusion

This chapter has dealt with a number of themes ranging from the historical and mythological origin of the Limbu to the political economic relations between the Limbu and the Nepali state, and between Limbu villagers and non-Limbu migrants during the 18th and 19th centuries. The central historical period outlined in this chapter is the Gorkha conquest of east Nepal. It is as a consequence of the Gorkha conquest that some of the most fundamental issues that this book deals with emerged in the first place. These include: the issue of Limbu political autonomy (resistance to the Gorkha state) which has strongly marked contemporary Limbu political and cultural self-awareness; and the expansion of non-Limbu migration into Limbuwan encouraged by land grants provided by the state, which resulted in a transformation of the rural economy (and culture) through new technological inputs and the monetization of land and social relations (e.g. usury). The arrival of non-Limbu migrants into the village set off a number of profound social, economic and ecological changes the effects of which are ongoing to this day. Paired with the somewhat more recent introduction of the high-value cardamom cash-crop, the village of Mamangkhe has been significantly transformed over the last 150 years from a subsistence-based community of Limbu villagers to a market-oriented—through both cash-crop production and labour-migration—community of Limbu and non-Limbu Nepalis. This shift of orientation towards the market (cash-cropping) and away from the village (labour-migration) has impacted the lives of villagers in different ways: some have benefited economically and with access to capital have been able to purchase property outside the village, pay for private education and finance more expensive (and lucrative) visas for work abroad; others have inevitably been drawn into increased debt and economic precariousness.

Chapter 3
Mamangkhe Village

Location, climate, and physical layout

Taplejung district lies in the far north-eastern corner of Nepal and shares borders with Sikkim (India) to the east and the Tibet Autonomous Region of China to the north. To the south lie the other three districts that make up the Mechi Zone, Panchthar, Ilam and Jhapa, and to the west the districts of Sankhuwasabha and Terhathum in the Koshi Zone. The district is located within latitude 27°16'00 to 27°57'00 N and longitude 87°27'00 to 88°12'00 E, and has a total area of 3,628 sq. km., almost half of which comprises the Kanchenjunga Conservation Area. 87% of the district's land is classified as either High Himalaya or High Mountain, with only 13% in the Middle Mountain range. In other words, much of the district is either uninhabited or sparsely and seasonally inhabited with much of the denser settlement distributions concentrated in the south-west of the district. Much of this high Himalayan land is traversed by snow-fed rivers that originate in the north, and with 70% of the land on slopes of 30 degrees or greater, rates of erosion are extremely high (TRPAP 2005: 10).

Climatic conditions in the district range from sub-tropical in the south to Alpine in the north and north-east. In 2004, the annual rainfall in Taplejung was 1,746 mm with a temperature ranging from 27.6 to 0.2 degrees centigrade (CBS 2006).[23] River valleys below 1,000m are characterized by dry winters and hot summers, and a generally warm but humid climate prevails up to 2,000m. Between 2,000m and 3,000m the mean annual temperature falls between 10 to 15 degrees centigrade, and anything above this experiences an Alpine climate with subzero

---

23 Data from the Department of Hydrology and Meteorology weather station in Taplejung bazaar.

temperatures for several months of the year. The village area is generally cooler throughout the summer months than villages downstream, receives a little more rainfall, and has a less severe winter than the next village up, Yamphudin. The district has one large river, the Tamur (or Tamor), and a number of smaller river or tributaries which all join the Tamur River and flow south-west to join the Arun River which eventually flows into the Ganges in India.

Figure 4: View of the village and the Himalayas facing north.

The Kabeli *kholā*, with its source in the eastern Himalayan peaks of the Nepal-Sikkim border, flows in a south-westerly direction until it joins the much larger River Tamur. Another river, the Khaksewa, flows in a south-easterly direction and joins the Kabeli *kholā* to the south of the village settlement before winding round a large ridge (*Phumphe ḍā̃ḍā*) and heading almost due south. It is from this ridge that one has the best view of the Mamangkhe village, nestled inside the V-shape created by the two rivers (Figure 4). The settlements of Pauwa and Mamangkhe, among others, are clustered along the slopes of the eastern side of the Khaksewa *kholā* valley. This steeply sloping hillside rises to a

Figure 5: View of Wards 3, 4 and 5 facing south.

Figure 6: Two houses in Ward 3 built by a Chhetri villager in 1958.

Figure 7: A much smaller newly built Limbu house in Ward 4.

height of 3,627 m. north of the settlements and provides the two natural resources fundamental to life in the village: water and forest. The more scattered settlements of Khandin, Sudap and Phumphe lie on the western side of the Khaskewa *kholā* on a more gently sloping hillside. With a total area of some 37 sq. km., the VDC has some 18 sq. km. with slopes in excess of 40 degrees, and 14.5 sq. km. with slopes of between 30 and 40 degrees. Only 4.5 sq. km. of land, equivalent to some 12% of the total area, is on a slope of less than 30 degrees (TRPAP 2005: 92).

There are 713 settlements in the district (TRPAP 2005: 8) divided into 50 Village Development Committees (VDC), 11 *Ilakas*, and two constituencies. As one of the VDC's, Mamangkhe is divided into nine wards, each with a specific name and boundary. The VDC occupies an area of 37.16 sq. km. (TRPAP 2005: 83). The settlements on the western side of the Khaksewa *kholā* come under two wards: Ward 8, which takes the name of the larger settlement of Sudap, and Ward 9 which is known as Phumphe. The focus of this book is almost entirely based on the people in the settlements of the seven remaining wards distributed along the south-facing slopes to the east of the Khaksewa *kholā* and north of the Kabeli *kholā.*[24]

These settlements are concentrated into four main areas which although physically close are divided by both natural boundaries and the difficulty of walking between. The settlements lie between latitude 27°24'00 to 27°26'00 N and longitude 87°52'00 to 87°53'00 E, with a distance of roughly three kilometres from one side of the village to the other. The Kabeli *kholā* runs through the village at an altitude of 1,500 metres, descending to 1320 metres before joining the Khaksewa *kholā.* Settlements are concentrated between 1,500 and 2,000 metres, with the largest school and shops located at 1,600 metres.

The first settlement reached after crossing the Khaksewa River, is Pauwa, with Ward 7 located above the main path through the village, and Ward 6 along and below this path. A relatively steep uphill walk through Ward 6 leads, after crossing two streams that cut the hillside and separate many of the wards on this side of the village, up to Ward 5. This is what most villagers refer to when they speak of "Mamangkhe" as a village, though it is formally referred to as *iskul ḍãḍā* (school ridge). The houses here mostly lie below the main path and there are multiple smaller paths that wind their way down towards the river. Safe access to the river, a 20 minute walk down a steep slippery path through cardamom forests, is only available from Ward 4. This ward, further around the hillside as it curves in a little, is one of the smallest and most of the houses are perched either above or below the main path. Part of Ward 3 is hidden from view by a large ridge slightly below the main path. This is the lower part of the ward, surrounded by rice paddy and is known as Tekadin. The other part of Ward 3 is below Ward 4, but further east. The main path to the village of Khewang, across the Kabeli *kholā* runs through this part of the village. The houses in both wards 1 and 2 lie mostly above the main path, in two settlement areas known as Totrua and Thumbimba, respectively. These settlements dot the hillside north and east of Ward 4. The most remote settlement is Thobabuk, still in Ward 1, separated from the main settlement area by the Hān *kholā* and a 30 to 40 minute walk from the school in Ward 5.

---

24 Throughout this book the terms "village" and "Mamangkhe" refer to these 7 wards, whereas the terms "VDC" or "Mamangkhe VDC" refer to the political entity which includes all 9 wards.

As with most villages in mountainous parts of the Himalayas, verticality is an important feature of life, both for ecological and cultural reasons.[25] Most of the natural resources used by villagers can be found along a vertical plane that runs from the river below the village, to the Alpine shrubs high above. The numerous streams that physically divide wards, are also the site of cardamom cultivation and clusters of bamboo plants. Apart from bamboo, alder and walnut trees, and small shrubs for fodder and fruit, most of the area surrounding settlements is terraced and cultivated. Both above and below the settlement areas are cardamom-planted forest and fairly dense uncultivated mixed forest. These are a source of year-round fodder for the livestock that most families keep. Above the upper forest, often between one to three hours walk, are the *mālingo* bamboo forests, source of a valuable and thin type of bamboo plant used for weaving baskets and sturdy mats. Below the village and the lowest forests runs the Kabeli *kholā*, an abundant source of fish, particularly *asalā* (*Schizothorax richardsonii*) and *tite* (*Psilorhynchus pseudecheneis*), named for its bitter flavour.[26]

History of Limbu settlement in the village

It was difficult to obtain exact information about the very early history of the village and of the Limbu in the area. However, from the genealogical charts collected, it appears that the Limbu arrived in the

---

25 Allen (1972) examined directionality in the Thulung Rai language, and Bickel (1997, 1999) examined spatial operations in the Belhare language. In the Limbu language, for example, a number of verbs include notions of direction within them. There are at least three different words for the verb 'to come': *phɛmma*, which contains no notion of verticality; *yuma*, which means 'to come down' and is used to describe descending to a lower area, as well as the verbs sitting and staying; and *thaŋma* which is used to describe ascending, or coming up from below. The same is true for verbs like 'to bring', with *yu:tma* meaning 'to bring down from above', and *thakma* meaning 'to bring up from below'.

26 The *tite* or bitter fish is particularly valued and appears only a few times during the rainy season. During the festival of *sāun sankrānti* (the first day of the fourth month *sāun*, July-August), children visit each other's homes and celebrate by eating cucumbers, *tite* fish, and singing about the abundance of the last few months: "*tite māchā khāyaū, phārsi khāyaū, iskus khāyaū...*" (we ate bitter fish, we ate pumpkin, we ate chayote). The other fish, *asalā*, is less prized but nonetheless appreciated—if only for the change it provides from buffalo and pig meat. While *tite* is only available for a few months a year, *asalā* is available almost year round, though a swollen river (after heavy rainfall) can make it harder to catch fish.

village between 15 and 16 generations ago, although there was no sense of an ancestral Limbu "founder" in the village.

Before living in their current houses, the Limbu lived in the forest, hunting and gathering wild fruits and yams. According to legends described to me by villagers in wards 4 and 5, the first settlement in Mamangkhe was a *yaksa* (L), or temporary shelter, made by leaning a bamboo and woven-leaf structure against a large boulder which is still visible today in the vicinity of two of the oldest houses in Ward 4 of the village. The first Chhetri ancestor, arriving around 1825, and thus well after the first Limbu, did not build a formal house structure until a few generations later, living in a *goṭ* (cattle shed) made of stones and wood. This must have been a little more substantial than the fairly impermanent *yaksa* structure. There is no clear data on the first permanent house structure built in the village. It seems likely that the Chhetri Kharel family who settled in lower Ward 3 around 1895, first built what is now the ubiquitous stone-wood-thatch structure that is seen everywhere in the village, and indeed in Nepal. Together with new agricultural technologies and techniques, Chhetri farmers arriving from across the Kabeli *kholā* must surely have brought this additional knowledge with them.

There are at least four houses which are thought of as the very first built by Limbu villagers. Makkhar Dhoj, six generations ago, built one of the earliest houses in what is now Tumbimba, in Ward 2, in 1893. Around this time Narayan Singh is said to have built his house just below the large boulder in Ward 4, in 1903. Sometime after this, two more houses were built, one in Ward 4, close to Narayan Singh's house, and one in Ward 5, slightly below the present-day school. Generally though, the area around this large boulder in Ward 4 is considered one of the first permanent settlements of the Limbu, together with the area by the main path in Tumbimba. The Chhetri may have built houses earlier than this, but did so some distance from the main Limbu settlements, in either upper Ward 2, or lower Ward 3.

Ward 4 may have been one of the first areas in the village to be permanently settled, with two of the four oldest houses. Also, the households are, with only one exception, all from the Mangar Mabo sub-clan,[27] the largest sub-clan in the village as a whole. This is the only

---

27 There are 21 households in Ward 4. There were five households which, for various reasons, had no adult male at the time of interview. The women in

ward in the village with just one sub-clan represented within it. Elsewhere, the Mangar Mabo are concentrated in wards 4 and 5, with some presence in all the other wards. The Hedungba Mabo sub-clan are concentrated in Ward 7, with only very few in the other wards, and none in wards 2, and 5. Finally, the last large sub-clan in the village, the Lungdoyu Mabo, are also mostly concentrated in Ward 7, with a few families in all the other wards except Ward 4. Non-Limbu families are concentrated into either wards 6 and 7, in the case of the Sārkī (cobbler caste) and Kāmī (blacksmith caste), Ward 5 for the Damai (tailor caste), and Ward 1 for the Gurung. The data gathered from the survey on sub-clan names and locations in the village do not necessarily correspond to the original distribution of the different sub-clans. Certainly in the case of the non-Limbu groups, families have not moved far from the land they inhabited when their ancestors first arrived. In the case of the Limbu though, there has been considerable movement within the village as the population size has continued to grow and families have sought land beyond the amount available to them from their parents and ancestors. In other words, it is quite likely that some 100 years ago there would have been more equivalence between the location of a household and the sub-clan it belonged to.

History of non-Limbu settlement

A more detailed history of the Bahun-Chhetri families who moved into the village is presented in Chapter 6, in which the lives of two Chhetri villagers, their ancestry and their relevance to contemporary lives is outlined. Briefly though, it is believed that one Chhetri villager, Ram Krishna Bhattarai, visited the village as early as 1789, eventually settling more permanently in 1825. Another Chhetri villager, Sirbelas Kharel, arrived approximately 70 years later, settling into lower Ward 3 in around 1895. There were very little data available on estimated dates of arrival of other Bahun-Chhetri families, and other non-Limbu families arrived much later, beginning possibly with the Gurung.

The first Gurung to arrive in the village was Man Bahadur Gurung, who bought land from a Sangraula (Chhetri) in 1945, before moving soon afterwards to a property in Ward 5, and leaving the village in 1983. The Gurung families who currently live in Ward 1 are only distantly

---

these households are all married to Mangar Mabo men.

related to Man B. Gurung, although they also moved to the village from a small settlement close to Yamphudin known as Yokhim. They are second generation inhabitants, arriving at a similar period to many of the lower-caste, or Dalit families such as the Kāmī and Sārkī. These Gurung families are said to have arrived with considerable wealth and were able to purchase large tracts of land above the main settlement areas. They were thus able to benefit from access to both agricultural land and pastoral land. The first Kāmī to arrive in the village was Bhirka Bahadur Gadaili, who came from Chyangthapu VDC in Panchthar district around 1943, some 65 years ago.[28] The five Kāmī households, all of whom are related to Bhirka B., all live in Ward 7. Unlike the Gurung, the Kāmī settled on small plots of land which have become still smaller over the generations since they arrived. Of all the Dalit households in the village, the Kāmī are by far the poorest. The Sārkī families are also all descended from one forefather who moved to the village in the 1940s, and all three households live just below the main path out of the village in Ward 6. Similarly to the Gurung, and unlike the Kāmī, the Sārkī were able to purchase considerable amounts of land when they originally settled in the village, as a result of which several Sārkī families are today among the wealthiest in the village. Finally, there are three Damai households in Ward 5. These are all descended from Chabi Lal, who also came to the village around 1940 and settled on a plot of land just below the school, which at the time belonged to a Chhetri, Lakshmi Prasad Koraria. Economically, the Damai lie somewhere between the Sārkī and Kāmī, having been able to purchase enough land to be somewhat self-sufficient: Damai households own double the per capita figure for land compared to the Kāmī, but half that of the Sārkī.

While it is difficult to obtain data for all the arrivals and departures of non-Limbu families since they first started to migrate to the area, there are two general points that emerge from this study. First, Bahun-

---

28 Although I had assumed that the Kāmī were also invited to the village, in the same way as the Khorel family had been, I was unable to verify this. The Kāmī men I spoke with said their ancestors had simply arrived in the village and bought some land, although a number of Limbu men in neighbouring houses said they thought that the subba who previously controlled land in the area had offered some land in return for tools and metal-work. No one seemed to know for certain how the Kāmī had ended up living in Ward 7 of the village, though it is most likely the case that their arrival was linked to the initiation of rice agriculture and the need for metal-tipped ploughs and other implements.

Chhetri families started to migrate and settle in the area as early as 1789, not long after the "Kirats were assured that the status quo would be maintained" by the then King of Nepal, Pritivi Narayan Shah in 1774 (Pradhan 1991: 183).[29] Second, all of the other non-Limbu families now living in various parts of the village, arrived within the first few years of the 1940s.

Overview of Village in 2007

Most of the data for this section was derived from the base-line survey covering the 201 households of wards 1 to 7 during August and September 2007. Supplementary data came from both the Nepal Census 2001, and a publication called the "Tourism Resource Mapping Profile" for Taplejung District (TRPAP 2005). The first section provides summary statistics on demography, household size, density of households by ward, and more general data on marriage, education and language use, infrastructure and services in the village. While the study focus is largely on wards 1 to 7, it occasionally makes us of VDC-wide data for comparative purposes.

Demography

The total population of Mamangkhe (wards 1 to 7) recorded as living in the village at the time of the survey was 968, in a total of 201 households, giving an average population of 4.8 persons per household. Although there are no figures available for life expectancy in the village, there are 15 household heads in wards 1 to 7 over the age of 70, and 6 villagers over the age of 80, which gives some indication of a reasonably high life expectancy.

Together with these figures though, one has to also consider the relatively high accidental death rate in the village. Again there are no exact figures for this but during the total period of 18 months in and out of the village, four male villagers died in accidents. Three of these men died while hunting, and one of them died slipping off a trail on a walk through the forest. In such a small village, these are extremely high

---

29 This assurance was reinforced by the *Tasali Patra ko Lal Mohor* [The agreement between "Kirat ministers of Bijaypur and the Gorkha Raja Prithvi Narayn Shah in 1774" (Chemjong 2003[1967]: 206-209)], mentioned in Chapter 1 (Nepal and the Limbu).

figures. The trails around the village, and even the main trail from the village, are steep, uneven, and frequently bounded to one side by a perilous drop or cliff.

Of the total 201 households in the village, 179 (almost 90%), were Limbu, and 23 households were non-Limbu. The largest non-Limbu ethnic group were the Chhetri, with six households. Table 1 shows this distribution more clearly:

Ethnic group or caste	Number of households	Population	Percentage of total population	Distribution (wards)
Rai (Sampang)	1	4	0.4	5
Sārkī (Bail Kuthi)	3	15	1.5	7
Damai -	4	25	2.6	5
Bardewa	-3-	-	-	-
Tatalo	-1-	-	-	-
Gurung (Raul)	4	21	2.2	1
Kāmī (Gadaili)	5	36	3.7	7
Chhetri -	6	22	2.3	
Bhattarai	-3-	-	-	1 & 2
Basnet	-1-	-	-	2
Gautam (Jaisi)	-1-	-	-	5
Siva koti	-1-	-	-	6
Limbu	178	845	87.3	All
Total	**201**	**968**	**100**	

Table 1: Number of households, population, percentage of total population and distribution of Limbu and non-Limbu households

Of the 178 Limbu households, 164 (92%) of them were of the Mabo clan. The next most frequent Limbu clans were Bhega, three households, and Thebe, also three households.[30] The remaining eight households

---

30 There is a definite sense—both within the village and outside it—that the Mabo clan is the most strongly associated with the history and identity of the village. Yet there was little evidence, besides very mild teasing by using sub-clan names as nicknames (either by adding the sub-clan name to a villager's forename—Lakshmi-Tamling—or by calling villagers by their sub-clan name—Lauti, in the case of Dil Kumari) of any tension or discrimination between sub-clans. Sub-clans are associated with geographical locations (villages, towns, valleys) and discussions about differences between sub-clans (dialect, behavioural habits) are always discussions about the differences between Limbus living in different parts of the district or country.

were all of other clans, including Lingden and Tamling. These were almost all households headed by women whose husband had either died or left the village. In one case, the Tamling household, the son of a Mabo woman returned to the village with his mother after his father married another woman. It was a "Tamling" household in the sense that the next generation born within that household would be of the Tamling clan. Five of the seven Mabo sub-clans were represented in the village: Mangar, Hedungba, Lungdoyu, Para, and Tumbangbe. The remaining two sub-clans not in the village were Lejenji, and Sabara. Mangar Mabo were by far the most predominant, with 100 Mangar Mabo households. The second and third most prevalent sub-clans were the Lungdoyu, with 36 households, and the Hedungba with 25. Table 2 shows this more clearly.

Limbu clans	Number of households	Distribution (wards)
Mabo -	164	All
Mangar	-100-	All
Lungdoyu	-36-	1-3, 5-7
Hedungba	-25-	1, 3, 4, 6, 7
Para	-2-	5
Tumbangbe	-1-	5
Bhega	3	4 & 6
Thebe	3	1 & 6
Lingden	1	2
Lauti	1	5
Murum-Bokhim	1	4
Neyong	1	1
Pandhak	1	1
Phempu	1	7
Tamling	1	4
Yongya	1	5
Non-Limbu groups	23	
Total	201	

Table 2: Limbu clan and sub-clan number of households and distribution in wards 1 to 7

The survey results demonstrate the fairly ethnically homogeneous nature of the village, despite the presence of a variety of Limbu clans and non-Limbu households. According to demographic data from

TRPAP, Mamangkhe VDC has a ratio of 344 non-Limbu to 1023 Limbu villagers; in other words, 75% of the VDC is Limbu. According to this same data set, only two other VDCs, of a total of 50 in the district of Taplejung, have a higher proportion of Limbu to non-Limbu inhabitants: Ikhabu VDC, with a 77% Limbu population; and Tapethok, with an 84% Limbu population—the highest in the district. This indicates two points: (i) the ethnically diverse nature of villages in Taplejung, which is common to many parts of Nepal; and (ii) the somewhat exceptional case of Mamangkhe where, despite a history of substantial immigration of non-Limbu settlers, the village has been able to hold onto, and create, a strong sense of cultural authenticity, partly as a result of the large proportion of Limbu households. This self-conscious sense of Limbu authenticity must have played a major role in convincing the Limbu cultural association, *Kirant Yakthum Chumlung,* to locate the first Limbu ethnic museum in this village, which was inaugurated on the 9th of May, 2007.

Marriage

There are two forms of marriage both in the village and prevalent throughout Limbu communities in Nepal: arranged marriages and marriage by free choice, or *lav bihāh* (love marriage).[31] These are defined as a marriage of agreement between the two families concerned, and marriage without the need for parental consent (Sagant 1996: 58). It is much easier to distinguish between an arranged marriage and marriage by free choice, than between a Western style love-marriage and the different degrees of "free choice" exercised by young Limbu villagers. A "free choice" marriage is not necessarily free, but an arranged marriage is definitely arranged. Of the 194 married household heads, 72 households were based on arranged marriages, while 122 had a "love marriage". While other researchers have written in more detail about marriage in the Himalayas (Jones and Jones 1976, Ahearn 2001, 2003,

---

31 This categorization of marriage into two types results from conversations with a large number of villagers about marriage practises, and is particularly prevalent in the way unmarried men talk about their future prospects and make plans. They clearly distinguish between two possibilities: an expensive and elaborate arranged marriage, or a cheaper and quicker love marriage. Younger adults tend to prefer the latter over the former, although the former carries considerably more prestige.

March 2002, Levine 2007, Ishii 1995), a few words on marriage in Mamangkhe will help to show how limiting surveys and categorizations of "marriage types" can sometimes be, when the reality, as always, is so much more complex and variable.

The main differences between arranged marriages and "free choice" marriages are that the former are almost always more expensive, are largely organized or orchestrated by the parents of the couple-to-be, and, more rarely today, can occur between couples who have never met. Free-choice or love marriages can take place without the parents approval and can be organized in a relatively short time. The latter type of marriage can occur for a variety of reasons, including: following an elopement, *phatca pekma* (L.); during a village market or festival; after a long romantic courtship; as a result of pressure on a son from a family following the death of a female member of the household; and following pressure on an elder son if his younger brother has married before him. While there are always different reasons for marriage, an arranged marriage is still considered more respectable, as it cannot be as spontaneous and haphazard as a love marriage (which can literally take place from one day to the next—often overnight: as with a *sɛtluppa* (L.). A number of elements are almost always a feature of a marriage: bride-wealth is paid by the groom to the bride's family, for both "free-choice" and arranged marriages; an examination of the bride's genealogical history is crucial, and any related ancestry within seven generations would make the marriage within the village impossible;[32] marriage celebrations, which occur in both the groom and bride's villages, are an important village-wide opportunity to gather and families often plan their weddings to occur in the winter months of reduced agricultural work.[33]

Although there have been very few inter-ethnic marriages in the village,[34] the Limbu raised no objections to a Limbu marrying a *kirant*

---

32 Several couples who married within closely related sub-clans or even married within the same sub-clan had to leave the village. In the past, this invariably meant migrating to Sikkim.

33 A number of couples have, in the past, chosen not to celebrate their wedding in any way. One of these was a young man and woman (he was 17 years old in 2007), who felt that it was an unnecessary extravagance.

34 Only 9 inter-ethnic marriages were counted in the 2007 survey. Most of these were between Limbu males and Rai females (6). The remaining three marriages were: a Sarki male to Para (Limbu) female; and two Lungdoyu

villager (i.e. Rai), as they were considered brothers. When questioned further about marriage, villagers might include the Gurung and Bhote in the category of "brother", but the strongest tie was always expressed as being between the Limbu and the Rai. Many villagers' definition of *kirant* included only these two ethnic groups. Interestingly, from the survey carried out, there were only six cases of Limbu men marrying non-Limbu women, and in all cases they were Rai women.[35]

Marriage to a Bahun or Chhetri would generally not be allowed by parents, let alone marriage to a lower-caste, Dalit villager. There were only a handful of other inter-ethnic marriages, some of which had resulted in the couple leaving the village. Of these, one was between the eldest daughter of a Jaisi Chhetri and a Limbu villager, both from Ward 5. They had run away from the village to get married and lived in Sikkim for seven years, only returning two years prior to the research survey. Limbu couples have had to leave if they married too closely within a shared genealogical history and, in the past, these couples had also travelled to and worked in Sikkim, often never returning. With few exceptions though, marriages in the village are intra-ethnic, exogamous[36] and virilocal. Just over 10% of male household heads have married a woman from within the 9 wards of Mamangkhe VDC. There are seven unmarried household heads in wards 1 to 7, only one of whom is male. The average age of marriage was 21.7 years.

Education and literacy

The first primary school in the village was established by Lakshmi Prasad Koraria in 1958. A Gurung teacher from Tellok VDC (downriver from Mamangkhe) had been asked to teach to the newly formed Class 1. Table 3 shows the history of the school from 1958 onwards. Villagers all contributed a small amount of money to pay for his salary initially and

---

(Limbu) males to Chhetri females. In all cases of inter-ethnic marriage, children have inherited their fathers' caste status, which has always been lower than their mothers' original caste status.

35 In only one of these households [115] did the youngest members of the household speak Limbu.

36 In the case of the Limbu, there must be, in theory, no endogamy within 7 maternal and paternal generations, though in practice it is hard to trace all sub-clan names for both parents for more than 4 or 5 ascendant generations.

the government eventually stepped in to support the expanding school.

Class	Year of introduction
1	1958
2	1959
3	1960
4	1984
5	1985
6	1996
7	1997
8	1998
9	2008
10	2009

Table 3: History of introduction of new classes in village primary school

Over half of the respondents (56%) in the survey had been to school, with only a third of those who hadn't attended able to read and write.[37] Only 16 households in the survey had children studying in private or boarding schools,[38] which often carry out classes in English and provide computer tuition. These two subjects were often cited to me by villagers in Mamangkhe as the main advantages of an expensive private education.

Knowledge of the English-language and computers was seen by many younger villagers, and particularly those who had already travelled abroad (beyond Sikkim), as essential skills for them to access lucrative employment opportunities abroad. It is believed that these

---

37 This indicates ability beyond just writing or signing one's own name.

38 During the survey it appeared that Sinam, a popular secondary school in a VDC one day's walk away, was a private school (from class 10-12) because families had to pay money for tuition. If children attended Sinam school (although it *is* private) the indicator "0" is used, as a means of differentiating between children who were being sent to expensive schools (boarding schools, such as those found in Jhapa) and those who had to pay a nominal fee to attend school (such as the one in Sinam). Those households who had children attending private schools where English was taught in parallel to Nepali, in other words all other schools except the ones in Sinam, Khewang VDC, and Taplejung Bazaar (unless a specifically private/expensive school) are indicated with "1".

tools could lead them and their families towards an imagined life of comfort and economic prosperity, towards a new social and economic class. They are strongly associated by many villagers in Mamangkhe to ideas of an advantageous life that can be lived in Jhapa.

Language use

For most of the people met outside Mamangkhe village on journeys across Taplejung district and in other villages along the Kabeli *kholā*, the perception of Mamangkhe seemed to be that of a village where almost everyone speaks Limbu. The audible presence of the Limbu language to any visitor travelling through the village is immediate. This is in part due, no doubt, to the remoteness of the village, being the last village upstream before reaching Yamphudin.[39] Yet data from the survey revealed that only half of household heads spoke Limbu regularly, while roughly a quarter spoke more Nepali and another quarter *ādhā ādhā*—half Nepali, half Limbu. Additionally the survey showed a considerable decline (compared to individual speaking) of families speaking Limbu with their children with only 55 respondents using Limbu, compared to 127 using Nepali, 17 both languages and 8 with children who don't speak any Limbu.

This seems to correspond well with impressions gained during participant observation. Limbu adults often speak Limbu with each other while working together or having conversations, choosing to use Nepali when the conversation shifts to political questions (villagers lack the vocabulary to continue the conversation in Limbu), or when younger or non-fluent Limbu villagers appear. Villagers tend to speak Nepali with children, though there are plenty of exceptions to this rule. Children of households where Limbu is spoken more regularly stand out in groups of Limbu adults for their fluency, often speaking the language better than adults who have learnt the language later in life.

There is a marked divergence of language use with age, with children tending to speak Nepali and older villagers tending to speak

---

39 Yet remoteness does not always correlate with the continued use of indigenous language. Some of the most fluent speakers of Limbu in the village were women who had grown up in Bharapa VDC, a village only a few kilometres north of Phidim, the district headquarters of Panchthar, where there is access to the main road and a large population of non-Limbu settlers.

Limbu. Children almost without exception use Nepali amongst each other, since even if Limbu is spoken at home, Nepali is taught and used in the school environment where children spend so much of their time. It is hard from this to make assumptions about language loss though, as it seems that even villagers who grew up in households with little or no spoken Limbu, started to become more comfortable with the Limbu language as they began to work and spend more time with older Limbu villagers, and less time in the school environment. While some younger children seemed to have very little knowledge of the language when I questioned their vocabulary informally, most Limbu teenagers or young adults understood almost everything spoken by others around them.

Despite the relatively high proportion of households regularly using the Limbu language, villagers note that more Limbu is spoken in, for example, villages surrounding Hellok[40] ("Even the Chhetri speak Limbu there!" is a common refrain) and in the villages of the Maiwa and Mewa *kholā* valleys to the west of the Tamur *kholā* (where both Sagant and Michailovsky did their fieldwork). A useful indicator of the vitality of a local language is the speaking-ability of non-local populations. In Mamangkhe for example, the ability to speak Limbu is particularly diffuse among the Dalit (particularly the Damai in Ward 5 and a number of Kāmī families in Ward 7), but not among the Chhetri or Gurung (who do not speak their own language).

A predictor for Limbu fluency or, in fact, lack of fluency, was whether the woman who had married into the household, or indeed the mother of a household head, had come from an area reputed for its "Limbu-ness" and use of the Limbu language. Women from Hellok in Tapethok VDC and villages along the Maiwa *kholā*, such as Thinglabu, who married into households in Mamangkhe all spoke fluent Limbu and, as a result, their children are also more familiar with the language and more comfortable speaking it from an early age. Women who came from villages along the Kabeli *kholā* such as in Ambegudin, Khewang, Pedang, and Tellok, tended not to speak much Limbu in their household and, as a result, their children don't speak Limbu as fluently as children from households where Limbu is usually spoken. These data are shown in the two tables below.

---

40 Hellok village is in Tapethok VDC, in the Tamur river valley one day walk north from Taplejung bazaar.

Village name	Number of households
Khewang	5
Mamangkhe	5
Pedang	4
Hellok - Tapethok	3
Lokudin	3
Tellok	3
Wayam - Panchthar	3
Ambegudin	2
Ankhop	2
Limbudin	2

Table 4: Origin of wife of male household head in households which speak Nepali (ranked by ten most frequently mentioned village of origin)

Village name	Frequency of households
Hellok - Tapethok	11
Tellok	10
Mamangkhe	10
Pedang	8
Chyanthapu - Panchthar	7
Yempang	5
Sikaicha	4
Kewang	3
Limbudin	3
Tinglabu	2

Table 5: Origin of wife of male household head in households which speak Limbu (ranked by ten most frequently mentioned village of origin)

Notions of traditionality can play an important role in, for example, a man's choice of wife. Several villagers joked that women from Hellok were the hardest working and always spoke fluent Limbu, these two factors making them good wives. Women from closer to home, from villages along the Kabeli *kholā* for example, were often described as less hard-working and usually not fluent in Limbu.

Economy
Infrastructure

The closest road to the village is an unsurfaced dirt road which connects Medibung bazaar, in Tharpu VDC, to Phidim in Panchthar. It takes most villagers half-a-day's walk, unloaded, to reach the road from the village down the river valley, though it can take up to two days to reach the village walking from Medibung. Mamangkhe VDC has three schools and the main one, built in 1958, has 10 classes. The other two schools are primary schools. There is a health clinic in Ward 6 which is staffed by one trained health worker and two assistants. It provides vaccines for babies, a limited number of pharmaceutical products, including male and female contraceptives, and first aid supplies such as bandages and sewing equipment. In February 2007 the first telephone was installed in the village, powered by solar energy, and it worked intermittently until the following year. By March 2008, a number of mobile phone companies, including Nepal Telecom, were installing mobile phone towers at points throughout Taplejung district and a number of CDMA phone sets were acquired by various families in several of the village wards, though reception can be extremely poor. There is also a twice-weekly post office service in the village, though money from abroad is either sent through a third-party (such as another villager or friend) or through one of the many money transfer services, of which the closest are all in Taplejung bazaar.

There are currently three micro hydro-electric generators in the village. The first of these was built in 1996 using money from an agricultural development bank loaned to a village fund.[41] This is a 1 kilowatt generator that produces electricity for 32 households in wards 4 and 5 who receive about 30 watts each, enough to power two 15 watt bulbs. The generator works intermittently, at best. The other two hydroelectric generators also produce 1 kilowatt each but broke down a month after they were installed in October 2007 and were still not working at the conclusion of the fieldwork studies. Ten households have installed solar panel systems for powering a small number of lights in their houses. The availability of electricity has had little impact on the daily lives of most villagers, since it is primarily used to replace kerosene lamps most households use in the evenings and night, and at

---

41 A committee was set up to manage the fund and villagers paid according to how many watts they wanted. The loan was repaid 3 years later.

25W, each bulb hardly produces more light than the lamps do. The biggest impact of electricity has been the use of amplification and music during village festivals and public events, which helps to draw people from neighbouring villages.

Water is supplied to all households through a network of 1 inch PVC pipes which tap natural streams above the settlement area. The network supplies a number of formal cement-masonry water drinking facilities that have been constructed in each ward of the village and these provide reliable and clean sources of water for all the households.

Similar to all VDCs in Nepal, Mamangkhe receives annual grant support for the school, health clinic and any development projects that the village as a whole decides to invest in.[42] The government pays for the salaries of six teachers in the main village school, the salary of the postman and the health worker, and provides small salaries to a number of individual social workers and social organizations. It also pays the salary of a government worker who administers VDC money and collects taxes. The salaries of the other six to eight teachers (numbers vary at different times of the year) are all paid with the VDC money. Approximately 400,000 of the 1 million rupees goes to maintain the three schools in the village. Part of this remaining money was used in 2007 to subsidize the installation of the micro hydroelectric project in all wards in the village, beginning with wards 1 to 3. The other wards were to receive money the following years but the project was dropped when the villagers realized that the hydroelectric generators were unreliable and discussions were held in mid-April 2008[43] concerning the next project that the VDC funds could support. One group in the village wanted to build a larger health centre and pay for the services of a more highly trained health worker than the current one. Another group wanted to partly subsidize the development, over a number of years, of a large hydroelectric generator to be placed in the Khasewa *kholā* that could generate enough electricity for the whole village. The final decision concerning the use of the surplus funds from the 2008 (2065 VS) budget was to support the enlargement of the secondary school so that Classes 9 and 10 (School Leaving Certificate level) would be available

---

42 In the case of Mamangkhe, this amounts to 1 million rupees.

43 At the start of the Nepali year.

over the next two years. The surplus funds would be used for the salaries of a number of new teachers hired from elsewhere in the district.

The agricultural cycle

Agricultural activity	Mar	Apr	May	Jun	Jul	Aug	Sep	Oct	Nov	Dec	Jan	Feb
Garden vegetables planted	■	■	■									
Maize planted	■											
Maize harvested						■	■					
Hoeing maize - first time		■										
Hoeing maize - second time				■								
Hoeing maize - third time					■							
Wheat and barley planted									■			
Wheat and barley harvested			■									
Millet planted			■									
Millet seedlings transplanted					■							
Millet harvested									■			
Rice planted			■									
Rice seedlings transplanted					■							
Rice harvested									■			
Potatoes planted									■			
Potatoes harvested	■											
Cardamom cleared and planted			■	■	■	■						
Cardamom harvested							■		■			

Table 6: The agricultural cycle in Mamangkhe village from March to February

Subsistence agriculture and the production of cardamom as a cash-crop form the core of the village economy. The agricultural cycle is made up of two main seasons, as is the work associated with agricultural operations: the high-work season during the spring, summer and autumn months from March to November, and the low-work season, or slack season, during the winter months from December to February.

The cardamom season, or *alaĭchi season*[44] as it is known in the village, refers specifically to the period of cardamom harvest from

---

44 Interestingly, villagers use the English term "season" when talking about

September to November. For some families, this can be one of the most labour-intensive periods of the whole year, with family members living for weeks at a time in the forests close to cardamom plantations. This also provides an opportunity for families with little or no cardamom of their own to earn money working for other families, either harvesting cardamom or transporting it to Tharpu for sale.[45] The period typically occurs just after the millet harvest, when millet-beer brewing is in full swing, and the end of the cardamom season, which is also the beginning of the colder winter months.

During the winter months or the dry season, work tends to focus on areas closer to the settlements. At this time, pit-sawyers prepare wooden planks for housing construction and for other buildings and temporary structures—which are regularly moved when mud and manure build up—are built by male villagers for their domestic animals. It is also a festive time when marriages take place and, as the millet has just been harvested, millet-beer is abundant. The winter months from October and November onwards are also the time for Limbu religious festivals and the performance of many of their important ceremonies: household rituals, ritual pig sacrifices, and rituals for specific deities. These months coincide with an increase in cash availability throughout the village following the sale of cardamom, and villagers usually travel to market towns to settle their accounts, buy market goods, and visit relatives. Before roads connected Taplejung district to the bazaar towns of the south (Phidim, Ilam, Birtamod), the winter months were also used for travelling long distances to sell butter, chickens, high-altitude plants, and home-made items, and to bring back salt, kerosene, cloth, iron tools and spices.

The agricultural year starts again in March when the temperatures warm a little and fields that have been resting during the winter are ploughed and planted with maize. Beans, cucumber, pumpkin and *iskus*

---

cardamom, but not with reference to other crops or climatic changes (e.g. the summer or winter seasons).

45 Tharpu is the small market village in Panchthar district, below the slightly larger market village of Medibung which has a direct bus service all the way to Birtamod in Jhapa district. There is a rough winding road that connects Medibung with Tharpu and is used by tractors to transport market goods between the two settlements. Villagers in Mamangkhe buy their supplies from Tharpu as it is an hour more uphill to Medibung and the prices are the same in both places.

(from the English word *squash*, or chayote, *Sechium edule*) are also planted in certain parts of these same terraces: beans normally close to the maize plants so their stalks will provide support for the winding bean plant; pumpkin and cucumber closer to the house; and *iskus*, which is a creeper and can produce large quantities of fruit, in a specially prepared area with bamboo supports. Potatoes, planted in November in the upper parts of the village, are dug out. In April, the few families that planted wheat or barley before the winter slowly harvest it either by picking the ears individually and gathering up the straw later, or by picking the whole plant and cutting off the ears at home. When the maize has been planted, firewood needs to be chopped and stacked in a convenient place before the rains commence again. Families with no access to forests of their own will usually pay a small fee for a tree in the forests high above the village. The job of carrying chopped wood in woven baskets down to the houses from the felling sites can take a week or more, even with many people helping.

Figure 8: A view of the village in March.

Between April and May, the Nepali month of *baisākh*, the maize which was planted in March is ready for its first hoeing to clear the weeds away. This is one of the most physically tiring and time consuming tasks, and is done three times in total during the maize growing period:

once in April, again in June, the month of *āsār*, and a final weeding during the transplanting of millet seedlings in July. Seedbeds for millet are also sown in May, normally in a single or small number of terraces. These are ploughed, fertilized and the millet seed is thickly scattered on the surface. Planting the millet in a seedbed enables the maize to be weeded twice before the millet is transplanted in the same terrace space in July. Rice seedbeds are also planted out in May, similarly to millet, for later transplantation in leveled terraces.

Figure 9: A view of the village in June.

The summer months are marked by an increase in both temperature and rainfall. In June, rice from the seedling bed is transplanted in specially prepared terraces in the lower parts of the village. Beans are planted on the edges of terraces to take advantage of the water in the irrigated terraces and to reduce erosion of the bank tops from rainfall. A second hoeing in the maize terraces is carried out and the millet planted the month before has to be carefully weeded. Some families begin to clear their cardamom plantations for the first time since harvesting cardamom and replant areas of non-productive or aged cardamom forest with transplants from neighbouring plots. These

Figure 10: Hoeing maize in April.

Figure 11: Harvesting wheat in May.

Figure 12: Preparing bundles of rice seedlings for transplanting in June.

Figure 13: Interplanting millet seedlings with maize in July.

activities, clearing and replanting cardamom, take place intermittently throughout the summer months. July is perhaps the most labour intensive month. The monsoon is at its peak, and working in the fields means getting drenched by the rain and splashed with mud. The millet is transplanted from the seedling bed between the mature maize plants. Labour is in high demand and groups of sometimes up to 15 or 16 *khetālā* are divided into two groups: the women and younger individuals plant the millet seedlings; and the men hoe the ground behind them in preparation for the seedlings. This is the final weeding of the terraces before the maize is picked in August.

Maize is harvested throughout August and into September. Maize growing in lower parts of the village is harvested as early as the beginning of August and maize either growing in higher parts of the village or that was planted later in the year is harvested in early to mid-September. Rice paddy is weeded in August, and some families plant *piṇḍalu* (*Colocasia esculenta*), a type of taro. By September, the rains have lightened a little and much of the more labour-intensive agricultural work is complete. The focus of work returns to cardamom as the *alaĩchi* season picks up. For most families with cardamom production, this means cutting weed growth back and clearing out leaves and detritus at the base of the plant that could reduce productivity. Some households build or improve their *bhatti*, the cardamom drying sheds. For families with cardamom plantations in lower parts of the village, harvesting of the cardamom fruit begins. Similarly to other labour-intensive tasks during the year such as planting millet, households try to hire as many *khetālā* as possible in order to finish the work rapidly. This helps to create a friendly work environment and close friends often plan to work together as *khetālā* for different households. *Mulā*, the daikon radish (*Raphanus sativus*), is also planted at this time in a specially prepared section of fertilized and stone-free land.

October is a month of abundance: families begin to harvest early planted millet and rice in some parts of the village, and vegetables abound. It is also the period of peak cardamom harvest and labour is much in demand for harvesting and transporting cardamom to markets. In November, later-planted millet and rice are harvested and after planting potatoes, wheat and barley, agricultural work comes to a close before the harsh winter months of December and January set in.

While a number of crops, including potatoes and the small amounts of buckwheat some families produce, tend to be planted at a slightly higher altitude and rice is grown below much of the village settlement, the sort of ecological verticality found in other Himalayan settings is absent. The concept of verticality emerged from the work of Murra (1972, 1985) and other scholars (Brush 1976, Brush 1977, Mayer 1985) who explored how communities in the Andes exploited altitudinal variation to increase crop diversity and pastoral opportunity across different microenvironments. The work of Stevens (1993) on Sherpa cultural ecology draws together the Andean concept of verticality with a study of the variation of productive systems and land-use practices. He shows how at increasing elevations in the Himalayas, both the food produced and productive system changes: between 1,000m and 2,000m irrigated and non-irrigated crop production result in rice, maize, millet and wheat production; up to 3,000m only non-irrigated production of buckwheat and barley in addition to maize and wheat; between 3,000m and 4,000m, summer production of potato, buckwheat and hay; and everything up to around 6,000m is limited to pasture for livestock grazing (Stevens 1993: 74). Unlike the Sherpa, verticality plays a minimal role in Mamangkhe since most of the settlements are situated between 1,500m and 2,000m, and almost the entirety of food production takes place below 3,000m—the "year-round crop production" zones in Stevens' categorization (Stevens 1993: 64).

Most non-agricultural tasks, such as basket and mat-weaving, and wood-chopping, are less strictly associated with particular seasons and are usually carried out when there is a particular need or spare time is available. Specific types of baskets are often woven just before harvesting cardamom. A small and circular handheld basket, known as *phurlung* or *coŋ'roŋ* (L.), is woven just before harvesting cardamom, and a larger version of the ubiquitous basket carried on the back and shoulders known as *ḍoko* or *sap* (L.), is often woven just before maize is harvested.

Division of labour

There is a clearly defined, though at times flexible, division of labour between adult men and women and children, which is expressed in and reinforced by the different wages received by them in most wards of the village. Women and young children[46] tend to earn 50 rupees per day while men get paid 100 rupees per day. The only tasks which are exclusively carried out by men are ploughing and basket weaving. Other tasks, usually carried out by men, are chopping wood, constructing houses or sheds, portering heavy loads, clearing cardamom land, preparing rice paddy terraces, and—at least during the period when millet is being planted—land preparation (hoeing) for millet. While many tasks associated with food preparation and house maintenance (including weaving mats, cleaning and dung-plastering the floors) are strongly associated with women's labour, men and children often have to prepare food for themselves when other family members are not available. In addition, a number of men in the village, both young and old, weave mats for their house or for sale. In summary, while two tasks in particular, ploughing and basket weaving, are exclusively carried out by men, there are no tasks usually carried out by women that men never carry out. Even the preparation of beer, which is almost always carried out by women, can be undertaken by men in the absence of women, or together with women if a large amount is being prepared.

Almost all agricultural tasks therefore have a general pattern of labour division but there is little strictness in adhering to this pattern. In relation to planting, most of the main crops—maize, millet and rice—are planted and transplanted by women. Certainly in the case of rice and millet, which require a large work force and the simultaneous preparation of the terrace by ploughing or hoeing (men's task) with the transplanting of seedlings, women and children are used for the planting while the men prepare the ground. Men regularly joke about how much slower they are than women, how much larger their hands are, and how not only is it better to have women planting because they are so much faster, but also because, in most wards, they receive half the wage rate of men (50 instead of 100 rupees). The preparation of terraces for millet and rice planting, for example, requires less labour input than the labour-intensive job of planting each seedling. As a result of this difference in labour demand for different tasks, women are in high demand during the months of peak agricultural activity, which in turn puts an added pressure on them at home where they are generally

---

46 Children begin to earn, or their labour is considered equivalent to that of adult men, when they show that they are able to work as much as an adult man. This is usually around the age of 15 or 16 years.

expected to carry out most tasks associated with food preparation. Generally, the men agree that women spend more of their time at work than the men, but they justify this by explaining that their work tends to be more physically tiring. For men, portering, chopping wood and digging are more physically demanding than grinding maize, planting millet and rice, and dehusking rice. However, from my observations living with two different families, it is clear that women work over a longer period of time, usually starting before men in the early morning and being responsible for cleaning up dinner in the evening. The work of Acharya and Bennett (1981), which examines the demographic and economic characteristics of eight villages across Nepal[47] in great detail, shows how in all the villages surveyed the burden of women's work was always higher than men's (1981: 160). They conclude that although women spend 80% of the time men spend in "economic activities" (as defined by national census categories), when this is expanded to include the provision of essential household supplies, such as fuel and water, and domestic activities such as childcare, women work on average 44% more hours than men per day (1981: 306).

In construction work and any of the tasks related to construction such as stone cutting and wood sawing, the division of labour is perhaps more explicit than for agricultural work. Although both women and men chop wood when it is needed for food preparation in the house, women are never hired by households for chopping wood. Tree-felling, pit-sawing, and stone-laying are also tasks strongly associated with male labour in the village. Similarly, men are responsible for building houses or toilets that make use of wood and carefully layered stones. When these tasks are needed for community construction projects, the women focus more on digging earth, transporting stones and providing food and drink for the male work team.

---

47   In Acharya and Bennett's (1981) study, eight villages in different regions of Nepal were chosen to reflect the diversity of ethnic composition of the country, from the Maithili of Eastern Tarai, to the Kham Magar of the Far Western Middle Hills. An earlier study of the gendered division of labour in Nepal was carried out by Acharya (1983), and a considerable amount of recent anthropological research has touched on this issue, particularly that of Cameron (1998). In her time-allocation study of high-caste and low-caste villagers, she shows how both high and low caste women spend more than double the amount of time working in productive and domestic activities than their male counterparts (Cameron 1998: 91-94).

Figure 14: Weaving straw mats on a makeshift loom.

Figure 15: Weaving a *ḍoko*.

Agriculture production: data from the survey

The survey contained 17 questions related to food production: six related directly to domestic animal production (ox, cow, buffalo, pig, goat, chicken); five more related to grain production (rice, millet, maize, wheat and barley); and the remaining six questions related to sale of grain production and the quantity of agricultural land either owned and/or farmed as a tenant. The data on agricultural land owned and tenant farming is discussed in more detail in the section on land below. Table 7 shows the percentage of households with different livestock in the village. Table 8 shows the distribution of livestock (excluding chicken) by ethnic/caste group and Table 9 compares the data with that of three other villages in Nepal.

	Ox	Cow	Buffalo	Pig	Goat	Chicken	Total
Percentage of households with livestock	27	42	43	84	82	91	97
Total number of livestock	96	240	136	247	596	848	2,163

Table 7: Percentage of households with different livestock

Ethnic/ caste group	Number of households	Total number of livestock	Average livestock per household	Average livestock per capita
Rai	1	4	4	1
Sārkī	3	24	8	1.6
Damai	4	26	6.5	1
Gurung	4	79	19.8	3.8
Kāmī	5	21	4.2	0.6
Chhetri	6	79	13.2	4.2
Limbu	178	1082	6.1	1.3
Total	**201**	**1315**	**6.5**	**1.4**

Table 8: Distribution of livestock in the village by ethnic/caste group (excluding chicken)

Animal	Mohoriya 1958*	Thak 1969**	Timling 1981***	Mamangkhe 2007
Buffalo	1.01	2.23	0.3	0.68
Cow	2.17	1.66	2.23	1.19
Ox	0.65	0.73	2.2	0.48
Goat	1.41	3.02	3.6	2.97

* Data from Pignède (1966: 134)[48]
** Data from Macfarlane (2003: 90)
*** Data from Fricke (1993: 72)

Table 9: Average household livestock in four villages

The village-wide data for livestock shows that while only around a quarter of households owned an ox, almost half the households in the village owned buffalos and cows. The most commonly owned livestock were pigs, goats and chickens. 97% of all households owned some form of livestock.[49] Table 8 shows a marked pattern of differentiation across ethnic groups with the Chhetri and Gurung owning almost four times as many livestock per capita than the Limbu. This is most likely due to the location of these Chhetri and Gurung households, situated in the upper section of the village settlement area, which provides better access to fodder in the forests above and to grazing land above that. It should be mentioned that unlike communities situated at higher altitudes where transhumance is the typical livestock management practice (Chakravarty-Kaul 1998, Brower 2003, Stevens 1996), villagers in Mamangkhe generally keep their livestock relatively close to their household, moving them from plot to plot every few weeks to spread the manure between sites. Three households keep buffalo and cows above the village settlement area in temporary sheds (*goṭ*), but the animals remain at the same altitude throughout the year.

---

48 Macfarlane incorrectly (I think) uses the figure of 94 households in his analysis of Pignède's data (2003: 90). As far as I can tell there are 98 households numbered on the village map (Pignède 1966: 63; Fig. 6) although Pignède himself simply writes "*Mohoriya groupe une centaine de maisons*" (1966: 60).

49 Only five households had no livestock. In the case of three households this is because the family has migrated but still owns property in the village. A further household belongs to a recently married couple who have yet to acquire livestock, and another household belongs to a disabled shaman who lives alone and relies on others for food (his land is cultivated by others in *adhiyã* but he does not have *adhiyã* livestock).

It should be mentioned that unlike communities situated at higher altitudes where transhumance is the typical livestock management practice (Chakravarty-Kaul 1998, Brower 2003, Stevens 1996), villagers in Mamangkhe generally keep their livestock relatively close to their household, moving them from plot to plot every few weeks to spread the manure between sites. Three households keep buffalo and cows above the village settlement area in temporary sheds (*goṭ*), but the animals remain at the same altitude throughout the year.

Table 9 presents comparative data for livestock in four villages located in a similar environment. The Tamang village of Timling appears to be the most pastoral with the largest number of cows, oxen and goats. The Gurung village of Mohoriya appears to be the most similar to Mamangkhe, both of which have a ratio of 1:2 buffalo to cow, and fewer oxen, whereas the Gurung village of Thak inverts this ratio which Fricke considers an "indication of orientation to more southern, "Hinduized" values" (Fricke 1993: 71).

	Rice (kg)	Millet (kg)	Maize (jhutta)	Wheat (kg)	Barley (kg)
Village-wide*	52	152	403	12	12
Grain producing households only	256	156	420	76	156
Total production village-wide	10,216	30,256	79,007	2,372	2,680
Number and percentage of productive households	40 (20%)	196 (98%)	193 (96%)	32 (16%)	17 (9%)

*Including non-producing households

Table 10: Average quantities of main crops produced throughout the village

	Total (NPR)	Number of households	Crop value per household (NPR)	Crop value per capita (NPR)
Rai	12,000	1	12,000	3,000
Sārkī	55,200	3	18,400	3,680
Damai	35,400	4	8,850	1,416
Gurung	128,400	4	32,100	6,114
Kāmī	21,600	5	4,320	600
Chhetri	63,600	6	10,600	3,347
Limbu	1,784,640	178	10,026	2,122

Table 11: Total food crop value (rice, millet and maize) by ethnic group

The data on crop production (Tables 10 and 11) shows that few households grow wheat and barley, though almost all households produce millet and maize. Five households do not grow millet and eight households do not grow maize, yet apart from these, a very large proportion of the village is able to produce at least some of the two staple crops. Rice is produced mostly by households in wards 1, 2 and 6 with only 40 households growing the crop. The total production of rice is 10,216 kg, equivalent to around 51 kg per household, and is only sufficient to feed a family of four for one month. Table 11 shows that the Gurung produce over three times more crops than all the other ethnic groups except for the Sārkī. Of the largest 10% of crop producers (20 households), one is a Sārkī household, two are Gurung and the remaining 17 are Limbu. Together they produce 41% of all the staple crops. The smallest 10% of producers, who account for barely 1% of the crop total, are also largely Limbu households, with the addition of one Damai and one Chhetri household.

Millet is either used for millet-beer preparation or, in the absence of rice and maize or to make other grains last longer, families also prepare ḍhĩḍo, a kind of polenta or porridge made from boiled millet flour. On occasions, maize flour also is used in this way. Two households, both in Ward 7 and among the poorest households in the village, stated that they never consume rice. They didn't grow it, couldn't afford to buy it and almost exclusively ate maize. During the two month strike in February and March 2008 by a number of Limbu political groups in east Nepal, the village's reserves of rice fell so severely that most families were forced to eat maize and millet ḍhĩḍo twice a day. Only a small number of families were able to continue eating rice throughout the strike. This period indicated both the degree to which most families depend on the market for their food supply, and the extent to which, despite not being self-sufficient, most families are self-reliant and adapt their diet in food scarcity situations.[50] In some ways, maize fulfils a more fundamental role in the diet than rice does being both the crop

---

50 Seddon et al. (2001) point out that the term "food self-sufficiency" is in any case misleading because it underestimates the role that off-farm and non-farm economic activities play in enabling households to aquire food (by buying it through other means). According to a study by Adhikari and Bohle (1999), the labour capacity of households is more likely to determine food security than figures for self-sufficiency.

that families rely on most during food scarcity, and also because of its fundamental role as a snack between meals. While rice is associated with economic well-being and is always served to guests, maize is associated with strength, stamina and physical toughness.

Cardamom production

At the time of the survey there were 147 producing (73%) and 54 non-producing households (27%). Some households were unable to provide data on production two years previously (2005) and only 10 households provided production figures for three years previously (2004). Table 12 shows the data related to cardamom production between 2005 and 2007.[51] There is a year on year fall in production of almost 50% over three years from an average of 208 kg in 2005 to 112 kg per household in 2007. This is probably due to a combination of factors including a general decrease in productivity due to crop disease, as well as an increased number of households starting to produce small amounts of cardamom (thus lowering the village-wide average).

	Cardamom produced in 2005 (kg)	Cardamom produced in 2006 (kg)	Cardamom production in 2007 (kg)
Total	**9,800**	**18,292**	**15,927**
Average household production	208	176	112
Number of households in sample	47	103	147

Table 12: Village-wide cardamom production over three years

---

51 Since the survey was carried out a few months before the 2007 cardamom harvest season began, the figures for cardamom production for 2007 were estimates of expected production for that year. I was able to verify over a dozen of these figures post-harvest and decided that although they were not always 100% accurate, when they were incorrect they were almost always within 0.5 of a *man* (40 kg). In other words, the estimates for production were extremely close to the final production figures.

Category of producer	Number of households	Percentage of households	Percentage of total production
No cardamom (0 kg)*	8	5.4	0
Very small (4 to 30 kg)	44	29.9	4.0
Small (40 to 100 kg)	47	32.0	17.7
Medium (120 to 160 kg)	24	16.3	20.8
Large (200 to 360 kg)	14	9.5	23.1
Very large (400 kg and above)	10	6.8	34.4
Total	103	100	100

*This refers to cardamom producers (households that have planted cardamom) producing no cardamom in 2007, as opposed to non-producers (households that have not planted cardamom).

Table 13: Distribution of cardamom production among cardamom-producing households in 2007 by category of producer and number of households

Ethnic/caste group	Total (kg)	Households	Per household (kg)
Rai	0	1	0
Sārkī	260	3	87
Damai	95	4	24
Gurung	685	4	171
Kāmī	0	5	0
Chhetri	1,260	6	210
Limbu	13,627	178	77

Table 14: Household and per capita cardamom production in 2007 by ethnic group

The tables above (Tables 13 and 14) show the unequal distribution of cardamom harvested in 2007. In Table 13, the categories defined are arbitrary and serve simply to describe the distribution of cardamom production across households. Local categories of production are exactly the same as the categories used to describe wealth: there are large producers (usually associated with rich households), small producers (usually associated with poor households), and non-producers (strongly associated with Ward 7 which is considered the poorest ward, and where two-thirds of all households are non-producers). At the lower end are 99 households with less than 120 kg of cardamom that produced only 21.7% of the total production. At the upper end are 10 households with very large production (400 kg and above) that produced

34.4% of the village total. Between these two extremes are the 38 'Medium' and 'Large' producers who together produced 43.9% of the total. Table 14 shows the distribution of production across ethnic/caste groups to show that the Chhetri produce almost three times more cardamom on average than the Limbu. The Gurung are the second largest producers, followed by the Sārkī.

Figures derived by subtracting the cost of each household's yearly rice consumption from the value of their cardamom production showed that only 45 households were able to cover their costs with the other 102 households producing less cardamom than the total cost of their yearly rice consumption.[52] This obviously does not include the 54 households (25% of the total population) who have no cardamom-producing land. In other words, while all producers benefit, to varying degrees, from cardamom cash-cropping, there is still a sizeable proportion of the village which produces no cardamom and, as with most households, is also unable to produce enough subsistence crops (maize, millet, and rice).

The main reason for not being able to produce cardamom is lack of cardamom-productive land, either in the form of access to forested land above or outside the village settlement, or too little agricultural land which could otherwise be partially converted to cardamom-producing land. As will be elaborated in Chapter 6, cardamom production allows households to access capital through credit and loans offered in lieu of future production. In addition, as a result of the high market value of cardamom, cardamom-productive land is often mortgaged by villagers to raise capital for expenses such as repaying large debts and financing work visas. Cardamom production acts as a double-edged sword: by increasing wealth and offering access to capital it also increases expenditure and therefore, in the long term, increases the sizes of debts households are willing burden themselves with.

Surplus production as a proxy for income

One rough estimate of the ability of households to support themselves is the difference between household production of subsistence food crops and the requirements for household consumption (Gregory and

---

52 Village prices in 2007 were used for this calculation: rice was 24 NPR per kg, and cardamom 200 NPR per kg.

Altman 1989: 172-73). Households with few members which produce a surplus of food find it easier to support, maintain and reproduce themselves economically than households with a deficit of food production—those which produce less than they consume. These data are only useful in subsistence economies which rely above all on food produced within the village. In the case of Mamangkhe, a large proportion of households either do not produce their own food (80% of households do not produce any rice—the staple food—and 4% produce no millet or maize) or produce far less than needed for year-round subsistence (only one household produces enough rice to satisfy its own household requirements). With the exception of only two households who claimed to never consume rice, all households in the village purchase or otherwise obtain rice from outside the village. This reliance on rice, supplemented by maize and millet in many households, means that households either have to have year-round access to cash, or are able to obtain rice on credit, eventually paying back their debt when cash becomes available—usually after the cardamom harvest.

Ideally, economic data related to cash (income or credit) would have been available for all households. Such data would have provided a useful insight into the distribution of wealth within the village and the relationship between wealth, land ownership, and productivity. In the absence of such data, which is extremely difficult to obtain let alone verify, a proxy for income is taken as the total value (at village prices in 2007) of all crop production (millet, maize, rice, and cardamom) in 2007. Surplus production is therefore the difference between the total value of crops produced and the cost of yearly rice consumption per household.[53]

Table 15 shows the distribution of these data across the village among both households with surplus and with deficit production figures. The categories defined below are similar to those used in Table

---

53 For example, in 2007, household 410 produced 720 kg of millet, 900 *jhutta* of maize and (predicted) 400 kg of cardamom (they have no rice production). At local prices this means a crop value of 10,800 NPR for millet, 10,800 NPR for maize and 80,000 NPR for cardamom: a total of 101,600 NPR. Household consumption of rice was approximately 75 kg per month, or 900 kg per year, which would cost around 21,600 NPR per year (at 24 rupees per kg). Surplus production is therefore the difference between 101,600 NPR and 21,600 NPR: in this case a surplus of 80,000 NPR.

13 above and, though arbitrary, provide a clear means of showing the skewed distribution of surplus throughout the village.

Category of surplus or deficit	Range surplus or deficit (NPR)	Number of households
Very large surplus	150,000 and above	1
Large surplus	100,000 to 149,999	4
Medium surplus	50,000 to 99,999	13
Small surplus	0 to 49,999	66
Small deficit	-1 to -50,000	117

Table 15: Distribution of surplus and deficit production figures across the village (n=201)

The figures for surplus production show that almost 60% of households had a deficit of production, i.e. the value of everything they produced was less than the cost of their consumption of rice. A further 33% of households had a surplus of between 0 and 49,999 NPR, with 9% (18 households) in the three highest surplus categories. Almost all the households (90%) in these three categories were also in the top 10% of cardamom producers. These high surplus producers were distributed throughout the village and although they were mostly Limbu households, there were also four Chhetri and Gurung households among them, more than double the proportion of non-Limbu households in the village as a whole. The tables below (Tables 16 and 17) show the ethnic/caste group composition of the top 10% (n=20) largest surplus and the top 10% largest deficit producing households in the village, as well as the average value of their household and per capita surplus/deficit.

Ethnic/caste group	Number of households (n=20)	Average household surplus (NPR)	Average per capita surplus (NPR)
Chhetri	3	82,667	36,640
Gurung	1	90,240	22,560
Mangar (Limbu)	10	88,992	16,553
Mangle (Limbu)	2	55,980	6,629

Table 16: Distribution of 10% largest surplus producers by ethnic/caste group

Ethnic/caste group	Number of households (n=20)	Average household deficit (NPR)	Average per capita deficit (NPR)
Kāmī	3	-29,200	-3,676
Lungdoyu (Limbu)	5	-33,408	-5,012
Mangar (Limbu)	8	-30,020	-4,180
Mangle (Limbu)	4	-28,595	-4,411

Table 17: Distribution of 10% largest deficit producers by ethnic/caste group

These data (Tables 16 and 17) emphasize the wide differentiation of production across the village, with a large number of households unable to produce a surplus, and a very small number of households producing very large surpluses. The 10% largest deficit producers include three of the five Kāmī households in the village (who own very little land) as well as a number of the poorest Limbu families. Even among the top 10% largest surplus producers, Chhetri and Gurung households had almost 50% higher per capita surplus figures than the Limbu. It is the large surplus-producing households, both Limbu and non-Limbu, that inevitably own large amounts of land and produce large amounts of cardamom—all of the large surplus producers in Table 16 harvested at least 240 kg of cardamom in 2006, and 90% harvested 320 kg or more. It is these households that form the backbone of an emerging "middle class", or at least, as we shall see, it is their ability to create such large surpluses which allows them to: access more lucrative work opportunities abroad; lend money and access larger amounts of credit; buy property elsewhere (usually in Jhapa); and send their children to English-medium schools.

Monetary and non-monetary economies in the village

There are times during the year, particularly the summer months before the cardamom harvest season begins, when villagers say there is no local cash available. People needing to collect money owed from the sale of pig or buffalo meat can spend up to a month or more repeatedly visiting the houses of the debtors. The latter villagers will, in turn, approach other households either to ask for similar debts to be repaid or to borrow money to cover their own debts. Such debt chains, involving many families, are usually made up of small interest-free loans of a couple of hundred rupees and they often remain unpaid for many months in the hope that they will be cancelled out by a reciprocated debt for something else. Families that kill an animal and sell the meat are sometimes able to settle the debt in kind with meat they ate from another family six months before. The example of a single household asked to list all of its smallest debts, both monetary (a couple of hundred rupees) and non-monetary (a certain amount of meat or a certain number of pumpkins), showed that it was in debt to almost every neighbouring house as well as other houses in the same ward and beyond, and that these households also owed something in return. During the sale of meat, the quantities of meat sold to different households are recorded in a notebook by the villager responsible for collecting the money for the meat at a later stage.[54] As a result, below the formal and larger debts and loans arranged between households, there is a constant reciprocation and negotiation of smaller credits and debts, often related to consumable and perishable items, but also related to labour, between these households. The following section will briefly describe some of the different characteristics of the monetary and non-monetary economies in the village.

Formal government employment

Any villager with either a part-time or full-time salary provided by the government is considered to have a government job, and these are largely valued as sources of regular and reliable cash. This includes six fully salaried teachers in the larger school in Ward 5, and one in Ward 8 outside the sample. All the other teachers and teaching assistants are given their salaries from VDC funds and were not entitled to pensions. Salaries are on a sliding scale, depending on the number of years a teacher has been working and the level of education achieved. The scale ranges between 2,500 for an assistant to 7,500 NPR per month for a secondary school teacher.

Other government employment in the village includes the health worker, the postman, one woman for her work in a village women's organization, and the *sarkārī karmachārī*, government worker, known as

---

54 A number of villagers usually help with the slaughter of animal, the weighing and distribution of the meat to other villagers, and the collection of payments for the meat. In return they receive a portion of meat for free.

sacīb (secretary), in charge of administering VDC money and receiving taxes for land.

Another category of government employment includes army and police work. One household has a son who joined the police, though no one from the village is currently in the army. There are also four older villagers receiving an army pension from the government having worked for the Nepal or Indian Armies, and one person receiving a half-pension having worked for the British Army. This would not strictly count as a government job, but the government administers the money. These, together with other government jobs, provide one of the few sources of cash in the village other than the sale of cardamom and the substantial level of remittances from villagers who have travelled abroad for work.

Finally, money is also made available to community organizations, or social clubs, in the village. There were 13 of these in 2007, most of them divided by wards and age group. There was a women's group, separate from the women's organization mentioned above, which was active in wards 4 and 5 and had received small amounts of money from the government, amounting to 20,000 NPR in 2006. VDC money also supports the Dalits, the "untouchable" castes in Nepali society, with 20,000 NPR being provided to the twelve Dalit households in the village, and a further 10,000 NPR were put aside for village festivities and sporting events. Exactly 40,675 NPR were given by the government in 2008 to help the village create a library in the main school and supply school-books to children.

Labour in the village

Village labour is part of both the monetary and non-monetary economy. There are fundamentally four types of labour in the village. First there is that of the *yāllik* (L.), *khetālā*, or farm worker. The term *khetālā* refers to a villager who is paid either in cash or in kind for labour carried out for a specific household for a specified length of time. Second, there is *thɔk yāllik* (L), *parma*, which is unpaid reciprocated labour, or the mutual exchange of labour (Campbell 2004, Messerschmidt 1981, Toffin 1986). These first two forms of labour are used daily in the village. Third, there is *thekkā*, which is paid contract-work or task-based work. This is usually used for construction projects such as building cardamom drying sheds or toilets and is sometimes used for cardamom cultivation and harvest.

Fourth, there is unpaid community work, *sārvajanik kām*, for village construction projects and every household in the concerned ward is expected to contribute labour. This form of labour was used for improving the village paths and building the steps up to the museum. Overall, therefore, there are two paid forms of labour, *khetālā* labour and *ṭhekkā* labour, and two unpaid forms of labour, *parma* labour and *sārvajanik kām*, or community work. Strictly speaking, all of these forms of labour (with the exception of *sārvajanik kām*) can be paid for in kind, and some *khetālā* workers regularly choose to receive food grain instead of money, particularly during periods of village-wide millet shortage in the months leading up to the millet harvest.

There is a village-wide agreement that adult men are paid more than women and children when they are hired as *khetālā*. Despite this, a number of households in wards 4 and 5 have recently decided to consider female and male labour equivalent if it is exchanged on a *parma* labour basis. In other words, if one household provides a female for a day's work on a *parma* labour basis, the household in which she works could provide either female or male labour in exchange at a later date.

Figure 16: Community work to repair a bridge across the Kabeli River in July 2007.

Figure 17: A large group of *khetālā* help with the cardamom harvest in September 2007.

This equivalence is only recognized by a small number of households and only if labour is exchanged. No household in the village pays the same for female labour as for male labour and for most agricultural tasks, men and young adults hired as *khetālā* are paid 100 NPR per day, while women and children are paid 50 NPR per day. The work day begins at 10am ending at 5.30pm in the summer, and between 10.30 to 11am ending at 6pm in the autumn and winter months. Snacks, usually of roasted maize and grain-beer, are usually provided between 2 and 3pm. Households with more labour intensive work such as wood chopping, pit-sawing, house construction, roof thatching, stone-laying, and cardamom planting, clearing and harvest, provide a meal at the end of the work day. All of the above tasks, except those associated with cardamom, are valued at 150 NPR per day for men. Some households pay for labour in kind with the equivalent of 100 or 50 NPR in maize or millet. This is particularly common for households with abundant food crop production, and for Chhetri households who produce millet but do not consume it.

Ṭhekkā labour provides the possibility for villagers to make more than the usual 100 NPR per day simply by working harder to conclude a particular task. During cardamom harvest season, some villagers are able to earn up to 200 NPR per day simply by arranging advantageous *ṭhekkā* contracts with their employing household.

The standardized salary of 100 NPR per day for a *khetālā* provides many households in the village with a low-level income with which they can buy basic food goods on a month-by-month basis. A family of four with one working adult man will consume an average of 45 kilos of rice per month. The cost of this rice can be met by working for nine days as a *khetālā*. Villagers visiting Mamangkhe from other villages in the Kabeli *kholā* valley commented that salaries in Mamangkhe are higher than elsewhere. In Sinam VDC, a standard *khetālā* salary is only 80 NPR per day. A number of young adults from Tellok VDC and Ambegudin VDC stayed in the village for a month during the cardamom clearing season in June 2007 simply because they could earn more money in Mamangkhe. However, the 20 NPR difference in wage rate is probably not a particularly strong incentive because there is no systematic pattern of labour migration to the village from other villages in the area.

Standard wage rates for men in Mamangkhe were 50 NPR per day around 20 years previously, increased to 60 NPR per day until 2000, and then rose to 100 NPR in 2001. This last increase occurred because of the concurrent expansion in cardamom production together with the highest recorded price of cardamom (16,000 NPR per 40 kg locally) which led villagers to agree on increasing wages. When the price of cardamom fell again the following year, a number of villagers tried to have the wage rate reduced again but they were unsuccessful.

Shops and merchants

There are seven small shops in the village, with the largest located along the main path through the village in Ward 5 and beside the main school. The oldest, and largest one, is run by Raj and his family since they moved to the village from Khewang VDC in 1992. A few years later, Lakshmi P., the head teacher of the larger school in the village, opened his much smaller shop on the opposite side of the school and recently installed a CDMA telephone set. In 1997, Chandra built a shop from the side of the house he was living in, and more recently a number of households, including Raj's daughter, have also opened shops in Ward 5 and one in Ward 7. Five of the seven shops are in Ward 5, and one each in Ward 4 and 7. Most of the smaller shops sell basic food items, such as oil, salt, sugar, and tea, as well as sweets and biscuits. They also stock a number of widely used, non-food products such as chewing tobacco, cigarettes, and soap. The two larger shops in the village, Raj's and Chandra's, also stock plastic jewellery, clothes, sandals and batteries. Raj's shop is the only one that sells rice and lentils.

Most households in the village depend on the shops for regularly consumed goods such as cigarettes, chewing tobacco and soap. Other goods, such as sugar and tea, are only occasionally purchased by households when guests arrive. Generally, because of the added cost for carrying the goods from Tharpu VDC, households prefer to buy such items themselves in Tharpu. Despite this, the purchase of only a few goods per week soon adds up on the credit notes maintained by the shopkeepers. These credit notes refer to the individuals who make purchases and the responsibility for repaying the debts in each shop falls on them rather than the household as a whole. However, such goods as meat are sold to households and resultant debts are considered the responsibility of the household as a whole.

Another more complex example is of loans of food goods or household items between households. These loans, known as thɛtloŋ (L.), or *sāpaṭi*, are given by one household to another and the same quantity of whatever was lent must be returned at a later date. Although the discussion and transaction normally only takes place between two individuals in two households, the responsibility for the loan normally falls on the entire household. A thɛtloŋ can sometimes be arranged more as an exchange between dissimilar goods if one household needs something and another household needs something else. Exchange of goods or *sāṭāsāṭ* does take place but is not formalized so that households that produce surpluses of different goods can exchange their surpluses for other goods. Normally, a quickly reciprocated form of a loan occurs and the goods returned are not the same as those received. This is slightly different to a straight barter between two individuals as the requirement for a particular good arises unexpectedly from only one side of the exchange. This is not the calculated exchange of surplus but a reorganized form of loan and loan-repayment.

The shops, and particularly G.P's shop, provide credit throughout the year to most of the households in the village. This allows households who have only infrequent access to cash, to continue to purchase foods and household goods until they are able (or forced) to repay the debt. Credit is extended interest-free until it amounts to more than 1,000 NPR, at which point the people concerned are asked for money to reduce the debt; the standard interest rate of 2.5 rupees per 100 per month is applied if they fail to reduce it. This can create a large debt burden on households who have cash-flow problems. As is shown in more detail in the chapter on Raj's life history, Raj managed to merge increased debts in his shop with the purchase of cardamom produced in the village. This resulted in households that accumulated debts throughout the year, by buying goods and borrowing small amounts of money, only able to sell their produce to him to cancel or reduce their debts. Two other villagers have emerged as village merchants by buying cardamom, usually from households that are indebted to them, and selling it in Tharpu or beyond when the market price is suitable.

This cycle of consumption, indebtedness, and cardamom production lies at the centre of this book. The cycle persists because, despite the increased wealth of a number of Limbu families, some of whom have migrated to other parts of Nepal and form a rudimentary middle class, a larger number remain trapped in debt. It is only by mortgaging their land or otherwise gambling with the resources available to them to raise capital, and then working abroad and sending remittances home, that individuals can ever hope to provide land and future opportunities for their families.

Land

Cadastral survey of 1985

Among the documents held at the land registry offices in Taplejung bazaar (Phungling village) is the *bhumi sudhār tathā byabasthā mantrālaya* or the 'Ministry of Land Reforms and Management' document containing data related to land use in all the VDCs of Taplejung district. The District cadastral survey began in 1985 with the VDC closest to the district headquarters and continued until completion in 1987. Before the cadastral survey, only *raikar* land had been registered with the government while kipat land was not recognized. After the survey, all land became government registered land and kipat, at least formally, ceased to exist. Informally, villagers still refer to their ancestral land plots, or land which had been farmed by their ancestors for several generations, as *their* kipat. For example, much of the land surrounding the old cluster of households in Ward 4, is considered kipat land by those who live on it because it has been continuously farmed by the same lineage of Mangar-Mabo and never been bought or sold (though it has been parceled up over several generations). In contrast, more recently bought land, or land which has no connected historical lineage of ownership or no family history, is described as *raikar*.

The cadastral survey of Mamangkhe village was conducted from 26th to 29th of May, 1986 and, according to the survey, 586 individuals were registered as land holders at that time. Land is therefore formally owned by individuals, who tend to be the oldest married male in the household. It is he who inherits land and who is identified throughout the survey as the household head.[55] A total of 1552 plots of land were registered throughout the VDC, occupying a total of 1,608.3 hectares. The government registered nine plots as government land, with a total area of 488.3 hectares. There was no *guṭhi* land and *khet* land was not measured, probably because there was little and it was of low quality. A total of 206 plots, measuring 64.5 hectares were registered as *chāhāra*, or fourth grade land with no water availability. Another category of land registered in the document were maize fields, of which there were 1,252 plots, occupying a total of 1,055.5805 hectares of land, or 66% of the total registered agricultural land. Another category in the document was cardamom. There were 234 registered plots of land, occupying a total of 4,473 *ropani*, 14 *ātā*, 2 *paisā*, and 1 *dān* of land, the only category for which the traditional Nepali measurement units had been used. An additional column seemed to have been added outside the table of data and referred to *sārvajanik* or community-owned land. This was marked in the document as a single plot which occupied 5 *ropani* and 3 *dān* of land.

The data on cardamom plots and land areas provides an interesting insight into the history of cardamom production in the village and a comparative perspective on production in other VDCs. It appears that, at the time of the cadastral survey, Mamangkhe had by far the largest

---

55 In cases when male inheritors have died, moved away from the village, or were not in the village at the time of the survey, the household head was assumed to be the oldest member of the house, usually the wife of the male household head. In unmarried households, the oldest person in the household was considered the household head.

cardamom area under production of any VDCs in the district. The villages with large amounts of cardamom production today, such as Yamphudin and Surungkhim, had only 49 plots/1415 *ropani* and 197 plots/3,255 *ropani* of land registered in 1985, considerably less than Mamangkhe. By contrast, in the period 2003 to 2004, Surungkhim VDC produced 207.59 metric tons (MT) of cardamom, over twice the 97.24 MT of cardamom produced by Mamangkhe VDC, and by far the largest amount of cardamom of any other VDCs in Taplejung district (District Agricultural Development Office document for 2003-2004). While production of cardamom is currently higher in Surungkhim, more cardamom land was originally registered in Mamangkhe and it is likely that originally more cardamom was produced there. This provides further support for the supposition that cardamom may have been first cultivated on a large scale in Mamangkhe, and spread from there to other villages in the locality.

The period just before the cadastral survey was crucial for families who wanted to prove that they had been farming particular plots of land. It was next to impossible to obtain accurate data about this period during fieldwork, but many villagers related stories about other villagers who had been wise enough to clear sections of forest, often far from the main settlement area, and then claim them as their own land. With the increasing encroachment on kipat land by non-Limbu villagers, it seems likely that most of the land within and outside the settlement area would have been claimed years before the cadastral survey took place. At the time of the survey, most of the large number of Chhetri households had already left the village and the land they had owned had been bought by other households. Therefore, although it is possible that a small number of plots were claimed by villagers through a last-minute effort, most of the village's land must have been parcelled and formally owned by individual households for some time before the survey. The cadastral survey was the last stage of a process of land privatization and absorption into the state's land ownership framework. It represented a final formalization of the shift from kipat and traditional land tenure to *raikar* which had been going on in some form since the Chhetri and other non-Limbu started living in the village, probably as far back as the early 1800s.

Village-wide data on total land area cultivated is available in the 1985 VDC-level survey, and household level data was collected during the 2007 survey. Documents in the land registry offices record land area in *ropani*, but many of the families interviewed did not know the area of their land in *ropani* as they usually talk of land more in terms of productivity, some land being of higher quality than other, and in terms of how many days it takes to plough it, the *hal* measurement. Data collected from land estimates by villagers in *hal* units is usually much less accurate than *ropani* measurements available from the land registry records, However, there are three advantages to using *hal* measurements in such a survey: first, this is the most commonly used form of measurement used by villagers when discussing land sale, purchases and agricultural production on plots; second, land has always been a politically sensitive issue and asking for measurements of land in *ropani* would have possibly antagonized the villagers and prejudiced my research; and finally, just as tracing the sale and purchase of land plots would have been immensely time consuming, adding together the tiny plots owned by different individuals would have been an equally time-consuming task and would have required written consent from all the individuals who owned land in the village.

Land in 2007

The survey focused on agricultural land used for growing maize and millet, the two staple crops. For rice paddy, production figures were taken as a proxy for land ownership largely because so few households produce it. With cardamom production, there are so many variables that influence productivity that even if figures had been available for the total area of cardamom fields owned, they would probably not have been as useful as the data on yearly productivity, which provides a much more accurate measure of inter-household variation. Three questions in the survey related to land: the first referred to the amount of land planted with maize and millet in 2007, recorded in *hal*; the second and third questions aimed to elucidate whether the household carried out any *adhiyā* agriculture (sharecropping) on anyone's land, and the area of such land, again in *hal* units. These last two variables relate more to issues of land tenure and indebtedness and are covered in more detail in Chapter 6. The two tables below show the results of the survey with respect to these variables. Table 18 shows the distribution of land areas (*hal*) across the village. Table 19 shows the average plot size per household distributed by ethnicity.

Category of plot size	Number of households	Percentage of total population	Total (hal)	Percentage of total land
No land (0 *hal*) *	5	0.8	0	0
Small (< 1 *hal*)	33	13.0	15	3.8
Medium (1 to 1.5 *hal*)	69	29.7	73	18.7
Large (2 to 4 *hal*)	80	43.0	206	52.8
Very large (5 *hal* and above)	14	13.5	96	24.6
Total	**201**	**100**	**390**	**100.0**

* Of the 5 households with no land: 2 are of villagers who spend most of their time in another village and have sold their land; 2 belong to older villagers who are unable to farm and have passed their land on to their children; and 1 belongs to an unmarried woman whose parents lost the land due to longstanding debts.

Table 18: Distribution of land ownership in the village by plot size

Ethnic/caste group	Average plot size (*hal*)	Number of households	Total land owned (*hal*)	Per capita plot size (*hal*)
Rai	1	1	1	0.25
Sārkī	2.67	3	8	0.5
Damai	1.56	4	6.25	0.25
Gurung	4	4	16	0.8
Kāmī	0.8	5	4	0.11
Chhetri	2.5	6	15	0.8
Non-Limbu total	*2.19*	*23*	*50.25*	*0.42*
Chhetri/Gurung/Sārkī	*3*	*13*	*39*	*0.7*
Limbu	1.90	178	339.75	0.4
Total	**1.94**	**201**	**390**	**0.4**

Table 19: Average plot size per household as distributed across all the ethnic groups in the village (hal)

Five households have no land, and 33 households have less than 1 *hal.* Almost 20% of the land is owned by 69 households with medium sized plots (from 1 to 1.5 *hal*). These households produce on average 244 *jhutta* of maize, which is only enough for a few months of subsistence each year. While 107 households with small, medium or no plots owned 22.5% of the land, the 94 households with large and very large plots owned 77.4% of all the land in the village. The most acute example of this unequal distribution of land relates to the households with very large (5 *hal* and above) plots: only 14 households, or 13.5% of the total population, own 24.6% of all the land in the village.

This unequal distribution of land is also reflected in the caste distribution table (Table 19). The village-wide average plot of land was 1.94 *hal*. Limbu households were the closest to this with an average plot size of 1.9 *hal*. Considerably below the average were the Kāmī, who own the smallest amount of land (0.8 *hal*) relative to their total population.[56] The three populations in the village with the largest per capita ownership of land are the Gurung, Chhetri and Sārkī who own an average of 0.7 *hal* per person, almost twice the Limbu and village-wide per capita figure of 0.4 *hal* per person.

This same survey would have shown an even more significant difference in the ownership pattern of land if it had been carried out before the larger proportion of the Chhetri population migrated from the village. The existing non-Limbu households own a total of 50.25 *hal* compared to the village-wide total of 390 *hal*. The land owned by the Chhetri households that migrated from the village, currently owned by a number of Limbu households and equivalent to most of the land in Ward 3 and several large plots in Ward 5, is approximately estimated as 57.5 *hal* of land. This, combined with the currently held non-Limbu land would amount to some 107.75 *hal*, more than one quarter of the total land farmed in the village today.

Landlessness

Results from the survey indicate that there are five households with no land. Two of these are households which have already divided their land and passed it on to their sons. Another two households are villagers who live mostly outside the village but still own cardamom-planted forest and occasionally visit the village for cardamom-related work. They still own their house but all their agricultural land had either been sold to other households (the case of one villager) or given to others to farm on a share-cropping basis (the other villager). The fifth landless

---

56 The Kāmī tend to have large families (their average household size is 7 compared to the village-wide mean of 4.8), own no cardamom, and earn money by working as blacksmiths and *khetālā* for other households. They are widely agreed to be among the poorest households in the village.

household is an unmarried woman who lives alone and survives by working as a *khetālā*. They are all Limbu households. Perhaps surprisingly no Dalit castes in the village were landless.

A related issue is that of share-cropping, known as *adhiyã*, where the tenant carries out all the labour and receives half of the produce. This is a fairly common practice in the village and many households supplement the food produced on their own land with some *adhiyã* farming. Results of the survey showed that 27 households carry out some *adhiyã*, although from observations and conversations it appears that many more households have either been involved in it in the past or were planning to do so in the next season. This, together with the finding that, for whatever reason, a certain number of households did in fact have some *adhiyã* when they claimed not to have any, leads one to believe that although only 27 households were identified formally, the number was probably closer to 40 or 50, equivalent to approximately a quarter of the total village households.

Overall, the data on landlessness and the extent of *adhiyã* farming shows that most households in the village have been able to reach some arrangement with other households so that only very few households have no land whatsoever (see above). As already noted, these few households are formed either by older villagers who have already given their land to their children or by villagers who spend most of their time outside the village. Not only are there a number of households with more land than they can farm with their own household members, and therefore provide it to others on a share-cropping or mortgaged basis, but there are also, and certainly were in the recent past, a significant number of villagers who migrated away from the village. In this highly agricultural village society, most households have access to land in one way or another, though its distribution, let alone the quality and legal or economic arrangement is by no means equal.

Communal land

The 1985 land registry indicated that a small plot of land, a little over 5 *ropani*, was communally owned land. This is a tiny proportion of the total land size in the village but an important shared resource for all households in the village. All of this land, which is forested, is located above the main village settlement, mostly around a cemetery in Ward 2. It serves primarily as a resource for wood to be used in the cremation of deceased villagers. Permission to use either fallen wood or to fell a tree is assumed by the household of a deceased villager. Households who have no access to wood for fuel during the year are also sometimes able to get permission to obtain wood from an area of communally owned land during the irregularly held, village-wide meetings. Fodder from this land area can also be taken by any households without the need for such approval.

Taxation

During the period before the cadastral survey of 1985, the Subbas, or Limbu clan chiefs, were primarily responsible for collecting land taxes. The two principal forms of land-ownership that existed, *raikar* and kipat, each had a different set of rules relating to taxation. The amount of tax paid by a household for *raikar* land was calculated in proportion to the total size of the land and households with large plots would therefore pay more than those with smaller ones. Kipat land owners, with rice land or *khet*, were exempt from taxation, and taxes were only levied on them for their house and any closely associated *bāri* fields (Regmi 1976: 91). As Regmi has indicated "the problem [of taxation] would have been less intractable had there existed a system of taxing Kipat lands...The Kipat landownership system thus deprived the government of resources in the form of both land and revenue...and prevented the government from establishing effective administrative control over the whole of its territory" (Regmi 1976: 92).

Since the 1985 survey, tax has been paid within the VDC to a government employee, who in turn deposits this money in the tax offices in Taplejung. According to staff of the land records office, since there is no longer any difference between land ownership types, every household has to pay the same amount of tax and this is set at 5 rupees per year for households with between 1 and 50 *ropani* of land. Larger landholders have to pay more. Whatever the formal situation is concerning land taxation, villagers rarely mentioned tax during the survey and, in the cases it was raised, they indicated that they had only started paying it again in 2006.[57] Before this, the Maoists had prevented

---

57 Since the 1960s, land tax ceased to be a serious source of revenue for the State and partly as a result of this the State came to rely far more on foreign aid and taxes on trade (particularly imports) than on the traditional (feudal) "squeeze the peasant" strategy of taxation.

taxes from being collected locally and villagers had had to pay their land tax secretly at the tax offices in Taplejung as they would have been fined for not paying regularly.

Interestingly, despite the conversion of all agricultural and forested lands into privately owned plots, there is still a significant amount of land that is illegally taxed by a group of "Subbas". These are either individuals who were Subbas in the past, or close relatives of Subbas who inherit the position (despite it not being recognized as a political position by either the government of most of the villagers) or, in some cases, other older men who take the place of deceased or uninterested Subbas. There are 29 Subbas, all from VDCs along the Kabeli *kholā*, who meet a few times each year to discuss arrangements made with tenants who use land high above the village area for grazing cattle. All this higher-altitude land, from Yamphudin in the north-east down to Tellok VDC, is used by pastoral farmers for grazing their buffalo and cows. As it gets colder in winter, they move their animals to lower altitudes in the valley and return in the summer. As a result of the long distances they travel across different VDCs, they make arrangements with this group of Subbas to pay a fixed fee for grazing rights. This fee is shared among the Subbas and while it usually amounts to not much more than one or two thousand rupees, it is enough to pay for the food and drink consumed during their meetings. This grazing land is nominally owned by the government but a modified form of the older kipat arrangements, where households within a patrilineal sub-clan could access land with permission from the Subba of that sub-clan, currently operates in the village.

Economic differentiation

In their study of landholding inequality in Nepal, Thapa and Chhetry (1997) use the Gini index to measure land concentration and its variation across the 75 districts of Nepal. They show that higher levels of landownership inequality are positively associated with certain indicators of socioeconomic development—such as lower infant mortality—and the amount of cultivable land in the district. Conversely land is generally more equally distributed in regions which have less cultivable land, are more topographically rugged and less economically developed such as Mugu and Humla district. The Gini indices for Mugu and Humla were 0.329 and 0.354 respectively, while the figure for Taplejung district was higher with 0.467 (1997: 136), but lower than the national average of 0.518. Within Mamangkhe village, the Gini index for the distribution of land plots was 0.412, comparable to the figure for the district as a whole.[58]

Fricke (1993: 158-165) compares the Gini indices of wealth distribution in a number of villages in Nepal and elsewhere. He shows how Macfarlane's data for the value of land, livestock and housing of 93 households in Thak produces a Gini index of 0.474—or 0.403 when the analysis includes non-Gurung households. The Gini index of "total wealth" in the Tamang village of Timling is 0.22, which represents a considerably more equal distribution of wealth than the village of Thak. Timling's Gini index matches that of the world's three lowest Gini index countries: Denmark (0.247), Japan (0.249) and Sweden (0.25) (UNDP 2009).

For Fricke, the lack of stratification of wealth in Timling is a result of the relative abundance of land in the village: 0.654 acres per person, considerably more than the figures provided by Banister and Thapa (1981) for per capita arable land in Nepal, 0.427 acres, and in the mountain and hill regions, 0.211 acres and 0.247 acres respectively. A rough conversion from *hal* to acres produces the significantly smaller figure of 0.15 acres per person in Mamangkhe,[59] which seems to match Fricke's assertion that abundance of land correlates with the reduced stratification of wealth. Yet the data from Thak contradict this: with an average of 0.64 acres of land per person—almost identical to the figure for Timling—the Gini index is more than double that of Timling (Fricke 1993: 68).

Stratification of wealth is unlikely to be simply the result of the (unequal) distribution of a single resource, although in subsistence societies land ownership always plays a key role. A number of resources

---

58 The Gini index was calculated using the Stata command *ginidesc*, and data from the variable for millet and maize land in 2007 (as presented in Table 11 above). While the data are by no means accurate, because they measure land in approximate *hal* figures and not in *ropani* or hectares, the variation within the dataset is considerable and reflective of the actual variation of land ownership within the village.

59 Fricke considers that one *hal* is roughly equivalent to three *ropani* (Fricke 1993: 68). One *ropani* is equivalent to 0.12571 acres. The final figure was derived from the total 390 *hal* and 968 people in the village in 2007.

are examined below (Tables 20 and 21) first by using the Gini coefficient, and second by looking at the top and bottom 10% of producers or owners of each resource.

Resource	Gini index
Land (*hal*)	0.412
Cardamom production in 2007 (NPR)	0.586
Food crops - rice, millet, and maize (NPR)	0.449
All crops - food crops and cardamom (NPR)	0.560
Livestock - including chickens (NPR)	0.339
Livestock and food crops (NPR)	0.425
Livestock, food crops and cardamom (NPR)	0.447

Table 20: Gini indices of different resources in Mamangkhe in 2007

The Gini indices listed in Table 20 clearly show the impact that cardamom production has on the unequal distribution of wealth in the village. While the amount of land and value of livestock and food crops have Gini indices of 0.412, 0.339, and 0.449 respectively, cardamom production has the highest Gini index of all with 0.586.

Another way of examining the distribution of wealth within the village is to compare the percentage of any given resource produced or owned by the top and bottom 10% of producers.

Resource	Largest 10% producers	Smallest 10% producers
Land (*hal*)	30.8%	1.5%
Cardamom production in 2007 (NPR)	52.5%	0.8%
Food crops - rice, millet, and maize (NPR)	31.8%	1.3%
All crops - food crops and cardamom (NPR)	40.9%	0.7%
Livestock - including chickens (NPR)	33.5%	1%
Livestock and food crops (NPR)	29.6%	2.3%
Livestock, food crops and cardamom (NPR)	31.3%	2%

Table 21: Percentage of total resource produced or owned by the largest and smallest 10% of producers in the village (n=20)

The data in Table 21 show that cardamom is by far the most unequally distributed resource in the village with the largest 10% of producers (20 households) producing over half of the village total compared to the smallest 10% producing only 0.8% of the village total. The other resources, including land, food crops and livestock, are also unequally distributed with almost a third of each resource produced or owned by the largest 10%, and 1% to 2% by the smallest 10% of producers.

In their economic and sociological analysis of women in Nepal, Acharya and Bennett (1981) note that although there is considerable variation in average household income levels between villages in eight different sites across Nepal, within each village "inter-stratum differences in household income level were relatively mild with the average annual income of top stratum households only three times that of bottom stratum households" (1981: 305-306). The evidence presented in this chapter, and particularly in this section, tells a very different story.

One of the most equally distributed resources in the village is livestock.[60] If the top stratum of households is defined as the largest 20 livestock-owning households (as in Table 21), and the bottom stratum as the smallest 20, then the top stratum owns roughly 3 times as many units of livestock as the bottom stratum, which seems to be equivalent to the figure offered by Acharya and Bennett above. Yet if the units of livestock are converted to their market value, the top stratum owns over 30 times the value of livestock owned by the bottom stratum.[61] The difference is even more acute with cardamom, where the top stratum of cardamom producers earned over 50 times what the bottom stratum produced. With regard to total production (livestock, food crops and cardamom), the top stratum produced a total value almost 17 times what the bottom stratum produced. This story of unequal distribution remains even when the top stratum is defined as the top 50% of producers and the bottom stratum as the bottom 50%. In this case top stratum producers of cardamom still produce 7 times the value of what the bottom stratum produced (23 times if one includes the non-producers).

These economic differences between the wealthiest and poorest households in the village are the outcome of a historical process of

---

60 The values of various livestock were derived from average village prices for adult animals in 2007: bull, 7000 NPR; cow, 6000 NPR; buffalo, 12000 NPR; pig, 5000 NPR; goat, 800 NPR; chicken, 300 NPR.

61 The top stratum owns an average of 95,535 NPR of livestock compared to 2,880 NPR of livestock for the bottom stratum.

changing production and distribution of resources. Cardamom production—the most unequally distributed and high-value resource in the village—has contributed to the accentuation of economic differentiation between households. Without cardamom (livestock and food crops only) the top 10% of households produce 14 times the value of the bottom 50% of households. With cardamom, the top 10% produce 17 times the value of the bottom 50%.

One of the contentions of this book is that while an ethnic or caste-based analysis is sufficient for understanding historical processes of economic and social change, a class-based analysis is much more useful for examining contemporary economic and social differentiation. In spite of this, the economic data presented above clearly shows a considerable degree of inter-ethnic/caste variation. Broadly speaking the Chhetri, Gurung, and Sārkī appear to be the wealthiest, while the Kāmī are among the poorest in the village, with the Damais somewhere in the middle. Much of this variation can be explained in relation to differences in land ownership. As was briefly described above, both the Gurung and Sārkī were able to purchase considerable amounts of land when they originally arrived in the village compared to the Damai and Kāmī who were less wealthy to begin with. Since their arrival, the Damai have been able to purchase land in the village and invest in property in Jhapa. The Kāmī, with their large families, small agricultural plots, and large production deficits (Table 17) have been unable to significantly change their economic circumstances since arrival.[62] It was reported that when they first arrived in the village in the 1940s, the Damai and

---

62 Höfer (1976: 354-359) describes how the Kāmī in a Tamang village to the west of Kathmandu were able to transform their economic and social condition (over a thirty year period) from one of a patron-client relation of dependence on the Tamang to one of independence (a result of post-Rana period legislation, economic development and the influence of the Indian indepence movement on returning ex-mercenaries) and increased food self-sufficiency (by purchasing their own land and increasingly switching from blacksmithing to agricultural work). Clearly, there are fewer economic opportunities in remote rural areas than in urban areas where occupational change from traditional to non-traditional sources of income are more common. Parajuli (2007: 72-73) outlines such a change among the Gaines of Pokhara showing how the households dependent on traditional occupations (such as fishing and itinerant musicians) fell from 70% to 19% between 1984 and 2004 as a larger proportion of Gaines took on non-traditional work as teachers, shopkeepers, factory workers and engineers (see also Chhetri 2007).

Kāmī were far and away the poorest households in the village. The transition from inter-ethnic or inter-caste economic differentiation to class-based differentiation is illustrated by the fact that the poorest households in the village today (as measured by deficit production figures) are no longer solely the Dalit groups, but include a large number of Limbu households: nine of the ten households with the highest deficit production figures are Limbu households.

In many ways Gurung and Sārkī households in the village are in a similar economic position to the Chhetri. For example, both Sārkī and Gurung households are involved in money-lending much as the Chhetri have done for generations. Yet, due to their comparatively recent arrival in the village (in the 1940s), and small population (historically never more than 7 households), this book focuses almost entirely on the Chhetri who began to arrive some 150 years before other non-Limbu groups, were once distributed across 28 households, and today play such a central role in the economy of the village as the largest cardamom merchants and money-lenders in the village.

Political organization

The village has had no political representative or representation since 2004, following Prime Minister Deuba's decision not to hold VDC elections because of the Maoist insurgency and not to prolong VDC elected members' tenure either (because the opposition UML party had a majority of these positions in the country as a whole). Following the national elections in 2008, two members of parliament for the two constituencies in the district of Taplejung were elected. Consistuency 1, which includes Mamangkhe VDC, was won by Suryaman Gurung of the Nepal Congress Party. There were supposed to be new village-wide elections in 2009, but these have been postponed as the drafting of a new constitution by the national constituent assembly is currently delayed.

Village meetings are held to discuss decisions that need to be taken by all the villagers and, usually, such decisions relate to how VDC money should be spent. The most politically active and vocal villagers are often also the village representatives of national political parties. Disputes in the village are resolved with the help of other villagers who are called to offer their perspective by both parties in the argument. Smaller disputes, which might be about cutting fodder without permission or goats eating a neighbour's maize plants, tend to be resolved quickly with the help of a number of villagers who are often relatives living nearby. More serious disputes, particularly related to boundaries between land or unpaid debts, are sometimes taken to Taplejung and eventually resolved legally.

In the lead-up to the elections for a constituent assembly in April 2008, political discussions in the village became a much more common activity. Groups of men and women interested in supporting or finding out more about a particular party would meet in someone's house. Representatives or supporters of political parties made the rounds of all the households trying to gain more support for their party and to gauge the distribution of political sentiment. Interest and enthusiasm died away fairly fast after the elections. The whole period leading up to the elections was also a period for many villagers to postpone jobs which needed to get done so when the elections passed the work load became particularly intense. This may in part explain the lack of interest in post-election political developments but it is probably not the whole story. The villagers' main viewpoint appeared to be that they were not interested in politics because they felt that governments never got anything done and never achieved what they set out or said they would do. For the villagers, life in the village and their continuous struggle to make ends meet was always at the forefront of their minds. Certainly, if the Maoists had had a more significant impact in the village, by recruiting more villagers to their army and perhaps having a permanent presence, more political discussions would have taken place in the village. However, in their absence and aside from the periodic interest in politics at a local and national level—particularly during the period before and after the elections—politics does not seem to be a subject that occupies widespread and frequent discussions.

Maoists

The Maoists' People's War, or Nepalese Civil War, began in the western districts of Rolpa and Rukum in 1996. During the period until the Comprehensive Peace Agreement signed on 21 November 2006, the Maoists controlled large parts of rural Nepal either directly, with the presence of Maoist legal courts and Maoist schools, or more indirectly with occasional rallies and taxation. Although Maoists were present in Taplejung district, and a large group of Maoists were stationed around the village of Yamphudin upriver from Mamangkhe, they made only periodic appearances in Mamangkhe and, overall, do not seem to have had strong political support within the village. They first appeared in 1995, travelling unarmed and in small groups of two or three people. They held small meetings, staying in a villager's house for one night, and then moving on to another village. These meetings, initially held in secrecy, were similar to the period during and after the People's Movement of 1990 when many villagers became involved with the Communist Party of Nepal (Unified Marxist-Leninist).

Figure 18: A Maoist banner at a pre-election rally in March 2008.

The last villager to represent the VDC at the district level had been and still was a staunch supporter of this UML party. It was only around the year 2000 and 2001 that armed Maoists became a visible, if irregular, presence in the village. Villagers in Mamangkhe said that in 2001 the *gā-vi-sa adhyakṣa* (chairman of the VDC) of Yamphudin, who was known to be a Maoist sympathizer, was killed by the Nepalese Army. One villager was severely beaten up by a group of Maoists, and several younger villagers were intimidated and, after being encouraged—in some cases threatened—to join the Maoist army, left the village to live in Jhapa until the war was over. Apart from these events and the stories about having to host small groups of Maoists who ate food without paying for it, there seemed to be little else that involved the Maoists in the village. They were never a permanent presence and one of the only lasting structural impacts was to ban the teaching of Sanskrit. The Maoists also banned the sale of *raksi*[63] and tried to stop villagers from paying Government land tax, while they themselves—from 2005 until 2007—taxed cardamom producers in relation to their estimates of total production. Since 2007, taxation has shifted from the producer to the merchant and anyone transporting cardamom from producing areas to large merchants in Jhapa has to pay a large number of official and unofficial (*ghus*) taxes including those levied by the Maoists, the Limbu political parties, the police, and various other government taxes.

Only constituency-level data from the elections in April 2007 is available, so it is difficult to judge political feelings within the village at the time of the elections. From the number of people at village meetings and impressions related to me by more politically engaged villagers, it seems that, although many villagers had moved to support the Maoists, with probably only marginal support for the Limbu political party and the Unified Marxist-Leninist party, the largest support remained for the Nepali Congress party. This support goes back to the 1950s anti-Rana revolution led by the party and the strong sense of loyalty the party has been able to maintain with its supporters over the decades since (Hachhethu 2006: 6-8). This is reflected by the result of the election at the constituency level, where the Nepali Congress won with 8,719 votes compared to the 8,407 votes for the Maoists.[64]

---

63 Villagers commented that as a result of Maoist pressure small village shops stopped selling raksi, but households nonetheless continued to buy and sell it amongst themselves.

64 For more discussion on the constitutent assembly elections, see the recent pamphlet edited by Holmberg et al. (2009). Holmberg analyzes the results of

Health, ritual and the role of shamans in the village
Health post and medicinal plants

There is one health post in the village which provides immunizations for babies, women's contraceptives, and a number of first-aid medicines for emergencies. For anything more serious, families have to walk to the hospital at Taplejung bazaar, a difficult two-day walk away. Almost one third of the survey respondents said neither they nor any other household members had ever been to the health post, and just over two thirds of respondents said no one in their household had ever been to a hospital. A few medicines such as sitamol, a form of paracetamol, are widely available in the shops and many villagers commonly use these. Although the study was not focused on first treatment choice, observations of the many instances when villagers became ill and had to decide what to do indicated that, generally as a first treatment, they would either visit, or someone would bring, a *phedangma*, the Limbu shaman. The shaman would first undertake a divination to determine the cause of the illness—usually which spirit had caused it—and would then perform a chant lasting between five and 20 minutes. Only very occasionally would medicinal plants be used as treatment, and villagers told me that only one of the shamans in the village was knowledgeable about them. Some plants, such as the extremely common *tite pati* (*Artemisia indica*) and roots of the yellow Himalayan raspberry (*Rubus ellipticus*), were often self-administered by villagers for minor illnesses.[65] Apart from these occasional uses of commonly available plants, the use of medicinal plants in the village was extremely limited. In the past, the medicinal plant *chiraita* (*Swertia chirata*), a biennial herb with fever-reducing properties, was wild-harvested from land above the village area. This plant has a high but fluctuating market value similar to that of cardamom; between 80 to 400 rupees per kilo. A number of villagers who had harvested it in the past mentioned that digging the whole

the elections in two constituencies and shows how although people "voted for change" they did so not simply by voting for political parties, but by voting through a combination of ethnic, kin and patronage lines.

65   *Artemisia indica* or *tite pati* (Manandhar 2002: 97) is extremely common and widely used during rituals. In the village it is considered useful as a poultice for body aches and sprains: a number of leaves, heated by placing them near a fire, are wrapped around the area needing treatment. A number of villagers mentioned that the roots of *Rubus ellipticus* (Manandhar 2002: 403), can be chewed to relieve fever and body weakness.

plant out was labour intensive and that recently the amount of it available had decreased due to over-harvesting. Although the market demand for this plant remains high, villagers rarely collect it any more and I never saw or heard of the plant being used as a remedy in the village.

Shamanism

Perhaps the most impressive aspect of the culture of traditional healing among the Limbu is the number of shamans available throughout the village, and distributed across all the wards. Although the term *phedangma* (L.) tends to be used to refer to a shaman, most of the shamans in the village are actually *yeba* (L.). According to Subba (1995) there are seven categories of Limbu priest: Phedangma, Samba, Yeba (male), Yema (female), Mangba, Yuma and Ongsi. Jones (1976) refers to all of the above except the last two. Sagant (1976) draws a main distinction between the *phedangma* and *bijuwā*. In Mamangkhe, villagers spoke of Phedangma, Samba, Yeba, Yuma, Maharani and Jhakri. According to Jones (1976: 31), all these categories of priest are capable of performing a number of set rituals but differentiate themselves when diagnosing and curing illnesses. He writes that a good *samba* "should know the entire *mundhum* [the totality of oral tradition] by heart" yet in Mamangkhe the villagers who knew most about these were *yeba* and not *samba*. Without getting into a long discussion about these categories and the division of labour within the religious and ritual domain, and because my fieldwork did not focus on this, it seems sufficient to observe that the high numbers of shamans in the village results in most of them hardly performing rituals at all. A small number, perhaps three or four respected shamans, are visited regularly by most households when an individual is ill, and one shaman, who claims he is both a *jhãkri* and a *yeba*, practises full-time.[66]

Generally speaking, the most common "shaman type" in the village is the *yeba* of which there are 16 distributed throughout the village. There are also three *samba*, one *Yuma-Phedangma* (who was 25 years old in 2008), and a female *jhãkri*. There is also one actual *phedangma*,

---

66 This particular shaman is physically disabled and although he can walk slowly on his own, usually has to be carried to households for any rituals. His inability to carry out agricultural work may in part explain why he is a full-time shaman.

although the term is constantly used in reference to all the other types. Not only was there an abundance of shamans and people available for performing rituals and healing illness, but several of these 22 shamans had only recently become "possessed" by the spirit that forced them to become shamans (see Sagant 1976a: 56-99).

Ritual practice

The performance of household and village rituals is still a widespread activity in the village. A large number of rituals are performed by households throughout the year, including the life-cycle rituals associated with birth, marriage, and death. Among them are: periodic rituals for the purification or appeasing of spirits (the *dung dunge* ritual); rituals associated with particular activities such as killing a pig, or agricultural rituals for good harvest (*tɔːk sok ti sok* ritual); rituals held at specific times of the year such as the village-wide ritual of *sansari pūjā* held on the three Saturdays after the Nepali New Year in April; and rituals specifically performed for curing the illness of an individual. Survey data on ritual practice at a household level was collected for all households. These data

Figure 19: Sansari Puja in April with a view to the south of the Kabeli River.

show that exactly 90% of the respondents (181 households) performed rituals, while 10% of respondents (20 households) have never performed rituals of any kind.[67] While these data, like much of the data collected

---

67 This does not include funeral and marriage rituals which are large-scale, village-wide events. The use of the word *puja* (worship or ceremony rite) in the survey was limited to household level rituals usually involving the

throughout the survey, are not completely reliable, they do show a pattern of widespread participation in ritual life throughout the village. It should be added that all the households which said they never performed rituals were referring to the rituals excluding those for healing illness which, without exception, everyone performs, though some more than others.

Figure 20: Preparing the altar for a *dung dunge* ritual.

Another variable was used to quantify the extent to which households carry out rituals as it appeared from initial observations that some households only carried out household-based rituals such as for the household or family deity *himsammaŋ* (L.)[68] (which they called *nayã ghar* or new house in Nepali). Other households carried these rituals out as well as such more elaborate, time-consuming and expensive rituals as the *dung dunge* ritual, which is considered even by Limbu villagers to be extremely "traditional" because it is fairly brutal in the method used to sacrifice a goat and is carried out by only a few households today. The results of this section of the survey show an interesting distribution. Just over 50% of the households were extremely

---

household, a shaman and a few close relatives.

68 In the Limbu language: *him* is house and *sammaŋ* is god.

involved in ritual performance and had performed all the household rituals and at least two other ones. Another 23% had performed all the household rituals and one other, such as the ritual to "raise one's head high" *maŋenna* (L.) or *sir uṭhāunu, sappok chomen* (L.), the ceremony preceding birth of a baby, and *nahaŋma* (L.) the ceremony for "anointing the family head". 15% of households had only performed household rituals such as *maŋenna* and *tɔːk sok ti sok* (L.), while the remaining 10% performed no rituals at all. In other words almost three quarters of the households in the village regularly perform one or more rituals, a clear sign of the continued survival of this aspect of cultural practice.

The data related to household ritual practice showed no significant statistical relationship with any of the data from cardamom production. However, the data related to frequency of ritual performance seemed to show an interesting relationship between the amount of ritual performance and language use. The highest frequencies of households which perform rituals (either household ritual only or more) were always those which reported speaking only Limbu in the household. Yet statistical tests such as the chi-square test run with data from Limbu day-to-day and frequency of ritual performance showed no significant relationships.

Ritual performance (in the last year)	Language use (frequency of households)			
	Nepali	Limbu	Nepal-Limbu	Total
No rituals	7	8	5	20
Household rituals	9	17	5	31
Household and one other ritual	17	19	11	47
Household and two other rituals	21	59	23	103
Total	**54**	**103**	**44**	**201**

Table 22: Language use and ritual performance by frequency of households

Data analysis in search of statistically significant relationships always risks hiding what is ethnographically interesting about the data and the background to it. In this particular case what is interesting is both that so many households still perform rituals, and that so many households still use the Limbu language more than Nepali in day-to-day conversations and activities. These patterns not only perfectly matched the impressions gained throughout the fieldwork research, but also matched the impressions that non-resident Limbu villagers had of Mamangkhe village. From the very first mention of the village during preliminary research to find a field site, Mamangkhe was spoken of as one of the true Limbu villages where people still spoke Limbu and knew about their traditions.

Conclusion

This chapter has covered a large amount of ethnographic ground by presenting data from a variety of sources related to the contemporary village. There are broadly two domains that this overview has concentrated on: the economic domain related to household level and village-wide production of subsistence and cash-crops, and the distribution of land ownership; and the cultural domain related to language use, marriage and ritual practises.

In relation to subsistence production, most households in the village are able to produce at least some of the two main subsistence crops—millet and maize—although this is, on average, only enough to feed families for roughly 6 to 8 months of the year. Though only a small proportion of households (20%) grow rice, as the staple crop it is one of the main components of household expenditure throughout the year. Since subsistence-crop production is only able to cover household needs for an average of 6 to 8 months of the year, most households acquire cash (to purchase rice) from two other productive processes: cardamom production and labour migration abroad.

In relation to cardamom production, almost three-quarters of households produce cardamom but the distribution of production figures varies widely with just over a third of households (the 'large' and 'very large' producers) producing 71.1% of all cardamom, and almost half of households (the 'very small' and 'small' producers) a mere 13%. While cardamom production enables all households to access capital to varying degrees, it is the small number of large producers who benefit significantly from this high value cash-crop. These are the households that can afford more expensive visa arrangements, purchase property outside the village, and send their children to English-medium schools. The ability of households to produce large amounts of cardamom strongly influences their capacity for social and economic mobility.

Another strong indicator of the economic condition of a household is its ability to produce a surplus above the cost of its reproduction (which in this chapter was taken to be the average yearly household consumption of rice). Again a wide differentiation of surplus production is found across the village with 60% of households in deficit—i.e. producing a total value of crops which was less than the cost of the household's reproduction. Among the top 10% of surplus producers the distribution along caste lines shows that the Chhetri and Gurung produced the largest per capita surpluses of 24,800 and 22,560 NPR respectively, considerably more than the Limbu average of 13,775 NPR.

This pattern of distribution is repeated in relation to land ownership. Over half the households in the village (107 households) with either no land or small to medium plots own only 22.5% of the total land in the village, while the 14 households with 'very large' plots owned 24.6% of all land. In addition, Chhetri and Gurung households have per capita plot sizes that are double the average figures for Limbu households (due to a combination of historical—they cleared large plot of forest upon arrival—and economic reasons—they purchased or otherwise obtained land from Limbu villagers).

With regard to the cultural domain, this overview of the village has shown that the use of the Limbu language and ritual practice, important expressions of Limbu identity and culture, are both very much alive in Mamangkhe today. The Limbu cultural association *Kirant Yakthum Chumlung* focuses its activities on these two "areas" of Limbu culture, working to raise awareness and knowledge of the Limbu language (through publications) and Limbu cultural celebrations. The section on marriage shows that while the majority, 63%, are described as "love marriage" or "free choice", not all these marriages follow the same western pattern of romantic courtship—some of the "free choice" marriages are more freely chosen than others. Whether a marriage is arranged or "free choice", the ceremony of marriage is still carried out by most villagers who marry clan-exogamously and almost always intra-ethnically (see footnote 36).

For a village that has undergone substantial socioeconomic transformations since cardamom was introduced over the last few decades, as well as an earlier and more profound change in lifestyle from semi-nomadic hunter-gatherers to shifting cultivators and finally to sedentary agricultural farmers, ritual performance (including traditional marriage ceremonies) and the use of the Limbu language remain extremely active. To some extent, the apparent persistence of Limbu cultural practises is a matter of perception and some might argue that what persists is only an external "shell" of a cultural domain or practice. With language for example, although Limbu is used by many villagers in day-to-day conversations, Limbu speakers increasingly borrow a large number of words from the Nepali language. In addition, although the written alphabet is used in some publications and taught in the village school, very few people read and write Limbu for either personal (letters) or public (political) purposes. Despite this, with the increasing awareness of the political implications of debates about ethnicity and the increased political voice that the Limbu have gained as a result of their association with the Maoists, initially, and various new ethnically based political parties since the peace process (2006), cultural expressions of "Limbu-ness" such as language use and ritual performance, will continue to be important markers of ethnic difference and distinction.

This chapter has shown how certain aspects of the village economy and society have changed more dramatically than others. Although it is impossible to gauge the distribution of resources throughout the village a hundred years ago, the introduction of highly marketable cardamom production has had a marked effect on the distribution of wealth in the contemporary village. This productive process (examined in more detail in the next chapter), together with international labour migration (addressed in Chapter 5), has enabled a section of society to gain access to increased social (e.g. education, prestige) and economic opportunities (e.g. international visas, new property). Historically these opportunities existed only for a minority: village chiefs (the Subbas); villagers recruited into foreign armies; and the few who, through a mixture of hard work and luck, managed to earn and save money working in Sikkim. Of all the non-Limbu ethnic groups who migrated to the village over the last 200 years, the Chhetri, Gurung and Sārkī in particular were able to take advantage of ecological and economic conditions in the village to become the largest per capita landowners and surplus producers despite their relatively small population. This unequal distribution of wealth and resources within the village is not limited to inter-ethnic boundaries. Increasingly among the Limbu, for example, some households are benefiting from cardamom production and

Chapter 4
Cardamom

Overview of cardamom

Large cardamom also known as Nepal cardamom (*Amomum subalatum* Roxb.) is a spice cultivated in the sub-Himalayan regions of eastern Nepal, Sikkim, Bhutan and parts of north and north-east India. The indigenous inhabitants of Sikkim, the Lepcha, are said to have collected wild cardamom and developed the first cultivated varieties. Subba points out that both the presence of wild species of cardamom (which are known as *churumpa* locally), and the ndance of cultivated varieties, support the view that Cardamom originated in Sikkim (Subba 1984, Ravindran and Madhusoodanan 2002). Yet Lepchas are thought to have inhabited parts of Taplejung as far back as several hundred years ago, and modern Sikkim and parts of eastern Nepal were frequently considered part of the same political territories, as well as being ecologically similar areas. Additionally, the term "Nepal cardamom" points to an unambiguously Nepali origin for the plant, and many villagers I have spoken to refer to Ilam as the area of origin. Terms for cardamom in the Limbu language point to obvious borrowings from the Nepali term, *alaĩchi*, with the Limbu words *arenji*, *irenji*, and the more unusual *tambut* (Chemjong 2003: 169), which I have never heard used by a Limbu and no one I asked recognised it. In Mamangkhe the Nepali term is almost always used, with the exception of a few Limbus who mentioned the term *siŋse* (L) as the original Limbu word for cardamom, though Michailovsky (2002: 68) translates this as "certain wild edible plants". Interestingly, wild varieties of cardamom which are not propagated because their fruits are smaller than the managed varieties, are found in small quantities throughout the forest in cardamom-growing areas and are reported by locals to have been in the area for hundreds of years.

Large cardamom (referred to simply as cardamom throughout this book) belongs to the Zingiberaceae family, together with the more commonly available, and expensive, small or green cardamom (*Elettaria cardamomum* Maton). While small cardamom is grown across Asia and parts of Central America and Africa, cardamom is grown solely in Bhutan, India and Nepal. Although the presence of cardamom as a locally produced spice in Nepal dates back around 200 years, it was only during the 1960s that the previously small-scale production expanded to become one of the major cash crops for farmers and families in the eastern hill area. While there had been considerable seasonal labour migration from Nepal to Sikkim for well over 100 years, in large part focused on the intensive labour required in the cardamom forests of Sikkim, which for a long time were reputed to produce the best-quality cardamom seed, there were strict border controls which, for the most part, prevented people bringing cardamom suckers (rhizomes) and seedlings back from Sikkim. The history of cardamom cultivation in Nepal is somewhat unclear. For a start, there is an almost complete lack of mention of cardamom in the numerous documents and reports published between the mid 19th century and early 20th century by botanists and Indian colonial administrators working in and visiting Nepal.

Hamilton (1819) is one of the few, and it seems the first, to mention cardamom in his *Account of the Kingdom of Nepal*, when he writes about "a most valuable article of cultivation", though it is unclear which part of Nepal he is referring to (Hamilton 1819: 74). Curiously there are no mentions of cardamom in the works of Hooker (1854), who travelled through the eastern Himalayan area, Campbell (1840) who was based in Darjeeling but wrote about east Nepal, or Caplan (1970),[69] Jones (1973), and Sagant (1976a, 1996), who worked as anthropologists in eastern Nepal during the 1960s and 70s.

---

69 Caplan (2000) mentions cardamom once in the postscript to the 2nd edition of his book *Land and Social Change in East Nepal* originally published in 1970: "...virtually all ten Limbu households which were receiving pensions...had managed to retain or regain most if not all of their lands...thus, they were able to buy or use their existing lands for the cultivation of cardamom, which had become a major cash crop in the area" (Caplan 2000: 205).

Interestingly, Regmi's Research Collection (Regmi 1980) of papers from sometimes over 100 years ago, are full of references to cardamom in many of the official appointments, orders, notifications and notes collected. One such note on "Nepal-Tirhut Trade, 1791" lists cardamom among the many goods imported from Nepal in 1790 (Regmi 1980: note 145), and another note entitled "The Goles of Eastern Nepal" (Regmi 1980: note 78) mentions how in 1913 VS (1857) "some producers and traders made an attempt to smuggle cardamom and other commodities to India." In a section titled "Cardamom Farming in Nepal" in Regmi Research series 15, Regmi notes that around 1812, cardamom was being cultivated in the Paudur area of Kaski district in the Gandaki zone west of Kathmandu. This, combined with considerable evidence of the export of cardamom to India, leads Regmi to conclude that "cardamom farming possibly dates back to the period before political unification, but that state-trading in this commodity through the Patna establishment started during the time of Maharaj Jung Bahadur [who ruled Nepal between 1846 and 1877]" (Regmi 1983).

It seems evident that although cardamom was being produced, taxed, traded and even smuggled as far back as 200 years ago, it was not until the 1960s when a boom in market demand and price, together with improved infrastructure, encouraged the rapid expansion of cardamom cultivation from the district of Ilam, traditionally associated with tea-gardens, to Taplejung in the north. Why was the cultivation of cardamom mentioned, together with ginger, as one of the important crops of the mountainous parts of Nepal by Hamilton in the early 1800s (Hamilton 1819: 74-75), and then ignored by botanists and administrators working in what would become the most cardamom-productive areas of the country? Perhaps cardamom, flourished in the 18th and 19th centuries, then died out, only to re-emerge (possibly through reintroduction from Sikkim) as an important crop in the 1960s.

Ratna Bahadur himself, who introduced cardamom to Mamangkhe and the Kabeli valley area, repeatedly told me that there was a complete absence of cardamom cultivation throughout Taplejung district in the 1960s. As far as he knows, there were pockets of cardamom in Ilam district, and a small group of traders in Ilam bazaar itself to whom he sold his produce during his first three years of cardamom production. When I asked him why no one had tried to bring rhizomes up from Ilam, since he had already explained how border guards prevented smuggling of plants from Sikkim, he said that it was both too far—the seedlings would have died on the long walk north from Ilam—and somehow too ambitious, that it required a particular way of thinking, a particular mind-set, particular cleverness (he said all this tapping the side of his head with one finger), and that it was only the *parbate*, the Brahman-Chhetri, who had this.

A recent document released by the International Trade Centre and produced by consultants working for the Asia Trust Fund (George et al. 2007), describes without mentioning sources, how cardamom was introduced into Ilam in 1865 by Nepalese migrant workers travelling between Nepal and Sikkim. They mention that it was not until the establishment of the Cardamom Development Centre in Fikkal, Ilam, in 1975, that the crop began its rapid development. While local versions of the history of cardamom vary, as will be seen again further below, the story of the introduction of cardamom into Mamangkhe by Ratna Bahadur just over 40 years ago, serves as an interesting case study.

Ratna Bahadur's story

I interviewed Ratna Bahadur (Ratna) three times using a semi-structured format with a particular focus on the history of cardamom in the village and wider area. I was able to spend several afternoons with him in a more informal setting, and managed to visit most of his scattered cardamom fields, including the plot he developed in the first 10 years solely for selling seedlings to other villagers.

Ratna Bahadur Mabo (Lungdoyu), or Jilla Babai as he is generally known, was born in 1928 in Mamangkhe. His father, Harka Bahadur, lived in Ward 2, and his grandfather, Kauman Singh was one of the first Limbu to live in a multi-floored house. Both his father and grandfather were familiar with the older "slash and burn" production method which is today only used in certain more remote pockets of potential agricultural land outside the village area. Ratna mentioned that he learnt Nepali as a child from the Chhetri families who lived in Ward 3. His father spoke "a little" Nepali and his grandfather spoke none at all—"he couldn't even say 'Namaskar'! [*greetings*]"[70]

---

70 Transcribed from a recorded interview with Ratna Bahadur on the 12/9/2007.

Ratna's great-grandfather, Lodu Man, lived in a *yaksa* (L.) or temporary shelter in the jungle and never saw a properly built house. It was during his father's lifetime that the wood-cutting saw arrived and was first used. Before that they had used axes to cut trunks down and the main construction beams were simply entire tree trunks. There are still a few houses in the village that have no saw-cut wood. Bir Bahadur's house in Ward 4 is one such case, and is considered by many to be the oldest, and first-constructed, house in the village. Ratna said that Bir B.'s house was probably between 150 to 200 years old. Bir B. himself said the house was built in 1904, making it over 100 years old.

Ratna didn't join the army like his contemporary Phul Bahadur (also born in 1928) because his father had forced him to marry early. His first marriage was in 1945 (aged 17), and he left his wife after 7 years because she was "*dherai dalli*" [very round] and had not produced any children. He immediately remarried in 1952 at the age of 24 and fathered three children (one son, who lives in the house opposite his, and two daughters, who have married and live in other villages). His wife died almost exactly one year before I started my interviews, and he currently lives with his eldest grandson, his grandson's wife and their two children. His only son, Indra is 53 years old, and is married with 10 children, 4 sons and 6 daughters. Indra travelled to Sikkim around 22 years ago, working there for a total of 6 years, but has never been to any other countries, unlike his eldest son, who is married and lives with Ratna, and travelled to Malaysia once where he worked in a bakery for 3 years. Ratna was able to trace his patrilineal ancestors back five generations, and owns one of the few copies of a Lungdoyu sub-clan genealogy produced by a Lungdoyu from Tharpu, in Panchthar. As is the pattern for most older adults in the village he speaks fluent Limbu but mainly uses it with other older adults, preferring Nepali for conversing with his extended family members and any younger adults.

He is considered fairly rich by other villagers, particularly since he was able to buy two houses and a considerable amount of land including rice and maize terraces and some cardamom forest, from the money he earned as a village representative and from the cardamom cuttings and seed he sold. While he is able to grow enough rice to feed his household (880 kg produced and 720 kg consumed), it is not enough for his son's household who has very little land and a large family. They share production and are therefore forced to buy rice for some 4 to 6 months of the year. They produce a large amount of millet for beer (12 *muri*, 960 kg), which Ratna stopped drinking a few years ago for health reasons, about 1200 *jhutta* (10 unpeeled maize cobs in a bundle) of maize, and some wheat (160 kg). The extended household, that is the one Ratna lives in together with the one opposite occupied by his only son, lives in two large tin-roofed houses built by a Chhetri family between 1902 and 1903 for a total cost of 1,500 NPR, where now 300,000 NPR would not be enough. At the time, there were only Chhetri living in "Tekadin", the name for the lower part of Ward 3 which Ratna moved to. They had originally come from Khewang, the village on the other side of the Kabeli River, around 1896. When I asked why they had come over, Ratna replied "We Limbus brought him over. We brought a man called Sirbelas Kharel, for the development of the village, to learn Nepali. [I interrupt: you spoke no Nepali at the time?] No, we only spoke Limbu and we had to learn Nepali. We Limbu sold him some land. We brought him because he was clever, for development."[71] The family moved to unused land in the lower part of the village and employed Limbu villagers to work on it. Sirbelas Kharel, one of the first non-Limbu to live in the village, had six sons. Ratna stated that Sirbelas K. had initially bought this land for a symbolic one rupee, which at the time was enough for a complete set of clothes.

The first house Sirbelas built is about 100 metres directly downhill from the house Ratna lives in today. The house Ratna lives in was built by Sirbelas' oldest son, Chandra Muni Kharel, in 1958, and sold to Ratna in 1980 for 150,000 NPR, though Ratna only began living in it the following year. The other two large houses in Tekadin were constructed by Sirbelas' other sons, and two more sons lived in other parts of the village, again building large houses in Ward 5 and 6. The first son to leave was Chandra Muni, in 1978, and two years later, in 1982, the whole family had left the village. The sons live either inside or near Birtamod bazaar, in Jhapa. The family as a whole is reported to have made a large amount of money with cardamom cultivation and by selling rice and millet to the Limbu on credit. They were able to sell their property and all their land to Limbu men who had earned money by working abroad for the British or Indian Army, or in Sikkim in cardamom. Ratna is one of the few men in the village who managed to buy a sizeable amount of

---

71 Transcribed from a recorded interview with Ratna Bahadur on the 9/9/2007.

land without having worked abroad in any capacity (another man, Chandra B.'s father, will be discussed further below).

It is necessary to go back a few years, to detail the story of how Ratna brought cardamom from Sikkim, and was able to earn enough money to buy several houses and a large amount of land in a totally Chhetri-developed area of the village. Ward 3 is today some 15-20 minutes' walk from the "old centre" where the first houses were said to have been built in what is today Ward 4 of the village, slightly east of the main school building.

In 1968, Ratna was working as a representative of the local *chettra*, a collection of 4 VDCs: Surunkhim (down the valley on the same side as Mamangkhe), Yamphudin (up the valley on the same side as Mamangkhe), Khewang (slightly higher than Mamangkhe and on the opposite side of the valley), and Mamangkhe. He started this job as *jilla chettra sadasya* in 1967, working until 1981, and said that it was his reputation and connections with people in the district headquarters that provided him with the necessary permission to cross the border into Sikkim, collect rhizomes and legally transport them back to Mamangkhe. Knowledge of cardamom cultivation and the economic benefits it provided was fairly widespread because seasonal migration to Sikkim for work on cardamom fields had been taking place for decades already. Ratna mentioned three reasons why no one had brought back cardamom and planted it on a large enough scale to have an impact before the late 1960s. They either didn't think about it as a viable economic possibility, were unable to cross the border carrying rhizomes as it was illegal, or tried to carry them but were unable to keep the cuttings alive for the length of the journey home. There are other local versions of the early history of cardamom, which I will return to later, but the overall impression one gets is that though there may have been very small plots of cardamom being cultivated, the lack of any large-scale cultivation, combined with limited infrastructure for transporting the crop, and a total lack of market demand in the area, meant that effectively cardamom cultivation in the area began when Ratna brought back rhizomes from Sikkim.

There was a Chhetri—Ratna referred to him as 'Ram Chandre's oldest son'—who lived in a village nearby, Ponpe (part of the Mamangkhe VDC), who mentioned to Ratna that cardamom should be developed, that it could provide a viable income just as it was doing in Sikkim.

During this same period, the district-level committee on which Ratna had been representing Mamangkhe, was having discussions about *vikas* (development). "Should we plant wheat?—they asked—Can we bring cardamom to Taplejung?"[72] The committee accepted Ratna's proposition to bring cardamom from Sikkim after sending a small team out to inspect the land he had suggested he would use to plant the first cuttings. They lent him 1,500 NPR, with an interest rate of 7 NPR per 100 per year, and he was told he had to pay back the 1,500 (plus interest) within 8 years. Ratna planned to travel immediately, within 1968, with Ram Chandre's oldest son to Sikkim after obtaining permission to leave Nepal from the same Taplejung district committee. Ratna said that no similar papers were needed for leaving Sikkim, just written permission from the seller of the rhizomes. Ram Chandre's oldest son had an elder sister who had married a Chhetri who lived in Uttare, West Sikkim, so they were able to visit, buy the rhizomes from him and receive the necessary permission to return to Taplejung. He bought a total of 3,400 cuttings, which he had cut to look like lumps of ginger by removing the stem. Ram Chandre's oldest son, together with a friend of his, bought 1,200 cuttings and the three of them carried the rhizomes back to Mamangkhe. In those days one hundred cuttings would cost 30 Nepali NPR, millet was one rupee for one *pāthi*, and butter was 15-16 NPR for a *dharni*.

Having planted his first cardamom rhizomes the next year in 1969, Ratna produced 40 kg of cardamom seeds after three years, 160 kg in the fourth year, and 320 kg in the fifth year. It was only five to six years after first planting the cuttings in 1969 that he began to sell cuttings to other villagers. He did this beginning around 1974, and selling to both Limbu and non-Limbu farmers throughout the surrounding villages in several VDCs up and down the valley. In total he sold 45,000 cuttings, a phenomenal number considering what he had started with only a few years back. He sold 100 or 200 rhizomes to many people, so doesn't remember their names. But he sold larger amounts to a few people only and remembers their names with encyclopaedic precision: "I sold the most to Babi Ram Bhattarai, Mohan's father—he bought 4,200 in that first year. Ughir Bahadur up in Ward 7 bought 4,000, Mabarna Limbu, in Ward 7 also bought 4,000, Phul Bahadur bought 1,700, Thule Damai,

---

72 Transcribed from a recorded interview with Ratna Bahadur on the 12/9/2007.

Antare's [5th oldest son] father, bought 1,700...a Chhetri man from Khewang bought 400 and another Chhetri from Taplejung bought 1,500..."[73] Overall in the first year, Ratna sold more than 200 seedlings to at least 17 people, three of whom lived outside Mamangkhe village.

Others had asked for money for particular projects, not only cardamom-related, but only a limited number of proposals were usually successful. The committee acted as a type of Grameen bank, lending small amounts of money to people who proposed reliable means by which the money would be paid back. Apparently, there was one other man who had received permission from Taplejung district headquarters to collect cardamom from Sikkim. They had given 1,100 NPR to a man known as Mansi, from Yamphudin. He went to Sikkim a little later than Ratna but only brought a few cuttings back.

Another man, Dharmananda Pradhan, a Newar, who lived in Tellok, a five-hour walk below Mamangkhe, was one of the few Ratna knows who had managed to successfully collect, transport and plant cardamom cuttings around the time Ratna travelled legitimately to Sikkim. Ratna says that he either brought back few plants, or few survived the journey, because he started with a mere 20 to 30 cuttings. After three years he transported 1 kg of cardamom seeds to Taplejung bazaar to distribute among various friends of his. He was one of the very first to produce and sell seeds to the district capital and surrounding villages. He reached an early peak of 800 kg of cardamom fruit production between the years 1974 and 1979, but was imprisoned because his eldest son had murdered his youngest son and he had to take the blame. After 20 years in prison, a large part of his land had been stolen and he now produces about half what he was able to in the late 1970s. He certainly could have been given more credit for expanding cardamom production in Taplejung had it not been for his imprisonment and the relative anonymity he lived in after he was released.

For the first three years of cardamom seed production, 1973, 1974, and 1975, Ratna had to transport the cardamom by foot all the way to Ilam bazaar, as there were no merchants interested or able to buy cardamom in the whole of both Taplejung and Panchthar. By the fourth year of production, 1976, a number of merchants had made their way north of Ilam and were buying cardamom in Phidim, the capital of

---

73 Transcribed from a recorded interview with Ratna Bahadur on the 21/7/2007

Panchthar, and in several trading or market points along the route from Tharpu up the Kabeli River valley, all the way up to Tellok. Ratna eventually found a merchant in Khewang to whom he still today sells his cardamom crop.

Ratna was able to carry the first year's harvest, 40 kg, by himself, but the following year he travelled with three other men, each carrying one bag. It was a 6-day walk to Ilam from Mamangkhe, and 6 days back, along a road known as the *sukha pokhari* (dry lake). On the way out they would carry cardamom, and on the way back rice, oil, salt, spices and cloth. The buying price at the time was 700 NPR per 40 kg. A Newar merchant bought his produce. The second time, carrying 160 kg of cardamom, the Newar paid a total of 2,800 NPR. One day's wage at the time was 12 NPR. Nowadays with the selling price around 10,000 NPR per 40 kg, and a daily wage of 100 NPR, the rise in the value of cardamom is significant. 30 years ago, with the value of cardamom around 18 NPR per kilo, a little under one and a half day's of work could buy 1 kilo of cardamom. Today, with the price of cardamom fluctuating around 250 NPR per kilo, two and a half days of work will buy 1 kilo. The following year the value of cardamom had shot up from 700 NPR to 2,000 NPR per 40 kg. The value stayed fairly high for a period until supply increased enough to bring it down a little, but from the first year of production, planting cardamom was the most profitable crop in terms of economic return to labour input.

There are several survey questions which provide an insight into the history of cardamom production in the village. Of 94 total responses, the average number of years since production had begun was 17.5 years with a range of 2 to 40 years. It seems likely that the single respondent who stated 40 years gave an incorrect estimate since it was her husband (who died in 1984) who first had planted the cardamom. Other figures collected refer to how long ago the parents of household heads started planting cardamom. Of the 23 responses, the mean figure was 21.4 years, with a range from 1 to 40 years. The 40 years reported here refer to Ratna himself, since the respondent was his son. According to Ratna, he began selling cardamom cuttings in 1974—35 years ago. This coincides with the later figures (excluding the single mention of 40 years) ranging from 26 to 35 years given by a total of 15 people. These figures show that while a sizeable number of people were beginning to farm cardamom during the first years that Ratna began selling cuttings, the real "boom" in production was around 20 years ago, with just over 10% of respondents beginning production within the last 10 years.

Early local history of cardamom in other villages

In Tribhuvan University, I found 24 masters theses dealing with cardamom. Almost all of them were case studies in a selected VDC in a district in east Nepal submitted as part of an MA in economics (e.g. Basnet 2002, Limbu 1996, Thapa 2003). While the studies themselves are fairly predictable and lack analysis—providing overviews of cardamom cultivation with some detail about botany, agricultural methods and marketing—some of them present a little detail about the local history of cardamom. These theses provide some perspective on Ratna's grandiose claim that he was among the very first to plant cardamom in the whole of Taplejung district, and perhaps further afield.

Limbu's (1996) study of cardamom cultivation in Morahang VDC, Tehrathum, describes how old farmers reported the existence of some cardamom cultivation as early as 1965/66, though it was only in 1971 that the market had developed sufficiently enough to encourage more farmers to grow the crop. Older farmers remember a price boom between 1978, when the price "per mound"[74] went from between 300 and 500 NPR to four times that amount in 1984 (Limbu 1996: 26).[75] In support of Ratna's version of history, Thapa's (2003) study in Tellok VDC, Taplejung district, mentions 1976 as the year cardamom was first planted. The local VDC representative at the time, much like Ratna, brought cardamom cuttings from a villager in Ilam, and another villager brought cuttings the following year from Panchthar.

---

74 The term "mound" probably refers to a *maund* which is equal to a *man*, or roughly 40 kg.

75 Basnet (2002), who studied Soyang VDC in Ilam district, describes a number of contradictory versions of the early history of cardamom in the village. One version tells of a Mr. Thapa who brought cardamom from Darjeeling as long ago as 1864. Another version describes a Mr.Niraula who brought the plants some 64 years before 1919. The author describes how "The history indicates the cardamom cultivation in 1925-26 B.S [1869]. Imported from Sikkim, this unique crop could not get any achievement up to 1975 B.S. [1919]. In late 1975 B.S, the present Rana government had opened a cardamom store in Patna (India) and then began to supply to other countries. Consequently, its production had increased, Indian businessmen used to come in Fikkal (Ilam, Nepal) and Dharan (Sunsari, Nepal) to buy cardamom" (Basnet 2002: 2).

Presumably there was an acceleration of cardamom cultivation throughout much of far-east Nepal starting around the late 1970s, particularly in Taplejung, which emerged to become the most productive district in Nepal. It seems likely that Ratna was among the first to introduce cardamom to the district as a whole, but others were close behind and since the plant already had a history of cultivation in Ilam, there were numerous sources for cuttings.

Knowledge and technology related to cardamom cultivation

While the agricultural technologies and techniques associated with cardamom cultivation seemed relatively simple when described to me initially, as with all crops there are factors that greatly influence the long-term productivity and yield of plants. By means of participant observation in cardamom fields, I noticed that there was tremendous variation in ecological and agricultural variables such as: soil quality or texture; tree density; water abundance; weed growth; distance from other agricultural crops; density of crop cultivation (spacing); depth of cultivation of cutting; gradient or slope of field; and genetic factors related to selection of cuttings from productive and healthy (disease-free) parents. Here there are both endogenous factors, which involve humans as involved agents, and exogenous factors, independent of humans, such as rainfall and variations in temperature. Many of the seemingly purely exogenous factors allow for some human involvement in determining the extent to which they can impact the agricultural process: rainfall, for example, will be more intense in a less forested area, and soil can be improved to some extent by allowing certain weeds and low bushes to grow, by terracing to reduce erosion, and by moving decaying leaves closer to cardamom plants to act as fertilizing mulch.

I was curious about the exchanges of information regarding cultivation techniques that had taken place in the past, particularly since the crop was introduced into an environment that had little cultural familiarity with it. Certainly many of the men in the villages who first bought the cuttings from Ratna, had worked in Sikkim at some point. Ratna insisted that it was all very easy. Many people knew about planting techniques and the technologies associated with cardamom cultivation from their experience working in Sikkim. He added that he had personally brought a *churi* (small knife used to trim and pick cardamom) from Sikkim. This tool, also known as an *aṅkus* (hook) was copied by the blacksmith in Ward 6. This was the only new piece of technology needed. The technical knowledge was picked up very quickly by exchanging bits of information related mostly to planting the cuttings themselves. A training session had been organized in Taplejung at the time that Ratna went over to get permission to bring back cuttings from Sikkim. A number of people who had worked in Sikkim were trying to encourage an interest in cardamom cultivation in the area. They gave basic advice to people attending:

> They had said that one needs to plant the cardamom 5 feet apart. That one had to clear the forest and dig up the soil a little. That a little thin forest was needed, not with no trees and not a thick jungle. That *uttis* [alder-tree *Alnus nepalensis*] were needed. That the plant had to be cut back after the fruiting, like a banana plant. That the *nala* produced *tusā* which produced the *dānā*.[76]

To people unfamiliar with the plant, these instructions seem somewhat vague. One would have expected more detail on the effect of soil types, forest cover, and water supply on productivity, not to mention training on the future management of the crop. This is important not because the farmers involved in cardamom production are ignorant about the methods to be employed, but because the crisis soon to unfold in Nepal, and one which has already occurred in Sikkim, could perhaps have been dealt with earlier or more efficiently if there had been a more standardised and systematic approach to cardamom cultivation in the region. This crisis relates to the increased spread of two viruses which have had a severe impact on Sikkim's total cardamom production, and which have now spread to Nepal.

While there is a particular period, which in 2007 stretched from mid-April to mid-August, when most people clear their cardamom forests of weeds and shrubs, some families carry out this task only once, whilst others carry it out three times, varying the exact nature of the task. Additionally, a whole series of factors are involved in the decision to carry out tasks on a certain day or week, and these can have a big influence on final productivity. Families with more cash and larger crop production can afford to invest in improved drying sheds, or *bhatti*, for

---

76 Transcribed from a recorded interview with Ratna Bahadur on the 21/7/2007.

post-harvest preparation of the fruit for the market. This can have a tremendous impact on the quality of the seed (George et al. 2007: 48) and therefore on the final price of the crop once it reaches the market. The larger cardamom producers in the village are usually families who have been growing cardamom for the longest period of time. In most cases they have worked in Sikkim consecutively over many years and acquired considerable technical knowledge potentially making their labour-input more effective and efficient. While no systematic study of the variation in technical knowledge and ability was carried out, it is interesting to hypothesize a positive relationship between years of work in Sikkim and cardamom productivity per unit area in Mamangkhe.

Even without systematically studying the variation in planting knowledge and techniques across villagers, it is clear from participant observation that the variation is tremendous. Where one farmer may cut 100 rhizomes leaving a complete stem, and plant them only in loamy soil with over 150 cm of spacing, another will cut 100 rhizomes down to their ginger-like bulb, plant them in pebbly and permanently wet soil at intervals of just over half a metre. When I asked villagers about this type of variation and whether different techniques would lead to different results, they replied that it was impossible to know, and that—in the case of one rhizome a villager had just planted—it might survive but it might also die. Their replies to my questions about planting knowledge seemed to suggest unfamiliarity with the plant, as if they were still finding out what worked and what didn't. This makes some sense in view of the fairly recent introduction of cardamom, and yet is also surprising given the long history of migration to Sikkim to work in the cardamom forests there. More broadly, a fatalistic attitude towards cardamom production is evident in villagers' evaluation of good and bad harvest years. The way they describe fluctuations of production focuses entirely on factors they consider beyond their control such as the amount of rainfall and prevalence of disease. As such, the impact of individual technical skill or the application of particular knowledge and technology goes unmentioned in discussions villagers have about cardamom production.[77]

---

77 The exception to this are discussions about drying technologies, although obviously these have nothing to do with the fluctuations of cardamom production as they are concerned with post-harvest processing for

Cardamom production

What marks cardamom out as a cash crop is that it is an extremely high-value, high-return, low-volume and non-perishable crop—the last two being of great advantage in remote parts of Nepal where transportation is limited. Cash crops which have had success in other parts of Nepal, such as apples[78] and tea, require a different climate, much more initial investment, and in the case of apples, are expensive to transport and are easily damaged. In other words, while quality control for cardamom at the national level remains low and improved drying-technologies remain outside the mainstream—few people in the village have these and the market has not developed sufficiently to provide an incentive to more farmers to install them—cardamom offers villagers a means to earn relatively large amounts of cash by working intensively only during the harvest and clearing seasons (which for a large producer can last about a month each). Research on agricultural systems in Nepal has shown that only intercropped rice with wheat can occasionally achieve such gross returns, but always using substantially higher inputs and labour costs (Timsina 1986).

According to the Nepal Department of Agriculture, cardamom is cultivated in 37 of the 75 districts of Nepal. Ilam, thought by many to be the original site of cardamom in Nepal, ranks second in productivity and third in amount of land under cultivation. Figures for 2005-2006 show a total of 13,193 hectares producing 6,951 metric tons (MT) of cardamom seed for the whole of Nepal. The Eastern region alone, comprising 12 districts including Morang in the Tarai or plains, produced almost all of this with 6,505 MT. Within the Eastern region, Taplejung produced the largest amount (2,118 MT), followed by Ilam (1,587 MT), and Panchthar (1,016 MT). The expansion of cardamom cultivation in Taplejung must have taken place extremely quickly considering that most reports estimate that widespread cultivation only began in the late 1960s.

During the decade between 1994-1995 and 2004-2005, cardamom production in Nepal more than doubled, from 3,010 metric tons (MT) to

---

improving the quality of the final product.

78 Vinding (1984) mentions how apple cultivation provided owners (Thakalis in Mustang District) with substantial extra income, although unlike cardamom, which is sold to a larger and international market, the apple market risks becoming oversaturated as production increases (1984: 74)

6,647 MT (Statistical Information of Nepalese Agriculture (SINA), quoted in George et al. 2007: 13). SINA estimates that the 6,647 MT of cardamom are grown on a total of 11,498 hectares of land, which support over 70,000 families directly and indirectly. Yearly prices have been fluctuating tremendously over the last decade. The national average price peaked to 300 NPR per kilo in 2000, and then dropped to 144 NPR per kilo in 2005. While prices were decreasing between 2000 and 2005, the total area of cardamom production was nonetheless increasing, as farmers tried to compensate for the fall in value. In 2007, the average price was 250 NPR per kilo and the government expects production to continue increasing to reach 10,000 MT by 2012-2013, an increase of around 50% in the next 5 years. In Mamangkhe, people generally described the value of a *man* (40 kg) of cardamom as fluctuating between 8,000 and 12,000 NPR per 40 kg (200 to 300 NPR per kilo). While the peak year is considered to have been in 2005, there has been a noticeable increase in the value of cardamom over the last decade, encouraging even families with very little land to plant the crop. 23 households stated that they expected to produce 10 kilos or less of fruit in the coming year (harvested in October and November 2007), and 10 of these stated figures of 4 or 5 kilograms total production. Keeping in mind that a single highly productive plant can potentially produce a couple of kilos of cardamom seed, some of the very small producers in the village literally have no more than 5 plants in their back garden. These 5 kilos of cardamom if sold at the current 250 NPR per kilo, would provide enough cash to buy a 50 kilogram sack of rice which would roughly last 1 month in a household of five individuals.

The increase in price of cardamom mentioned above is not linked to a surge in market demand, as much as a decrease in overall production. Together with Nepal there are two other countries that produce cardamom: India and Bhutan. Due to the increasing spread of disease, combined with lack of proper attention to crop regeneration—replanting old or less-productive plants—production in both Sikkim and Bhutan has been declining. Production in India (mostly in Sikkim) which stood at 6,154 MT in 2003-2004 fell to 5,185 MT in 2005-2006, and a preliminary estimate for production in 2006-2007 predicts another fall to 4,303 MT— a fall of 30% from the 2003-2004 figures (George et al. 2007: 8).

While productivity has overall been increasing in Nepal, there are scattered cases of production decline due to crop disease, and, certainly within Mamangkhe, increasing concern about the long-term impact of this on the household and local economy. Much of the village economy is based on a cash-equivalent exchange system, in other words, people keep track of how much money they owe and are owed and eventually the books are balanced. This is in large part because of the almost chronic lack of cash within the village, and relates also to the large-scale and long-term debt many families are in. Government salaries are paid quarterly and it is one villager's responsibility to travel to the district headquarters and return with all the cash to be handed out to the local school teachers, health post workers, postmen, committees and youth clubs. Much of this cash leaves the village to pay for food goods and supplies bought on credit in Tharpu bazaar or elsewhere, as well as, for example, being sent to support secondary school students living away for many consecutive months. The little cash that is left in the village is constantly circulated by the villagers in a perpetuating and enormous balance book of credit and debit accounts.

To give an idea of the difficulty of collecting money from villagers during these times of cash shortage, one has only to consider the local "meat market". When a household decides to kill a buffalo, for example, several other villagers are invited to help. Usually at least two of them will help kill the animal, cut and weigh the meat and distribute meat to villagers who were unable to attend the event but have "reserved" a certain amount. These villagers will receive their portion of meat for free (usually one *dhārni* in the case of buffalo meat). Usually these same villagers, together with members of their households, will be in charge of collecting money from all the villagers who had bought meat that day—a literate member of the household would have noted everyone's name down and the quantity bought. Typically, one month after the animal was killed, these villagers will begin to visit other households to collect the money. Often the first visit is a reminder, and several more are needed until the money actually appears. This process can last up to a full month, if not more in some cases, with all the money collected finally returning to the original buffalo owner 2 to 3 months after the animal was killed. Villagers who are asked for this "meat money" often have to go on their own round of the village in order to make this money, *paisā banāunu*, by borrowing it, or often partially reducing a debt from other villagers who in turn borrow it from others and so forth.

The months after the harvest of cardamom, from November onwards, are thought of as months of abundance. Not only is there the tremendous injection of cash into the local economy as a result of the sale of cardamom, but the millet has also been harvested and beer-making and drinking become an almost full-time activity. Weddings and many village rituals take place during these months. The sale of cardamom enables many debt-ridden families to pay back the debt incurred over the last year, a debt which forces families to mix their rice with maize during meal-times, and others to eat no rice whatsoever. Cardamom production is the economic life-source of the village.[79] Either directly so, by providing a yearly source of cash, or indirectly through cardamom productive land being pledged to creditors as a means of raising capital. This will be demonstrated by examining the increased prosperity allowed to a section of the village by the development of a cardamom-based economic system. Before this, it is important to examine in more detail the process of cardamom production as it occurs within the village, as well as some more of the data collected during the village-wide survey.

Cardamom production in the village

The various activities necessary for cardamom production can be defined as associated with: clearing, planting, harvesting or selling, which are detailed separately below. Broadly speaking both males and females are involved in all the activities of cardamom cultivation. In part, the nature of the village's system of mutual labour-exchange, *thɔk yāllik* (L), encourages this, by forcing households with different proportions of male and female members to exchange labour with each other. The potential to earn their own cash, all or part of which they can manage privately, encourages women to work in any of the village's labour-intensive agricultural and productive tasks, and thus is perhaps one of the main reasons why so many of the labour-intensive tasks

---

79 In the village of Tingchim in Sikkim, surplus cash generated from expanded cardamom production since the 1960s, and surplus time created by increasingly employing Nepali labourers to work on their land, have allowed Lhopo villagers to invest in the practice and study of Buddhism— considerably more prestigious than their shamanic religious practices— as well as pay for biomedical health care and secular education for their children (Balikci 2008: 63).

traditionally associated with men, except ploughing which is exclusively carried out by men, are increasingly carried out by both men and women. Of all the activities I witnessed associated with the cardamom production cycle, women were most frequently involved in the collection of cardamom and the tasks associated with post-harvest processing.

One household, with whom several days of participant observation was carried out during the cardamom harvest period, will be used as an example of how household composition affects gendered distribution of labour. The household of what used to be the village representative in Taplejung district, nicknamed "Gavisa",[80] household #538 in Ward 5, is made up of six permanent residents: Gavisa himself, who is 56, his wife, his father, his unmarried daughter, and his daughter-in-law and her son. Labour for any large agricultural tasks is usually paid for as the small size of the household, and the age of its inhabitants, limits the possibility for labour-exchange. The neighbouring household, #537, on the same extended terrace, belongs to one of Gavisa's five married sons.

Figure 21: Where rice paddy meets cardamom forest.

80 This nickname is derived from the words *gaon vikas samiti*, or local council committee.

In it lives his daughter-in-law with her two sons. Gavisa's sons in households #537 and #538, have been working abroad until recently but spend most of their time since they returned, building their house near Birtamod, in Jhapa. This leaves household #538, which has not formally divided its cardamom fields between sons, with a labour force of one adult male and three adult females (Gavisa's father is too old to engage in any agricultural labour and his wife does not work in any cardamom-related activity).

Figure 22: View of a cardamom plantation shaded by alder trees.

On one of the days that participant observation was carried out, 17ᵗʰ September 2007, the three women had invited, or "hired", female friends from neighbouring houses in the same ward, to begin harvesting the cardamom on the lower sloping fields closer to the river, which ripen earlier than those further above. A total of 10 women, including Gavisa's unmarried daughter and one of his daughters-in-law participated, together with Gavisa's third-eldest son, *sāila*, who had come up from Jhapa specially to help out during the harvest season (see Figure 17). Of the eight non-household women, three were unmarried but of marriageable age, and three of the remaining five women had husbands who were currently working abroad. Both unmarried women and women whose husbands are abroad are both more economically independent and financially insecure. Lack of regular income is a strong incentive for them to earn money by working on other people's land. Most of the women on this day stated that they would be working for Gavisa for the rest of the week (from Monday through to Saturday) as Gavisa had planned to harvest all his Ward 5 cardamom plants in one go. While earning money is a strong incentive, doing this with friends from the area, all the while joking, laughing, teasing each other and relating anecdotes, makes it much more enjoyable. If a fieldworker had happened upon this particular work group, he would have been excused for thinking that among the Limbu, harvesting cardamom is a predominately female task.

Clearing cardamom

Clearing forest is both the first task for the development of any new cardamom field, and the first task for old fields as the cardamom season picks up. For new cardamom fields, trees may be thinned or planted depending on whether the field is being converted from forest or

Figure 23: Clearing a cardamom plant in May.

previously agricultural land, and weeds, shrubs and undergrowth are cut back. In old cardamom fields, non-productive plant "stacks" might be removed, using the same sickle which is used for weeding. In both old and new fields, clearing, known as *alaĩchi phãḍnu*, or *arenji lɛːŋma* (L), can take place any time after the start of the monsoon, and is thought of as one of the most physically demanding tasks of the year. Usually the undergrowth will have had almost a year to grow back since it was last cleared and brambles, snakes, and leeches are abundant.

Figure 24: View of a cleared cardamom stack in flower.

Many households have already begun clearing their fields in early June, while others have not yet carried this task out even once by late August. In addition, some households clear their cardamom fields up to three times and others only once, or, if the plants are well-established, not even once. Below is an extract from a day of participant observation during a forest-clearing activity which took place early in the cardamom season. The clearing was carried out by three of the four sons in household #413, who are aged 13, 16, and 18.

Extract from field notes: 23rd May, 2007:

Spent the day clearing the forest: from 11pm to around 1pm, when a longish break was taken, of perhaps 40mins. Then more clearing until 3.30pm, then a long break, perhaps 1hr. Then from 4.30 to around 5.45pm. About 5-6 hours of work.

The technique is to chop-clear away anything on the ground that stands up, but not as intensively as if we were preparing the ground for planting. Small sized trees are cleared away, slightly larger trees (2 years' growth perhaps) have their branches chopped. The aim is to clear-clarify-simplify the forest, even though the actual planting of cardamom is very sparse/thin. There are plants spaced about 3-5 metres apart. I am sure it could have been more intensively farmed. The trees are also thinly spread, having sprouted alone, they look like 10-year growth or so, but I am told they are only 4-5 years old (having emerged after the landslide that wiped away the maize planting land, and made them decide to plant alaïchi instead).

The trick is to clear the land as much as possible without being too low-to-the-ground, and make a particularly good job of clearing the area immediately around the alaïchi plant. This is done, in one case (Dhan A.) by pulling up all the stems and leaves that have gathered, or fallen away (a large number have dried up or died), and, holding them together, leaning them against the shoulder while clearing the area just around the plant bulbs with the left hand, as the right hand holds the sickle used to clear (in Dhan A.'s case this is the opposite as he is left-handed). There are a large number of leaves that have fallen into the middle of the bundle of huddling flower-bulbs, many rotted away and blocking the flowers from getting pollinated or benefiting from light and air flow.
In this regard it seems important that the clearing is done at this early stage, since the bulbs have only just started to flower and need to be pollinated: but most people are leaving the clearing to later (a month or so ahead of now), and even expressed surprise that they (Bir B.'s children) were going so soon.

The leaves, having been cleared (and initially I was told not to do this as snakes are known to hide in the bundle of bulbs) are chucked away, whilst stones and larger rocks that have slid into place at the bottom of the plant, by the bulbs, are also removed. Some have become quite firmly lodged. This is, after all, a year after the harvest and, I think, no work has been done since then.

At first sighting of the plants, Dhan A. said that although the plants were doing well physically (not too much disease which is what causes the leaves to die out: which has happened on a large scale in Sikkim and therefore, apparently, the work there, the demand for labour, has fallen dramatically); although they were doing well, the fruits themselves had become too wet, because of the recent heavy rainfall, which would reduce the amount of final fruit harvested.

Planting cardamom

All the villagers use cuttings from other cardamom plants to propagate their own plant population. Large cardamom propagation can take place through seeds, rhizomes (cuttings) and tissue culture techniques, but propagation through rhizomes is the only method employed in the village, and throughout most of Nepal. Seeds are used by research centres and cardamom nurseries. In the village, households begin planting new cardamom cutting from early June through to mid-July 2007. Finally there is the post-planting "mulching" of soil by placing leaves and dead weeds around seedling to help conserve soil moisture and increase local soil fertility. This ideal procedure for planting cardamom—perfect location, precise digging and planting, and localised mulching—is somewhat far from the reality of how people in Mamangkhe carry out this activity. Observing villagers at work brought out not only the considerable variation of technique from one person to another, but even as a participant, I was given very little direction except being told to take care whilst clearing leaves from cardamom fruits as snakes liked to nestle there. Often I worked beside children as young as 8 years old, who were never told how to do things, but simply copied the older people around them.

There are five main varieties or cultivars of large cardamom: Ramsey, Sawney, Golsey, Varlangey and Bebo (Nair 2005: 406). There are also a number of subcultivars such as Ramnag, Ramla, and Madhusey grown in Sikkim. The most widely grown variety in Mamangkhe is Ramla, followed by Golsey and what villagers call "Chibesay". Golsey is only grown in small quantities, individual producers often harvesting between 1 and 5 kg. Within the village, there is a price difference of 200 to 300 NPR between the Golsey, the more expensive variety, and the Ramla. There is some speculation that Ramla, which grows similarly to Ramsey and has capsule characters like Golsey, could be a natural hybrid between Golsey and Ramsey (Varadarasan and Biswas 2002: 303).

Figure 25: Carrying bundles of cardamom cuttings for transplanting elsewhere.

Figure 26: Preparing a hole before planting a cardamom cutting.

Golsey, which is also known as Dzongu Golsey, is especially cultivated at low altitudes (below 1500-1300m) and found in the Dzongu area of North Sikkim, the "traditional lands" of the Lepcha. Cultivation of Ramla in Sikkim is restricted to a few mid-altitude plantations in North Sikkim. The two most common varieties of cardamom in the village area are therefore varieties native to the Dzongu and North Sikkim area.

Below is another extract from a day of participant observation during cardamom planting which took place at the height of the monsoon season. This task was carried out by the three sons of household #413 mentioned above, together with the father who joined later in the day.

Extract from field notes: 27th June, 2007:

Cardamom planting was an almost spontaneous decision on the part of the three eldest sons of BirB, as the night before I had asked what they were going to do the next day and they (L at least) didn't know. It seems often like this with them, he has told me many times that he would have to see what occurs the next day—what needs to be done. We eventually set off at around 11am, after drinking a large bowl of water. *khājā* was carried together with those long sickles (which they call *sikel*)...Borrowed some rope from Tika's on the way to the *alaĭchi bagān.*

As we headed down to Sikten [Ward 3], through the thickly *alaĭchi*-planted forest, we passed Tika's fields, which were mostly on terraces (previously rice land). The plants were largish and thickly planted, perhaps 1.5/2m distant from each other, but a large proportion of the buds were not going to flower. They had rotted due to too much rain, wetness, or some other condition that L and D were not sure about. They just said that there were not many fruits, that the fruits had broken. The seed-bundle that becomes fruits was large on most plants and abundant. Where the flower had gone to fruit, lower down on the cone, the flower had in a manner, closed in and hardened to show a red lid: in other words it was easy to identify gone-to-fruit flowers, and most of the cones I saw up close were not fruiting and not going to fruit.

Parts of the field were very wet, with channels from the river coming through in strange places. Lokendra said that was good for the plants, but the manual I read describes well-irrigated (properly drained) loose soil, but not soaking soil.

The plan was to collect seedlings from Tika's plants and transport them to their own fields further across the side of the mountain, where we had cleared the weeds a month back. This is often done to thicken plantations, and to replant the seedlings that don't make it, that don't grow well. D said that he was constantly replanting seedlings. No wonder they seemed so cheap to me: 100 seedlings for 30 NPR.

And 100 seedlings are estimated to be able to produce a *man* of cardamom worth around 10,000 NPR. So an enormous profit if the seedlings grow well. D said that around 25% of the plants would not make it. Perhaps the number is larger, particularly considering the almost haphazard way that the plants were planted, in such different types of soil it seemed to me.

To pick the seedlings out, the idea is to select a plant that has a large number of cones/potential fruits, bundled together, but to not cut out a seedling that is actually in fruit. A non-fruiting cone, or rotten cone is fine. The sickle cuts away at the side of the large stack of nodules so as to pick out a small collection of seedlings, hopefully with young sprouting leaves. Two stalks of leaves or three are a good size to aim for. The nodule should be smallish but big enough to be already producing one or two cones. That is the ideal. The roots can be mostly cut away, leaving the nodule with almost nothing except a short section of root and the sprouting leaf stalks. The older, thicker leaf-stalks must be cut, as they will probably die anyway in transport, make the load heavier, and after transplanting reduce the speed of growth of new shoots/stalks.

200 seedlings are needed. We collect them all from a relatively close clump of plants. Sometimes one of us cuts an actual fruit away with the plant. Sometimes we cut too far into the stack and destroy some plants. L does this once (the first) and says that this is not good, laughing, and that Tika would get angry if he saw. I badly cut a plant myself with D and ask him if Tika sees it, if he would get angry? He says "no", then "maybe yes", "best you hide the plant a little", he says.

We collect all the seedlings and walk across the side of the mountain to a lower part, initially getting the directions to the planting area wrong: L knew the right area, it was higher up, his father had said.

For planting, once we reach the field that we had cleared a month back, (after drinking tea but leaving the corn for later), D makes a few pointed sticks to poke holes in the ground to help plant. Ideally the heavy iron rod-pole would be used here, particularly as some parts of the field are so stony. BirB eventually appears, with the rod and gives it to me. He seems happy to see me at work on his field, and announces his classic refrain: "*hāmro nepāl mā yesto cha iān-bhāi!*" [This is what it's like in our Nepal, younger-brother Ian!].

The idea is to find spaces between the already planted *alaĭchi*, to replant the 200 seedlings. Clear a small area and poke a hole that's big enough and loose enough to cover the seedling. Placing the seedling in, pack the soil around it—Saila emphasises that it should be well-packed after coming across a badly planted one. Dhane seems to plant many of his at an angle, sort of asleep/resting. I ask whether this is okay and he says "fine, they will straighten up". What will probably happen is the stalks already there will die off (many of them were bent in the transporting process in any case), and new stalks/shoots will emerge, for which it doesn't matter what the angle is. We plant 80 or so and take a corn break.

The other 120 or so we plant in about 1.5 hrs, till just past 5.30, and it starts to rain a little.

Harvesting cardamom

The first crop from a newly planted cardamom cutting produces fruit between two to three years after planting. Yields may double for the first few years, for example from 1 kg to 2 kg to 4 kg, until reaching a stable yield which is maintained over the next decade or more. Non-productive old plants are then removed and replanted. Harvest generally starts around late August and early September at lower altitudes, continuing through until December at higher altitudes.

In 2007, the first day of cardamom harvest in Mamangkhe took place on the 17th of September, in a field slightly below the main village settlements.[81] By the end of September many families in wards 4 and 5

---

81 Balikci (2007) describes how among the Tingchim Lhopo of Sikkim, the village shaman, or *bongthing*, performs a pre-harvest ritual for the cardamom deity known as Lenji Anya, a Lepcha ancestor and guardian of the cardamom plant. A goat or chicken is offered to appease the supernatural being (*nöpa*) that owns a particular plot of land (Balikci 2007: 210). Considering that the Limbu have their own extensive ritual traditions, and considerable

had begun harvesting any cardamom they had in fields at lower altitudes. Usually harvesting takes place in one round in a particular cardamom field unless the variation in elevation is severe. Some cardamom fields stretch vertically several hundred metres up a hill side which causes cardamom plants located higher up to ripen sometimes even up to a month later. Harvesting in one round has the advantage of finishing the job quickly, which is preferred if many people need to be hired and there is a labour shortage, and also ensures that fruits can be processed roughly at the same time, reducing the total amount of time spent during the post-harvest phase. The disadvantage of harvesting cardamom from a large field in one round is that the produce will often contain fruits of varying maturity and size, which will reduce the quality of the final product.

Harvesting begins when the seeds in the upper section of the fruit capsules in each spike become dark red, and when the flower has since dried or fallen off. Seeds are pulled off, cracked open and tasted. The flesh inside should be sweet, something like strawberries, if it is ready for harvest. The *churi*, mentioned above, is used to cut the stalk of the spike below the capsule. These are tossed into specially designed baskets kept close at hand. A couple of hours are kept free at the end of the day for separating the seeds, which are thrown into an enormous pile on clear ground, from the capsules, which are simply discarded. The following day, or soon after the harvest, the seeds are transported to the *bhatti*, and the seeds are cured to reduce moisture content from an average of between 70 to 80% moisture content to below 10%. The curing process brings out the aroma of the seed and increases its shelf life by killing any fungus infections (Mande et al. 1999: 465).

---

experience working with cardamom in Sikkim, it is surprising that no such pre-harvest ritual is performed in Mamangkhe. This is perhaps explained by the relatively recent introduction of the crop and conceptual separation of subsistence food crops, for which harvest rituals are performed, from cash crops such as cardamom.

Figure 27: On the way to harvesting cardamom in September 2007.

Although there are many modern versions of the *bhatti* (Mande et al. 1999, Rao et al. 2001, Nair 2005: 424) which use less firewood and produce a higher quality product, there is little incentive to depart in any particularly radical way from the standard or slightly adapted *bhatti* technology in the village. Most production is bought by local traders at prices they themselves have set, and villagers have neither the economic security nor the organization to develop their own connections with markets that would pay much more for better quality cardamom seeds.

Figure 28: Harvesting cardamom and cutting down old cardamom shoots.

Figure 29: Harvesting cardamom.

Figure 30: Sorting through the fruit capsules and extracting the seeds.

Figure 31: An old *bhatti* used for drying cardamom. The man to the left is Ratna Bahadur, mentioned at the start of this chapter.

The basic *bhatti* system, used by all save the smallest cardamom producers who borrow someone else's *bhatti* (usually a close relative's), is a small hut with walls on four sides and a roof placed above the walls. There is an opening in the front wall, often no wider than 1 metre, and a tightly woven mesh is placed on top of horizontal beams, to resemble a bed frame, which can be anything from 4 m² to 9 m². This mesh structure is placed some 2 metres above the ground and the separated cardamom seeds are spread evenly on top of this. A fire is prepared below and stoked, often for up to three days non-stop, until the seeds are properly dried. Obviously large quantities of wood, both green and dry, are burned and these need to be already cut and available nearby. The large amounts of smoke generated by green and wet wood mean the final product will inevitably fetch a lower market price (Karibasappa et al. 1987). Before moving onto the final phase, selling cardamom, the problem of disease on cardamom crops will be examined below.

Problem of disease

Cardamom plants are susceptible to diseases, usually of viral or fungal origin. Viral diseases such as Chirke and Foorkey, and fungal diseases such as wilt, leaf streak, clump rot and flower rot, are all fairly widespread problems in older cardamom-producing areas such as Bhutan, Sikkim and east Nepal (Nair 2005: 420). Curled, pale and streaky leaves are a common sight in Mamangkhe. Flower rot usually affects the flowers before the plant is able to produce capsules, and wilt, prevalent in either swampy or overly dry conditions, causes the cardamom plant to dry up. As a non-specialist, it would be hard to say exactly what the most prevalent diseases were in the village, but it was clearly a major concern for the villagers, who refer to all these diseases as *rog* (sickness, disease). Symptoms of wilt seemed fairly common among cardamom plants in the village. When asked about the rotted fruitless capsules (clump rot, flower rot) I was always told that it was caused by too much rainfall or swampy soil, and dried-up plants (wilt) were either too old or had not survived transplantation (from rhizome cuttings). According to one study, although diseases such as fungal and viral wilt had existed for many years in Bhutan, it was only in more recent years that a combination of ecological factors (prolonged high humidity, acidification of soils, and age of plantations) and human factors (poor management) combined to make it possible for this disease to cause economic damage (ibid.).

Cardamom production in Sikkim, where the spice crops ginger, turmeric, and garlic are also grown, has experienced a severe reduction since around 2002. A number of organizations working together, including the Horticulture Department, the Spices Board, Central Integrated Pest Management and Indian Council of Agricultural Research, claim to have successfully combated the problem. Yet as was noted earlier, total production of cardamom in India has fallen dramatically in the last few years, and the villagers in Mamangkhe, many of whom have worked in Sikkim, frequently describe how cardamom plantations in North and West Sikkim have been overwhelmed by disease.

In Mamangkhe there are signs that the disease will become a more serious problem in the near future. A local cardamom buyer said that it had only been two years since the disease really began to affect production in the village.[82] Before this period, the factors most likely to affect production were the location of the plantation and its suitability as a site in terms of tree shade. Villagers believe that most other factors such as the soil quality, presence of rocks, amount of water, slope gradient, weeds, and so forth, are less important considerations.

One of the important elements of cardamom production in the long term is the role human activity (the poor management alluded to earlier) can play in averting a potentially disastrous collapse in cardamom production. From several days of participant observation during the transplanting and replanting of cardamom plants, it seemed that there were no particularly explicit rules being followed to make sure that disease would not spread from infected plants to new plantations. The Spices Board recommends three key management practises that should be adopted to minimize potential loss due to viral diseases. These include "constant vigil to detect disease affected plants", "regular roughing of infected plants as soon as symptoms appear (uproot and destroy)", and using "seedlings produced in certified nurseries". The uprooting and burning of infected plants is cited by several documents as the only effective treatment for preventing the spread of disease in a cardamom plantation but there has not been a

---

82 Data about disease, productivity and cardamom varieties in this sub-section comes mostly from a long interview conducted with Raj, 24/5/2008, as well as participant observation of the various stages of cardamom production with four separate households.

single case, as far as I am aware, of someone carrying this out in the village.

From the little research I carried out specifically on this issue, it seemed that the general perception of the disease was that it was something inevitable. As it had already reduced production significantly in Sikkim, and people in the village were acutely aware of this, many villagers replied that it was only a matter of time before the *rog* would ruin production in their area. When prompted to provide solutions, no one mentioned any specific technical means by which the impact of the disease might be reduced. This is unsurprising when one considers that the damage caused by various diseases has only been in the last two years, and that even in Sikkim it became a widespread problem only around 5 years ago. During this same period the focus of labour migration has shifted from Sikkim and other Indian states to the Gulf states and Malaysia. Any technical knowledge that might have been absorbed by working with cardamom in Sikkim, including the implementation of research recommendations carried out by the Centre for Integrated Pest Management in Gangtok, would not have been brought back by seasonal migrants.

Although most individuals in the village describe how much cardamom production figures have fluctuated over the years, the total amount of cardamom being produced in Mamangkhe and beyond continues to grow, in line with market demand. It is this inexhaustible demand for cardamom, and its high market value, that pushes villagers to produce what they can, and increases the number of merchants who trade cardamom from remote villages to the cities of the southern plains.

Selling Cardamom

The smoke-dried seeds are gathered into jute bags and carried home for storage. There is no clear relationship between the amount of cardamom seed produced and the amount sold immediately after harvest. My initial assumption was that small-scale producers, those with between 5 kg and 20 kg perhaps, would be either forced by debts to sell their cardamom quickly or encouraged to sell for the purpose of buying consumer goods. Large-scale producers, I had imagined, would be more flexible. They would perhaps store the cardamom and take advantage of the rise in market price a few months after the harvesting season. As will be seen below, both large and small-scale producers are susceptible to debt, and generally speaking, most cardamom is sold immediately after the harvest. The cardamom harvesting season generally extends from early October through to December at higher elevations. At lower elevations, closer to the river, cardamom harvesting begins as early as mid-September.

It is particularly during the harvest and post-harvest (portering and selling) phases that both producers and non-producers have the possibility of quickly earning a significant income. Producers obviously earn money or reduce their debts by selling their produce to merchants. Non-producers, and many of the small-scale producers, are able to earn money as wage labourers both during the agricultural growing season, and in post-harvest activities by carrying the produce to market.[83] Many households in the village are able to significantly reduce their debts through labour contracts (*thekka*), and portering the cardamom for sale.

Generally speaking, there are two ways that cardamom is sold. The first is independently, outside the village area, and the second is to a local merchant. Those selling independently will carry their own produce, usually to Tharpu, but sometimes further afield. Some of these families may have an exchange relationship with a merchant who lives along the Kabeli valley between Mamangkhe and Tharpu. Others may know their way round the cardamom offices in Birtamod and travel there themselves while visiting relatives. A significant proportion of households sell their produce inside the village to one of three individuals. The largest buyer is the shopkeeper and former school teacher known as Raj. Another school teacher and shop-keeper known as Lakshmi and the tailor Indra also started buying cardamom about two years ago. In 2007, the estimated total amount of cardamom produced was 15,927 kg. Of this, Raj bought approximately 3,600 kg (23% of the village's total production), Lakshmi 720 kg (4.5%) and Indra 360 kg (just over 2%). This means that approximately 70.5% of the village's total cardamom production is sold independently of local merchants.

---

83 Since porters who transport cardamom to market usually also bring rice back to the village, they earn more than double the usual portering fee. Some villagers earn up to 900 NPR per trip, and travel up to 20 times during the three months of cardamom season.

Cardamom and debt

Data related to debt was collected from a series of in-depth interviews with a number of villagers. This relates specifically to large debts, *r̄n* not the short-term and usually interest-free loans known as *sāpaṭ, thɛtloŋ* (L.). These figures are not exact as debt is a delicate topic to talk about and I was rarely able to make a systematic record of a household's total debt. In most cases, debt was talked about with reference to a particular relationship, that is between one individual and another (i.e. a merchant, shopkeeper, fellow villager) or one individual and a commodity (i.e. cattle, land, visa-expenses). In this particular case, most of the debts related to money borrowed for the payment of work visas, and/or market goods bought locally or through a merchant. Table 23 depicts the distribution of these debts. Some households cited two reasons for the loan, hence the total number of cases is higher than the number of households.

Reason for the loan	Number of cases	Percentage
Market goods	10	45.46
Visa expenses	5	22.73
Purchase of land	3	13.64
Marriage	2	9.09
Construction of house	1	4.55
Inherited	1	4.55

Table 23: Distribution of debts among 15 households

Sagant's (1983: 194) much more detailed study of debt reveals the three most frequent reasons for loans as "justice of the *subbā*" (21.94%), indebtedness, "with the Sherpa" (16.20%) and, "funeral rites" (13.69%). Sagant was able to document an impressive 401 cases of indebtedness in his village-based study during the year 1966, and relate debt to four categories of loan (1983: 193): "loans related to one of the major events in the life cycle; following judicial proceedings; arising out of increasing impoverishment; [and] indebtedness involving the extension of dependency relations, where the mortgage is a cheap form of land endowment." Although the sample above is tiny in comparison, a number of important points emerge from the data. First, while Sagant documented 15 different reasons for the loan, none of them include indebtedness through participation in the market (45.46%), the most prevalent reason cited in the data above (Table 23). Furthermore, although Sagant does mention "departure for migration" as a reason for the loan in 12 cases (2.99% of total), this is significantly less than the 5 cases (22.73% of total) cited above. These two elements, visa expenditure for travel abroad and debt through the purchase of market goods, are characteristic of the tremendous changes that have come about since Sagant carried out his fieldwork in the late 1960s. Not only this, but the most cited reason for a loan in Sagant's work, "justice of the *subbā*", no longer applies as the Subbas who occupied such a crucial role in Limbu society right through to the 1970s, hold only symbolic power in most Limbu villages now.

To return to debt and cardamom in Mamangkhe, a closer examination of the relationship between these 15 households and their cardamom production suggests that both large-scale and small-scale producers are equally likely to become indebted. Table 24 shows debt and cardamom production figures over two years for these 15 households.

Participant	Debt (NPR)	Mean cardamom produced in 2006 & 2007 (kg)
50531	18,000	220
42031	25,000	30
60531	70,000	80
10131	78,000	15
30731	80,000	360
40831	100,000	360
41531	114,000	60
50230	118,000	180
41331	120,000	160
31331	130,000	180
41731	136,000	280
51131	250,000	0
32731	260,000	100
51831	300,000	170
40731	323,000	540

Table 24: Participant (coded), debt, and mean cardamom production for 2006-7; ranked by debt

A scatterplot of the variables for debt and mean production (2006-7) shows no marked linear relationship, and only a weak correlation[84] between the two variables. Overall then, there seems to be no strong relationship between debt and cardamom production. While it is generally true that households with larger-scale cardamom production will be able to borrow money from local or non-local merchants, those with either no cardamom or only small-scale production have their own means of borrowing money. They tend to raise capital by borrowing smaller sums from more people, mortgaging or offering as collateral plots of land, or, in rare cases, selling plots of land. This relationship between land and debt will be returned to in Chapter 6.

Cardamom merchants
History of the merchants

During several weeks of fieldwork in the city of Birtamod in Jhapa,[85] I carried out three semi-structured interviews with cardamom merchants. Four main points emerged from these interviews. These were related to: (1) the history of merchants; (2) profit margins of cardamom trade; (3) fluctuations of market prices; and (4) lack of knowledge about the cardamom market by producers.

The first point relates to the ethnicity and ancestry of the merchants. There are ten larger merchants in Birtamod. Of these, three are Marwari with a long history of cardamom trading (the other merchants are Bahun-Chhetri and Newar who became involved in cardamom trading in the 1990s).[86] One of these merchants, DB, claimed to have been "in the business" for four generations, having begun in Ilam around 50 years ago. In the early days, there was a total of 8,000 kg being bought by his great-grandfather. It was a side-business, which occupied the family for one or two months at the most. In the period leading up to 1977 (when another merchant's family [SD] started

---

84 Pearson's correlation showed only a slight relationship (non-significant) between these two variables (r=0.381, p= 0.244).

85 23/09/2007 to 30/09/2007, and 24/02/2008 to 01/03/2008

86 Originally from Rajasthan in India and considered to be successful businessmen, Marwaris have played an important role in the Nepalese economy, both as merchants and as financers for industrial development (Whelpton 2005: 145, 186; Zivetz 1992: 83-96).

trading), production had increased to 800,000 kg and there were four families, all of them Marwari, involved in buying cardamom and selling it on. SD's family moved down to Jhapa 24 years ago, to take advantage of both the increase in production in all the districts north of Ilam, and the improved infrastructure connecting these points with Jhapa. Work on a road connecting Ilam to Gopetar to the north was started in 1992 and the road connecting Ilam with Birtamod to the south had been fully surfaced by 1991.

The second point relates to the profit margin merchants make and the costs along the market chain as a whole. SD's margin is roughly 100 NPR per 40 kg of cardamom. This is the same profit margin for a smaller merchant who was at the offices during the interview, and who buys cardamom locally (in Phidim, Panchthar). There are multiple costs (Table 25) involved in transporting the cardamom from any of the market towns which act as the first selling post for most producers, and further costs "down-stream" including export taxes and shipping costs.

Item	Cost
Local tax in harvest area	Variable
District-level tax in harvest area	120 NPR per 40 kg
Limbuwan-affiliated groups tax	50 NPR per sack (80 kg) or 2,000 per truck
Young Communist League activists tax	75 NPR per sack
Police tax	Anything from 200 NPR to 1,000 per consignment
Packaging and transport costs	100 NPR per sack
Labour costs of cleaning, sorting, re-bagging, loading	Variable
Labour costs of loading and unloading	50 NPR per consignment
Jhapa district tax	25 NPR per bag
Consignment cost	571 NPR per delivery
Export tax	Variable
Cost of shipping abroad	Variable

Table 25: List of taxes and costs incurred by cardamom merchants from harvest to sale abroad

In short, the market chain is full of taxes, payments, labour arrangements and so forth, making the process of independently selling cardamom in Jhapa for a producer based in a remote village in Taplejung, almost impossible. Merchants are well-educated, literate, experienced in dealing with businessmen, bureaucrats, and politicians, and have a large amount of capital at their disposal which enables them to buy up and store cardamom to resell it subsequently at the most convenient time. Raj is such a merchant and his life and business will be discussed in more detail in Chapter 6.

Year	Price of cardamom (NPR per kilo)
1975	15
1976	40-50
1977	75
1980	105
1983	75
1985	100-150
1990	200
1992	300
1999	300-400
2001	137.5-550
2002	102.5

*Data collected from interviews with two cardamom merchants in Birtamod.

Table 26: Price trend of cardamom in Birtamod and Ilam Bazaar from 1975 to 2002

The third point relates to the fluctuation of market prices. There are the historical or longer-term fluctuations, and the short-term fluctuations over a few days to months. The first producer to sell to SD when his grandparents were living and working in Ilam, was a Rai villager from Yamphudin[87] who had first planted cardamom in 1970. In 1975 he had carried 80 kg to Ilam and sold them for 1,200 NPR (15 NPR per kg). He decided it wasn't worth it and says he uprooted all his cardamom after returning to the village. In 1976, the market price started to increase from 15 NPR per kg and he decided to plant cardamom once again. Before this, any cardamom producer, and there were several in Ilam he says, would have been producing cardamom at a loss. The

87 By a stroke of good luck, this villager, P.B. Rai, was in the office at the time of the interview. He had come to sell 1.5 kg of cardamom seeds (seeds inside the capsules) and ask about the current market price.

price continued to rise over the next few decades (Table 26), reaching 550 NPR per kg in 2001. The price collapsed to 102.5 NPR per kilo with the "9/11" attacks on the World Trade Centre. A terrorist attack on the other side of the world had an immediate impact on the price of cardamom in east Nepal.

Below is a transcription from part of an interview with one cardamom merchant (DB mentioned above) which deals with the question of market prices, the effect of the "9/11" attacks and what cardamom is used for: [88]

> *ICF - Do you have any history of market prices with you?*
> DB - No.
> *ICF - But approximately?*
> DB - Approximately, for example, 500 per kg in 2000, eight years ago, that was the highest, and the lowest, when the US towers collapsed, that was in...
> *ICF - 2001?*
> DB - No no! 2003! 2058 VS [which was 2001]. Bin Laden put the plane in towers in 2003. 11th Sept, that time the rate was 4100 for a *man*.
> *ICF - For a man?!*
> DB - Yes. This means 100 NPR per kg.
> *ICF - Why?*
> DB - Because that year the crop was more and everyone was frightened, everyone got frightened, not the farmers, but the buyers in Pakistan. US is the king of the world, that year there was a large production that year, and people were scared, Third World War or what will happen.
> *ICF - But only for 1 month?*
> DB - For 3 months. That year, the price never went above 6000 per *man*. 6500 per *man* something like that. Now the rate is in these four years, highest is 10,000, lowest is 6,500, in these last five years.
> *ICF - Will it reach 20,000 again?*
> DB - Who knows! If demand increases, there is a chance.
> *ICF - Where does the most demand come from?*
> DB - All over India, Delhi, Kanpur, Amritsar, Indore

---

88 Carried out on 25/02/2008 and conducted in both Nepali and English.

ICF - *What is Indore?*

DB - A city's name, Chennai, Calcutta...Every big city contains the big cardamom. What is its use do you know?

ICF - *No?*

DB - It is for meat spice, meat *masala*. Muslims eat a lot of this. Muslims use it in meat.

ICF - *The largest use is this? How much meat do they eat?!*

DB - How much do they eat? Now, let's see how many Muslims there are in the world. And another thing is, this cardamom is only grown in 2 places...in 3 places, Bhutan, Sikkim and Nepal, in no other places is it grown, in the whole world only here. In Sikkim it has become zero production, in Bhutan the production has also decreased significantly, now, in the world, the first producer is Nepal.

ICF - *Nepal is the largest?*

DB - Nepal's production is high, every year the total production is increasing

ICF - *But in the villages it seems to be decreasing?*

DB - This is why: in the village, at an individual level it is decreasing but new farmers are increasing, the product and quality of Nepal cardamom is increasing. Another example is that farmers used to produce 100 *man*, and now they have started produce 50 *man*, but the total number of farmers has increased. Where there used to be 2 farmers there are now 10 farmers. Now, before, in Kagbari, there didn't used to be cardamom. It has only been about 10 years that we have started working there [buying cardamom]. We have been working for 50 years, and now the most cardamom is coming from there. In other words, we have to say that they have won. Khandbari. North of Dhankuta [Sankhuwasabha district]. You have to go and visit once. It is a nice place.

Short-term fluctuations, of a couple of hundred NPR during any one week, have a smaller effect on cardamom producers in the village who usually sell cardamom immediately after harvesting or keep small amounts in storage to be able to sell it when they face a shortage of cash later in the spring and summer months. During one week of interviews in Birtamod, the price of cardamom fluctuated from 8800 rpm to 9200 rpm. The Rai villager from Yamphudin (P.B. Rai) explained how he had brought all his cardamom down to Birtamod, and was only going to sell if the price went over 10,000 rpm. Raj, the largest cardamom buyer in Mamangkhe, stores most of the cardamom he buys in Tharpu in the house of the merchant who supplies him with market goods for his shop in Mamangkhe. Even as late as June, Raj was selling several *man* of cardamom he had left in his house in the village, hoping to take advantage of the slight rise in market price.

In one interview with Raj,[89] he explained how when he started to buy cardamom in 1991, the local cost of cardamom was 2250 rpm. He bought a total of 50 *man* and sold them in Birtamod for 3500-4000 rpm that year, making a profit of 77.8%. There were fewer taxes along the road, and villagers were less experienced with the cardamom market. Over the years, both the number and level of taxes have increased, and villagers have become more economically aware. With improved communications, everyone immediately knows the market value of cardamom anywhere along the market chain and although no one except Raj sells cardamom directly to the merchants in Birtamod, this widespread knowledge of costs has meant that Raj's margin has been reduced dramatically. When the cost of cardamom in Birtamod was 9000 rpm, Raj's price in the village was 7800, a reduction in the profit margin from 77.8 to 15.4%.

Figure 32: Porters resting on sacks of cardamom outside a merchant's office in Birtamod.

89 Carried out on 09/03/2008, as part of a series of three successive interviews with Raj.

Figure 33: Cleaning and cutting the tops of individual cardamom pods in a merchant's storeroom in Birtamod.

Figure 34: Weighing and repackaging cardamom into 25 kg sacks for export.

Figure 35: Sacks of cardamom in storage before being exported.

The final point about cardamom that emerged from the interviews with the merchants relates to the lack of knowledge about the demand for cardamom. Considering what a tremendously valuable crop it is, it seemed surprising that not a single villager had any specific ideas about either where cardamom was sold or what it was used for. Some villagers mentioned that they knew most cardamom was exported to India and they assumed it would be used to spice tea. In the village a few households occasionally use ground cardamom seeds, removed from the pods, to spice tea, but this is only very rarely served and only to guests. Freshly picked cardamom is sometimes eaten by children, who suck the flesh—which tastes like strawberries—surrounding the seeds inside each pod. I observed adult villagers occasionally tasting a couple but the general understanding is that eating too many will cause a headache, which although potentially true is nevertheless a useful concept to prevent pickers from eating too many.

A broader point should be made in relation to the relatively low level of assistance and attention given to cardamom by the Nepali Agriculture Department. A report on the cardamom sector in Nepal

(George et al. 2007) points out that there is very little training given to farmers on how to control crop pests and improve seed drying technologies to increase the quality of the final product. The report outlines a long list of recommendations to the Agriculture Department and district level development officers, ranging from "produce and distribute quality planting materials in large scale" to "introduce an auction system" with the aim of improving prices for both growers and buyers (George et al. 2007: 48-50). In comparison with India, which has a Sikkim branch for both the Indian Cardamom Research Institute and the Indian Council of Agricultural Research, the Nepali State is decidedly uninvolved with the development of a crop that has become so central to the lives of many farmers across east Nepal.

Conclusion

This chapter has examined one of the most important productive processes within the village. Since cardamom was first planted by a local villager in 1969, it has been adopted by almost three-quarters of all households in the village. The sale of cardamom has directly benefited both small and large producers by providing them with a relatively secure yearly income. It has also benefited households by providing them with access to capital through credit and loans offered in exchange for future production, and through usufructuary mortgage arrangements of cardamom-producing land. Cardamom production in the village has also benefited non-producers and small producers by increasing the demand for labour both in the cardamom forests and for transporting cardamom to market.

The somewhat ambiguous origin of cardamom—some evidence suggested that it had existed in Nepal over 200 years ago but never on a large scale—and its fairly recent introduction into the village are reflected in the low level of technical knowledge most of the villagers seem to have about the crop. At all stages of the production process, from clearing the forest to harvesting the crop, the tools used today are the same as those used over 30 years ago. Improved drying technologies, introduced in other parts of east Nepal by international NGOs, have yet to arrive in the village despite the impact such technology would have on the quality of the final product as well as the reduction in fuel wood required to dry the seed capsules. The recent introduction of the crop, and the laissez-faire attitude with which villagers produce cardamom, is not only reflected in the lack of technological innovation and entrepreneurship. It is reflected, for example, in the heterogeneous nature of technical knowledge related to any of the stages of cardamom production. Authoritative botanical and agronomic manuals (Nair 2005, Ravindran and Madhusoodanan 2002) indicate that some of the essential considerations for successful cardamom cultivation include: tree cover, soil type, spacing between plants, varieties of plants, and the replacement of infected plants with healthy plants. Very few of these were mentioned by villagers when asked about cardamom growing techniques. Most of the factors they considered important, such as rainfall and the gradient of slope (the probability of a landslide), are exogenous factors. In other words, many of the villagers I worked with and interviewed seemed to consider the success of cardamom crops to be more a result of exogenous ecological conditions than any technical or practical input by the cultivator.

Despite this variation in technical and practical knowledge and the seeming unfamiliarity with cash crop cultivation—most notably expressed by the lack of entrepreneurship in adopting new technologies and seeking more profitable relations with merchants further down the market chain than the village merchants and those based in Tharpu— the extremely high value of cardamom has benefited a large proportion of the village. The figures presented in Chapter 3 showed that 22% of the households in the village produced enough cardamom to pay for the cost of their rice consumption. Small and very small cardamom producers are still able to benefit from the high market value of cardamom. Even a couple of *man* of cardamom can support a small family with several months' worth of rice, or longer by mixing the rice with maize.

While smaller producers certainly benefit from their cardamom, and the opportunity to work for larger cardamom producers and porter the sacks of cardamom out of the village, the real impact of cardamom as a high-value cash crop is experienced by the large and very large producers. At some 40% of the total village population, these account for 70% of the total cardamom production in the village—a disproportionate amount of the cardamom in relation to their population size. Such larger producers, who more than cover the costs of their yearly rice consumption with the cardamom, are able to invest their surplus capital both inside the village (e.g. lending it out at high interest rates) and outside (by investing in work visas abroad or purchasing property). This is not to say that smaller-scale producers do not also invest in visas, property, and money-lending, among other things. The data related to debt (Table 24) indicated that both large and small scale producers accumulated large debts which are often related to these kinds of investments. The difference between smaller and larger producers lies not in the kinds of investments, but the amount of investment they are able to make. Both small and large producers are able to put money aside and pay for work visas abroad, for example, but larger producers can afford to pay for the more expensive and secure work visas which in turn enable them to earn more money. The difference can be as significant as paying 80,000 NPR for a work visa with a guaranteed salary of 10,000 NPR per month, and paying 150,000 NPR for a work visa with a guaranteed salary of 30,000 NPR per month—significantly more in proportion to the original cost of the visa.

These differences are also highlighted by the ability of households to purchase property: smaller producers—or indeed poorer households, whether they produce cardamom or not—are still able to purchase a small piece of land, such as 1 *khaṭṭhā*, in Jhapa, with little agricultural land, for as little as 35,000 NPR; large producers with substantial capital have invested as much as 200,000 NPR for 3 *khaṭṭhā*, a sum of money that would take a small producer (40-100 kg) at least 10 years to make, but a very large producer (400 kg and above) barely 1 to 2 years.

These examples point to the different kinds of access—to property, visas, credit, agricultural land, etc.—which are enabled by income resulting from the sale of cardamom. Access to capital and the ability to purchase property had of course existed before the introduction of cardamom. A small number of villagers had worked for the Indian and British Armies, earning substantial pensions which enabled them to purchase land within the village and increase both their subsistence and cash crop productive capacity. Also long before the introduction of cardamom, villagers had carried out seasonal labour migration to Sikkim and other parts of India. This seasonal economic migration continues to this day—although fewer travel to Sikkim than did in the past. Both of these extra-village economic activities have played a part in increasing the wealth of a number of households in the village. Employment in the Indian or British army in particular has significantly benefited the handful of households who still receive a pension (e.g. the case of Phul Bhahahur presented in Chapter 5), while only a limited number of the countless villagers who worked in Sikkim were able to purchase new property.

The economic impact of cardamom production has been widespread, benefiting both producers (large and small) and non-producers, but the high value of cardamom has particularly suited the few large and very large producers. To put the value of cardamom into perspective, the largest producers of rice in the village produce around 800 kg of rice, over fifteen times the village-wide average of 52 kg. This has a local value of approximately 20,000 NPR. The largest cardamom growers in the village produced between 600 and 1,200 kg of cardamom over the last two years. Taking the average figure of 896 kg, the total value of this production is roughly 180,000 NPR, many times more than the value of a large rice crop. In other words, the value of cardamom has little relation to the value of subsistence-produced crops. It is this extremely high value of cardamom which has driven a wedge between the large and very large producers on the one hand, and smaller producers and non-producers on the other. Unlike non-producers, small and very small producers (those producing between 4 and 100 kg of cardamom) do generate some capital (between 800 and 20,000 NPR) but this is not sufficient to cover the costs of household food consumption. In other words, while small and very small producers do benefit from both additional capital provided by the sale of cardamom, as well as the potential to mortgage cardamom productive land should the need arise, the income they make from cardamom plays only a subsidiary role.

If the unequal distribution of land and subsistence production created fault lines or cracks within the village which historically contributed to the economic and social differentiation of households—initially predominantly along ethnic lines but more recently also within ethnic groups—then cardamom production acted (and continues to act) as a wedge within those cracks to push apart and heighten this economic and social differentiation. The concept of *rural class formation* can be applied to describe this process of differentiation which has created groups of households with diverging economic and social conditions; households with differing degrees of access to resources and opportunities for changing their social and economic condition.

The final section of the chapter described the history of cardamom merchants and the cardamom market. This section emphasized how the combined effects of increased crop disease (which has already devastated production in Sikkim and, to a lesser extent, Bhutan), increased production in other parts of Nepal, and decreased productivity of old production sites (due in large part to the improper management of cardamom plants) have contributed to an fluctuating market price and an uncertain and potentially unsustainable future for cardamom production in the village. This uncertainty neatly coincides with the emergence and increased importance of international labour migration as an additional productive process—the other two being subsistence production and cardamom cash crop production. As will be shown in the next chapter, the growth of international labour migration is closely tied to the history of cardamom production. In the contemporary village, this relationship can take different forms. For example, for some households it is the income from cardamom production which covers the cost of the work visa. For others, it is the ability to mortgage cardamom productive land which either directly pays for the visa or is used in a loan agreement as collateral should the borrower fail to pay back the debt. Whatever the specific process or relationship is, cardamom provides a significant boost of income to a certain proportion of the households in the village who are thereby able to travel and work abroad. However uncertain the future of cardamom production is today, it has played a crucial role in securing, for a certain proportion of village population, opportunities for economic and social change. As a result of this, it has also been responsible for the increased socioeconomic differentiation which is visible in the village today and which will no doubt continue to increase as the benefits of cardamom production are allied with the economic benefits—at least to some—that come from working abroad.

Chapter 5

Migration

*Of all the migrations from Nepal, those of the soldiers are the best known...
While the soldier is abroad, his farm survives without him. His father, uncle,
eldest brother, a cousin or sometimes his wife, do the sowing, transplanting,
weeding, harvesting. When at last he returns at the end of his service, one
thing is proven: the village has managed quite well without him... But land
has become scarce. In most cases, the farms are already too small to be
further subdivided. Conversely, a small number of notables, political leaders
or moneylenders, jump on the least false step in order to increase their 'vast
domains'. The soldier's return, as those who have stayed behind are well
aware, represents a threat. Looking beyond the happy reunion, the village
prepares, with time-honoured experience, for confrontation. <u>Eastern Nepal
is saturated, and has been for a long time, with men hungry for land.</u>*
Philippe Sagant - The Dozing Shaman (1996 [1978]: 278-279, my
emphasis)

Situating a dispersed village

In the final chapter of *Resources and Population*, Macfarlane wrote that
the estimated 2% annual population growth rate in the village of Thak
would result in an ecological disaster within a generation, as well as
increased under-employment and scarcity of cash (Macfarlane 2003
[1976]: 294). Thirty years later this ecological disaster had been avoided
largely as a result of "extensive and permanent out-migration"
(Macfarlane 2003: xvi), something Macfarlane claims was not possible
to predict in 1969, and the growth of urban centres, both of which
contributed to reducing rural populations and production intensity on
hill environments (Campbell 2004: 153). High levels of out-migration
from Thak might actually have been predictable if analysed in the
context of the "decline" of hill villages and rural communities around
the world. Rural-to-urban migration and the "progressive subordination

of small communities to the dynamics of the wider economy and society" (Seddon 2001: 119) have been a feature of rural change in both developed and developing countries for centuries. Many of the families which migrated from Thak settled either in clusters along the road from Thak to Pokhara, Nepal's third largest city, or in Pokhara itself. In 1969 there were only three Thak households in Pokhara, but the number of households had grown to 43 by 1992, and 58 in 1999 (Pettigrew 2000: 81).

The formation of a community outside, but of equal size to, the original village of Thak is described by Seddon as an example of a "dispersed" village. Focusing only on the "core" village of Thak, as Macfarlane does, rather than on the "dynamic, changing, and spatially as well as socially extended "community" of "the people of Thak" (ibid.: 121), produces only a partial understanding of social and economic change. Both the "core" and the "dispersed" villages must be included in contemporary village-based studies to avoid the bias of an "emphasis on the least dynamic part" of a community (ibid.). While I disagree that only households that move from their home village to new settlements can be considered part of a "dynamic" model of social change, it is certainly the case that there is both a "core" and a "dispersed" village of Mamangkhe. In this book, the core refers to the village settlement along the Kabeli River in Taplejung, Mamangkhe proper. The "dispersed" village can be conceptualized in two ways: first, as households scattered across districts and in India with often no contact with Mamangkhe; second, as households concentrated in specific sites with continuous contact with Mamangkhe. The first would include all the households which were originally based in Mamangkhe proper and have moved permanently to a number of new settlement areas either along the Kabeli River, or in the district capital of Phungling or other districts in Nepal, or to Sikkim and beyond.

The second more concrete "dispersed" village refers specifically to households in and around the settlement of Happenchowk, about 20 km north of the town of Birtamod in Jhapa District (see Figure 2). These are the households that have migrated either permanently or temporarily from Mamangkhe and are clustered around two new settlement areas, Aitabare and Happenchowk, along or close to the main road that runs north from Birtamod to Taplejung. These include 18 and 12 households respectively, all of which have a household head from Mamangkhe. In addition to these two main settlement areas, there are two households located about 2 km west of Happenchowk in Hadiya, and three households in or close to the settlement of Budhabare, about 5 km south of Happenchowk. All of these households except one are ethnically Limbu and have moved to the area within the last ten years. A small number of non-Limbu families have also migrated or bought property outside Mamangkhe in Phungling, Ilam bazaar, Birtamod and Kathmandu, but were not included in the Jhapa survey as they form part of the "scattered" rather than "concentrated" or "concrete" model of the dispersed village mentioned above. The dispersed village therefore includes 35 households. A base-line survey was carried out using 29 of the 35 households: the sample included all 18 of the households in Aitabare and 11 of the 12 households in Happenchowk.

Theories of migration

Generally speaking, the study of migration and human mobility is characterized by a focus on a particular migration typology. This includes: distance—internal versus international migration; direction—rural to urban, urban to rural, or rural to rural migration; and period—short-term versus long-term or permanent migration. Research tends to focus on specific types of migration to the exclusion of others such that a study of international migration will make little reference to internal migration, and research on rural to urban migration will overlook urban to rural migration. As Osella and Gardner remark:

> Within academic circles...the focus has tended to be on international migration, with a growing emphasis upon how places and people are interconnected... In focusing overly upon movement which transverses and transgresses national boundaries, then, we are in danger of failing to recognize important social and historical continuities between different types of migration, as well as prioritizing contact with foreign countries as the major agent of cultural change (Osella and Gardner 2004: xi-xii).

While it is certainly the case that scholars have tended to focus on international migration, often overlooking movements within national borders which are usually important precursors to international migration, theories which have been developed to explain the causes and consequences of international migration can sometimes be applied or adopted to understand migration at many different levels.

One of the oldest theories of international migration, which stems from neoclassical economic theory, originally had its roots in models developed to understand the relationship between economic development and internal labour migration (Lewis 1954, Todaro 1976, Massey et al. 1998: 18). This theory considers migration to be caused by regional and international differences in wage rates. The flow of workers from low-wage, labour-surplus areas to high-wage, labour-deficit areas would, theoretically, be matched by an opposite flow of capital which would ultimately lead to the equilibrium of wage rates and labour. The corresponding micro-level theories of migration emphasize individual choice and conceive of migration as a form of rationalized (following a cost-benefit calculation) investment in "human capital". These two approaches have been characterized as "push-pull" theories, conceiving migration to be caused by a combination of "push" factors, such as the lack of economic opportunities and social and political marginalization or repression, and "pull" factors, such as demand for labour, high salaries and social or political acceptance (Castles and Miller 2003: 22). These theories have been criticized for being overly individualistic, ahistorical and unrealistic in their representation of decision-making processes.

The "new economics of labour migration" approach was developed in the 1980s to deal with some of the criticisms of neoclassical theory (Stark and Bloom 1985, Stark 1991, Taylor 1999). The main suggestion of the theory is that "people act collectively not only to maximize expected income, but also to minimize risks and to loosen constraints associated with various kinds of market failures, apart from those in the labour market" (Massey et al. 1988: 21). According to the "new economics" theory, families self-insure by reorganizing their household labour so that some individuals work in productive activities closer to home or elsewhere in the country, while others travel abroad. Although both the new economics and the neoclassical theories of migration differ in what they consider to be the causes of migration, they are both based on the idea that individuals, or households, follow a similar process of decision-making to maximize income (or minimize risk). In this way these theories are about micro-level processes and do not take into account either the wider political economic context or the social networks that tie individuals and households together across geographical and social spaces.

A number of macro-level theories have offered alternative explanations of the causes and consequences of migration. These theories, developed in the 1970s, share with the Marxist political economy approach a conception of the unequal economic and political power wielded by developed countries over developing countries. Historical-structural theorists such as Portes and Walton (1981), Petras (1981), and Sassen (1988), describe international migration as the result not of individual or households decisions, but as a "natural response to the penetration of weaker societies by the political and economic institutions of the developed world" (Castles and Wise 2008: 21). The penetration of capitalist economic relations coincides with the proletarianization and increased landlessness of peasants, the growth of foreign-owned industries, exploitation of natural resources, and development of infrastructure for the transportation of market goods. All of which leads to creation of large mobile work forces which become increasingly detached from their agrarian communities and willing to migrate abroad (Massey et al. 1998: 36-38).

Where neoclassical theories of migration failed to take into account larger-scale processes of economic and social upheaval caused by the increasing involvement of industrial capitalism on land-based populations, historical-structural theories (also known as historical-functional or neo-Marxist theories) were criticized for considering capital to be all-determining and for failing to take into account individual, household or group decision making.

"Migration systems theory" (Castles and Miller 2003: 26-29) attempts to account for the failings of previous theories by examining migration from both ends and including both macro-structures, such as the international market and the legal and structural behaviour of the state, and micro-structures, such as the social networks that migrants create and rely on to support themselves and their communities. This theory makes considerable use of the concept of social networks and explores how they develop and are used by migrants to negotiate their way around the various economic, social, geographical and legal hurdles which they face both in their own communities and the receiving country or area. It is this focus on social networks, and in particular the ways in which migration creates and extends linkages between sending and receiving communities, which has led to the emergence of a theory known as "transnationalism" (Glick Schiller et al. 1992, Basch et al. 1994).

The globalization of new technologies of transport and communication has led to the increasingly circular or repetitive migration patterns of migrants who are able to stay in contact with their communities, and visit more frequently than had been possible in the past. Transnationalism or transnational processes "emphasize the ongoing interconnection or flow of people, ideas, objects, and capital across the borders of nation-states, in contexts in which the state shapes but does not contain such linkages and movements" (Glick Schiller 2004: 449).

Transnationalism criticizes the view of culture as a discrete unit, separated from other units by geographical boundaries and its own historical contingencies. This view, initially propounded by functionalists and structural-functionalists (with their notoriously ahistorical conceptualization of culture and society), was nonetheless compounded by the popularization of Geertzian-influenced anthropology which continued to view culture as a discrete and bounded unit with its own internal system of meaning (Glick Schiller 2004: 450). Transnationalism, defined as "the processes by which immigrants forge and sustain multi-stranded social relations that link together their societies of origin and settlement" (Basch et al. 1994: 7) straddles, as a theory, both the micro-level decision-making processes of individuals and groups within social networks, and the macro-level effects of global capitalism on the integration of the world by both transnational corporations and international labour.

All of these theories have strengths and weaknesses. Transnationalism and "migrations systems theory" both attempt to integrate the important concept of social networks with larger-scale structural issues related to the state, capital and the market. Yet they fail to acknowledge the importance of internal migration, usually a precursor to international movements, and the role of non-migrants, or those who have not yet migrated, within larger social networks. Additionally these theories, and particularly the "new economics of labour migration" theory, can be criticized for viewing migration as largely framed by economic interests and for overlooking its social and cultural dimensions.

Scholars who have included non-economic dimensions in their studies have shown how migration can be seen as a status symbol and younger generations may be attracted to labour migration as a way of avoiding agricultural work (Thieme 2006: 11). Migration can also be a rite of passage to adulthood for adolescents (e.g. the practice of *bhāgne* described in detail by Sharma 2007: 199-200), a means to escape political conflict or difficult relationships in the family or community of the migrant, or form part of an "identity project" for individuals (Osella and Osella 2000).

The recurrent theme of this overview of migration theory can be seen as the relationship between the structures that cause and shape migration, be they historical, political, social, or economic, and the agency of migrants—i.e. whether they migrate following a cost-benefit analysis, as a means of increasing their prestige, or as a rite of passage. In many ways transnationalism and "migration systems theory" have forged a compromise between these two positions by examining both ends of migration and making social networks a central part of their analysis; yet they have failed to get away from the "international bias" of migration theory.

The approach taken in this chapter is neatly summarised by Osella and Gardner (2004):

> Relationships between places are structured first and foremost by global capital, but within this framework there is much room—literally and metaphorically—for movement. Thus, while migration occurs in the context of power relations between people and between localities which shape the circumstances of people's movements, at the same time migrants continuously interpret, negotiate and subvert these constraints within the unfolding of specific migratory practises the outcome of which cannot be predicted (2004: *xlii*).

A number of separate points emerge from this extract. First, global capital, or local capital in the case of smaller-scale migrations, plays a primary role in structuring the framework (or power relations) of migration. Second, this framework shapes the relations people create and rely on—their social networks—for the migrations they undertake. Third, migrants are not only affected by this framework, or (economically) determined by it, but are themselves involved in shaping it. Osella and Gardner's use of the terms *locality* and *movement* are particularly suited to the experiences of migration detailed in this chapter which range from intra-village movements of individuals and households (these can hardly be called migrations), regional movements from the core village to the dispersed village, and international movements to India, the Gulf states and Malaysia.

While recognizing the contribution the theories discussed above make to debates about the causes and consequences of migration, this chapter, and the book as a whole, considers the term *mobility* to be more suitable for a study that examines multiple categories of migration. This is more than simply a means of escaping the "international bias" of the term *migration*. The term *mobility* includes both the geographical and socio-economic aspects of movement and therefore ties in with the sense of change entailed in the conception of migration as *"projects of transformation,* either by individuals or groups or even states" (Osella and Gardner 2004: xl). The term mobility dovetails with the approach taken in this chapter of dealing with multiple types of movement between different localities—some local and some international. Finally, while the term *migration* refers to an actual movement, *mobility* implies both actual and potential movement. By considering migration *as* mobility, migration in this book can be studied using several levels of analysis, each with different economic and social causes and consequences.

The first level of analysis will be the household and the movement of households within the village. The second level of analysis relates specifically to households which form part of the "dispersed" village and have settled in or around Happenchowk in Jhapa. Finally the analysis will focus on international labour migration. These levels are differentiated primarily by geographical focus; that is, they look at increasingly larger geographical areas. Beginning with wards within the village, the focus enlarges to the whole village and moving upwards through districts and regions eventually encompasses the whole Asian continent—or at least the countries in it that form part of the analysis.

Migration not only takes place on both the micro-level, within a village, and the macro-level, to another country, but can be a temporary or permanent movement. Temporary movement can either refer to short-term or seasonal migration, or to the movement of individuals and families which lasts only a few months, weeks or days. While a journey of a few days cannot strictly speaking be described as a migration, if the focus of the analysis remains on the ability to move, or *mobility*, it is certainly an important expression of economic and social status, and very much linked, ultimately, to migrations for longer periods of time. As such, it forms part of a continuum which places permanent long-distance migration at one end and extremely short-term and short-distance movements at another. The capacity to move— be it within the village, between villages, between villages and towns, or between countries—always relates to particular economic and social conditions within and between households which create or encourage such movement. Social networks play an important role in supporting individuals and households who intend to move or have recently done so.

The integration of Nepal's rural economy and society into the national and international political economy is marked more by the circulation of people and commodities than the unilinear flows associated with many development and migration oriented studies. An example of this is cyclical labour migration and the flow of remittances sent home which contribute to the development of communities (Aubriot 2009: 50, Castles and Wise 2008: 24, Graner 2009: 28-31).

While the analysis presented in this chapter makes use of the migration typology presented above (rural/urban and internal/ international), it shows that although such categorizations are conceptually useful for research purposes, the boundaries between categories are far from static and people, information and commodities constantly circulate within and between them.

Village-level mobility

The most significant movement of households within the village results from household fission after the marriage of a son in the same patriline as the household head. Households may be partitioned because of quarreling between in-marrying females or in-marrying females and unmarried sisters in the household (Jones and Jones 1976: 51, Parry 1979: 174-5).[90] Certain recently married men may take advantage of available land and resources to establish a new household. In these cases, the son of the parent household takes on his share of the parent

---

90 Parry describes how household partition in Kangra, in north-west India "is almost always blamed on quarrels between the women-folk" (1979: 174).

household's total available agricultural land as well as total family debt. A number of households, particularly those with larger holdings, do not formally divide their cardamom plantations between the sons if the eldest male, that is the formal owner of the land, is still alive. Rather, the profits from the sale of cardamom are divided among eligible members of related households. Increased segmentation from population growth and post-marital household fission resulted in the closely clustered distribution of households typical of many parts of the village today. Households with little land are often unable to provide entirely new plots for a newly married son. Such households might build an extension to the main house or the newly married couple might live temporarily or permanently in a smaller house (usually the *maṭān*), if this is available, on the same plot as the main house.

The ability to separate quickly from the parent household after marriage is strongly linked to the economic status of the household. Newly married couples who either continue to live with the main household or live in an adjoining property are perceived as having a low economic status by other villagers. This does not apply to youngest sons who typically remain and inherit the parent house and surrounding land while older brothers move out. As the social, economic and political "hub" of the village increasingly becomes the area around the primary school and small shops in Ward 5, the ability to live near either this hub, or alongside the main path which bisects the village, is also perceived as a sign of relatively high economic status.

Before the first primary school was built in 1958, and before the establishment of the main village shop next door to the school in 1978, it appears that there was no sense of a village centre, as there is today, and that remoter households might even have been better off as they had improved access to fodder and food supplies from the forest and river. With the recent inauguration of a Limbu museum near the school, the repaving of the main path through the village, increased tourism in the last few decades, and recent discussions about building a new health post on land between the Limbu museum and the main primary school, the focus of village social activities and of the sense of "the village" has shifted more than ever to this central area. This shift, combined with most households' increased dependence on market goods, has meant that many villagers consider it economically, socially and physically beneficial to live closer to this central area. Here, villagers tend to be more visible in formal and informal social gatherings and village meetings. Villagers who live in Thobabuk, for example, which is the furthest settlement to the northeast of the main primary school and almost an hour's walk from the shops, are seldom seen in the "centre" and are considered by other villagers to be of fairly low economic status. As will be shown in the section below, which analyses the history of household movements in Ward 4, all the houses currently closest to the main path moved to their current locations shortly after marrying and are considered by other villagers to be of relatively high economic status.

The movement of households within the village, either as a result of marriage-related household fission or for other reasons, is sometimes explicitly linked to extra-village migration. Households which are either unable or unwilling to sell their property before migrating will often mortgage their house and any bordering agricultural land in exchange for a deposit or *bandhaki* arrangement. The location of the household, as well as the amount of agricultural land, will affect the cost of the *bandhaki* and the ability of the migrant to find someone willing to take on the property. There are often multiple families interested in houses which are located close to the village "centre", whereas it can be more difficult to find people willing to move into remoter houses such as those located in Ward 1, lower Ward 3, and Ward 8. A closer look at the history of some of the households in Ward 4 provides more detail on intra-village household movement and its relationship to migration.

Case study of Ward 4

Ward 4 is one of the smallest and oldest wards in the village, and is the only one where every household produces cardamom. It is also the only ward where every household, with the exception of household 8, belongs to the same sub-clan of Mangar-Mabo. Figure 36 shows both the rough location of households and elements of household mobility.

The most important information portrayed in Figure 36 is the location of original houses, including those that are now over 50 years old and were generally built during the first decades of the 20th century. There are nine of these older houses, five of which were originally

Ward 4: Gairi Gau

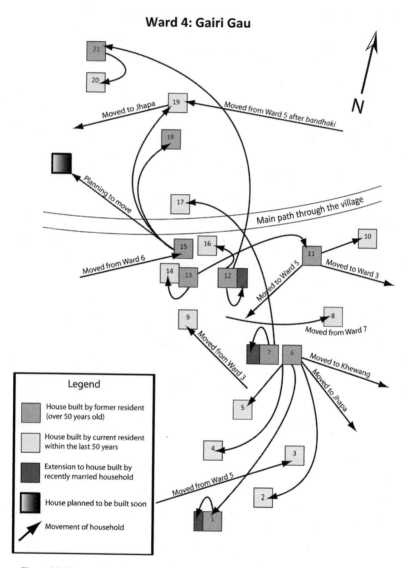

Figure 36: Diagram showing the location of houses within the ward and movement between households, wards and other parts of Nepal

by Bahun-Chhetris and then rebuilt or expanded by Limbu families. The twelve remaining houses were all built within the last 50 years by households who separated from their parent houses in Ward 4 or, in the case of four houses, from elsewhere in the village. Household 19 moved to Jhapa and is the only household to have a *bandhaki* arrangement in Ward 4. Three households built extensions to the original house after marrying and in two of these cases (households 1 and 12), this was done because they were poor (*garīb*) and had little land, therefore nowhere for the new couple to move to. In the third case (household 7), an extension was built by the youngest son who has six children and he will eventually inherit the main house from his father.

Although land is usually the limiting factor in household partitions, households with little land nevertheless often move to new plots and build their own houses. Two of the poorest households in Ward 4, households 16 and 20, built tiny single story bamboo huts despite having very little agricultural land. There are usually a number of factors which influence decisions about whether to move and build a new house or simply add an extension. The availability of land is clearly an important factor, as is economic capacity, the physical and demographic size of the main house, and relationships between family members.

While Figure 36 provides no economic and very little historical information, it does provide a broader sense of household movement and shows how settlements expand as a result of population growth—or household fission—and migration. It provides a micro-scale perspective on movement and mobility within a single ward in a village and thus demonstrates both the importance of viewing villages and households as dynamic structures, and shows how long-distance migration is connected to intra-village migration.

Household mobility within Nepal

Mobility plays a fundamental economic and social role in the lives of villagers. Most households for example are dependent on the market for basic foods such as rice, salt and oil. Since these goods must be portered to the village, households unable to carry heavy loads themselves must pay a fixed rate of 10 NPR per kilo to a local porter. The two-day walk up to or down from the village to the market in Tharpu is marked by constant pauses en route to talk to fellow villagers coming from the opposite direction. Usually, the villagers one meets on the path are either carrying goods (typically 50 kg packs of rice) uphill from Tharpu, or on their way downhill to pick goods up. At certain times of the year, in addition to the porters, there are groups of students on their way to or from the secondary school in Tellok. These two characteristics, mobility related to education and market-related mobility, are the most prevalent forms of mobility from the village to other sites. They are also intimately tied to the economic conditions of individual households.

Although the village recently decided to make classes 9 and 10 available in the local school, Khewang, Tellok and Sinam are the only villages close to Mamangkhe with provision for the last two years of secondary school. Daily journeys between these schools and Mamangkhe village are not possible and, as a result, students in classes 11 and 12 live away from the village for two to three months at a time, depending on the schedule of classes and exams. Many of these students have arrangements with families in these villages to provide them with free accommodation, but their food, clothing, books and other school equipment, and a minimal school fee still have to be financed by the students. Holidays and study breaks are timed so that students can help their families with work in the village during times of intensive agricultural activity, but these breaks do not coincide with, for example, the period of cardamom harvesting from September to November. Not all the households in the village are able to support their children to go to secondary school. Those who are able to do so could be considered part of the more economically mobile section of the village, usually with more access to cash and credit than families who cannot afford to send their children to neighbouring villages. More wealthy households find it easier to compensate for any reduction in the total pool of household labour either by hiring *khetālā* or relying more on the market for their household consumption.[91]

Market-oriented mobility refers above all to the relationships households have with the market in Tharpu, the settlement closest to the main road and the source of almost all commodities consumed

---

91 During fieldwork, there were several cases of households that, faced with the prospect of a number of younger adults leaving the village for an extended period (in most cases for study, in some cases as labour migrants), decided to reduce, by either selling or killing, the total number of livestock they owned. Household heads explained that there would not be enough help within the household to carry out the time consuming task of fodder-collection.

within the village. This includes the purchase of foods and implements used for agricultural work and food preparation, as well as selling cardamom to local merchants. Villagers visiting more distant settlements, such as Phungling in Taplejung or Birtamod in Jhapa, will also usually return with items purchased in these markets where the costs of certain goods are considerably lower. While education and market-oriented mobility are the most common forms of individual mobility within Nepal, there are a number of other important forms related to marriage, employment, pilgrimage and travel to visit friends and relatives.

Marriage-related mobility usually refers to women, as they generally marry outside the village, but in a few cases can refer to men from the village who move away from the village immediately or soon after marrying. Work-related mobility refers to individuals or households who move as a result of work outside the village, but inside Nepal. This is usually a result of government sector employment, as there are so few employment opportunities in the private sector in Nepal. Teachers are usually employed within the village and there are no teachers from Mamangkhe working elsewhere at the moment. The two main external employment opportunities are with the Nepal army or police and on road-building work. There are only two individuals employed with the Nepal police, and another three who were in the Maoist army and remained in it after the peace accords in November 2006. One of the villagers employed with the police recently got married and has moved to Dharan in Sunsari district. The other is unmarried but reported he would move out of the village in the next few years. Of the three villagers who were in the Maoist army, one left the army in 2007 and returned to the village and the other two are still in the army but unmarried.

In addition, the government employs a large number of villagers to work periodically on two roads: One of these will run from Phungling bazaar towards the Kabeli River and the other will run from Tharpu up along the Kabeli River to Yamphudin, with both roads meeting in Tellok. Groups of between 10 and 20 adult men from Mamangkhe village work on different sections of the road in Tellok and Sikaicha VDCs for a few months at a time, earning on average 150 NPR per day. Work groups are also organized for bridge building and other infrastructural projects within the VDC such as the installation of the small hydroelectric systems in wards 1 to 3 in September 2007. During the survey, eleven respondents said their main source of income was road or bridge building and most of these villagers were from wards 1 to 3 where a bridge had recently been built. The survey figures for employment are not accurate because most villagers who do not have permanent or stable employment carry out a wide range of different jobs including road-building, portering, working as *khetālā*, and cardamom cultivation.

Another form of mobility relates to pilgrimages or visits made by individuals or households to sites outside the village. The most frequent sites for pilgrimage are the Pathibhara Devi site in Taplejung, the sacred lake of Timbung along the Nepal-Sikkim border east of the village, and the Larumba village of Ilam which is the headquarters of the Satyahang religious movement (Gaenszle 2002: 335-6). Visit-related mobility includes pilgrimages, travelling to visit a relative, accompanying a groom to the village of his bride, and travelling for pleasure with friends. Most of these types of mobility are relatively infrequent, but nevertheless form part of an important continuum of mobility which ties shorter and temporary movements to larger and permanent ones. Young adults visiting Jhapa, for example, often also make inquiries into working abroad at one of the many manpower offices in Birtamod. Unmarried adults visiting relatives in other villages may find their marriage partner and, for females visiting villages, a short visit can become a long permanent stay.

Where mobility has a specific purpose such as purchasing goods, visiting a pilgrimage site, or travelling to school, there is always a strong awareness of how the traveller is perceived by fellow villagers. Villagers travelling to Taplejung to receive remittance money from a family member or relative will often tell other villagers they are visiting a friend. Perhaps there is a case to be made for *conspicuous mobility* within the other kinds of mobility. That is, people displaying their economic status by being mobile in particular ways. Villagers returning from visits to market towns will be careful about which items to make visible and which to hide. Items they want to show others they have bought they will strap onto the outside of their bags or carry by hand. Mobility is intimately tied to economic and social status. Political figures, such as villagers involved in local or regional political parties, are often on the move, travelling between villages and to the district capital in Phungling. Villagers with business interests such as cardamom trading or money lending, regularly travel to districts south of Taplejung. Raj for example, the largest cardamom merchant in the village, travels to Ilam and Jhapa at least once every two months. In the dispersed village, many villagers either have close relatives or their own property in both Mamangkhe and Jhapa and therefore part of longer distance mobility is related to travel between these two points.

One final type of mobility was caused directly by the increased Maoist presence in and around the village in the last few years of the People's War. As will be shown below in the section on the dispersed village, a number of the households now living in Jhapa cited this Maoist presence as one of the reasons they migrated. In addition to this, a number of individuals moved to Jhapa during the last years of the war to avoid recruitment into the Maoist army. These villagers were young adults in their last years of secondary education that lived with relatives in and around Happenchowk and studied at a secondary school there.

Survey data on mobility provides a rough sense of the total number of households involved in movement to sites outside the district of Taplejung. This includes pilgrimages, visits to relatives, health-related travel and travel for work and study. Of a total 201 respondents, only 58 (29%) stated that they had travelled outside Taplejung at least once in the last year.

A majority of the villagers who have travelled during the last year have been to Jhapa, usually to the Limbu settlements in or around Happenchowk. While some 62% of respondents indicated Jhapa as being their only travel destination, the majority of villagers travelling to points beyond Jhapa also tend to visit relatives or friends in these settlements. Although it was expected that wealthier villagers would be more mobile, there were no correlations between mobility and any of the indicators of income such as average cardamom production over the last two years, total value of crop, surplus value, number of livestock, or the amount of land owned.

Their destinations are listed in the table below:

Destination	Number of households	Percentage
Jhapa	36	62.1
Kathmandu	5	8.6
Sikkim	4	6.9
Dharan	3	5.2
Qatar	2	3.5
Chitwan	1	1.7
Ilam	1	1.7
Jhapa/Kathmandu	1	1.7
Kathmandu/Malaysia	1	1.7
Manipur	1	1.7
Panchthar	1	1.7
Phidim	1	1.7
Phidim/Jhapa	1	1.7
Total	**58**	**100**

Table 27: Travel destinations outside Taplejung in the last year by household heads, ranked by frequency and percentage

Survey in Jhapa

As a result of the central role that the dispersed village in Jhapa plays in mobility outside the village of Mamangkhe, further research was carried out specifically in these settlements. There are a wide variety of households in the dispersed village, from the complete extended family to the single-householder family, and similarly to households in Mamangkhe, their size and composition constantly changes as household members come and go, returning to Mamangkhe or travelling further afield. Almost every Limbu in Mamangkhe has at least a distant relative in Jhapa, and relatives as well as friends constantly visit Jhapa either to study, to visit cardamom merchants and buy goods, to visit the manpower offices in Birtamod, or to travel east to Kathmandu or west to Sikkim. The journey down to Jhapa usually takes approximately 14 hours from Tharpu by bus, leaving before dawn and arriving after dusk. Tickets cost between 400 and 600 NPR per person one-way, a considerable sum for villagers who earn around 100 NPR per day for wage labour.

The survey in Jhapa focused particularly on household demography, economics and mobility. Table 28 compares some of the demographic data collected in Jhapa and Mamangkhe. The only significant difference between the two sites are the figures for children per household—and consequently the size of the household—with households being markedly larger in Mamangkhe.

Demographic data (averages)	Jhapa	Mamangkhe
Age of household head	40	44
Age of marriage	23	21.8
Size of household	3.8	4.8
Children per household	3.1	4.4

Table 28: Comparison of average figures for demographic data of households in Jhapa and Mamangkhe

Of the 29 households surveyed, most had moved to the area within the last five years and 90% of households owned their own house. Plots surrounding each house tended to be relatively small: the average plot of land was 1.9 *khaṭṭhā*[92] (642.2 square metres), which for most households was not enough for agricultural production. There was no correlation though between either the amount of money invested or the total size of property and number of years since arrival. While land and houses in the main settlement area cost more now than they did ten years ago, it is possible to buy a bamboo and thatch house today with a small amount of land for as little as 25,000 NPR some distance from the main road. Again, as is the case in the core village of Mamangkhe, distance from the road and main settlement cluster, as well as the materials used for the main house (whether cement or bamboo), are both associated with a certain degree of prestige.

The fact that some households invested as little as 10,000 NPR on their property while others invested 500,000 NPR, points to the large degree of economic heterogeneity within the dispersed village. This heterogeneity is neatly matched by the figures related to cardamom production since roughly half the sample still owned cardamom (14 households) in Mamangkhe and half did not (15 households). In addition, almost two-thirds of households sent their children to private English-

92 1 *khaṭṭhā* equals around 338 square metres.

language schools while only one-third sent them to Nepali government schools. While there was a fairly strong correlation between living in Jhapa and attending private schools, there were no correlations between schooling and any of the other variables such as cardamom production, amount of money invested in property, or size of property.

The variation of data related to property size (all land including agricultural) and type of house, the amount of money invested, cardamom production and the education of children all point to the fairly varied economic conditions of households in the dispersed village. This apparent economic heterogeneity contrasts with a number of common patterns in data related to work and migration abroad.

5The majority of household heads (79%), 10% more than the household heads living in Mamangkhe, had travelled abroad in some capacity, either for service in the Indian or British armies, in Sikkim, or on work visas to Malaysia or one of the Gulf countries. In addition, more than half (55%) of households in Jhapa had members who were working abroad at the time of the survey. Data collected on work carried out prior to migrating to Jhapa shows that while cardamom production in Mamangkhe and cardamom-related labour in Sikkim both played an important role in allowing families to generate enough money to invest in property in Jhapa, the international labour market has become more important in the last few years.

In many ways the settlement in Jhapa acts as a hub for both internal mobility—for example villagers travelling to Kathmandu often stay with relatives in Jhapa to break up the journey—and, more crucially, for the many migrants who travel down from Mamangkhe and stay with relatives before travelling abroad. As a result of circular migration and the increased flow of remittances to households in Jhapa, the physical hub of the dispersed village in Jhapa has also become a central node in the social networks which migrants and non-migrants create and rely on in their efforts to transform their social and economic conditions. These social networks are made up of villagers who have already migrated and returned, those who are still abroad, and those who intend to migrate, as well as those who have no immediate intention to migrate. Many of these villagers continue to be based in Mamangkhe—since they travel directly from there and return to their village after working abroad—but considerable numbers of villagers have moved to Jhapa in recent years and many more stated their intention to move to Jhapa in the near future.[93]

The importance of Jhapa in these social networks is not simply related to the number of villagers who have settled there with experiences of labour migration abroad. It is the combination of the economic and human capital which exists as a result of the flow of migrants into and out of Jhapa. This human capital includes, for example, the knowledge certain villagers might have of more reliable, affordable or efficient "manpower" agencies, as well as familiarity with the process of applications and job interviews. Some villagers are able to bypass manpower agencies by getting relatives who are already abroad to organize visas for them. This procedure, known as "pulling" (*tānnu*) or "inviting" (*bolāunu*), saves villagers considerable time and money and ensures they know their salaries and job conditions before they travel abroad. Combined with this human capital, is the economic capital available in the dispersed village in the form of remittances, savings and property. Villagers hoping to travel abroad increasingly rely on loans from relatives living in Jhapa who have either accumulated savings by working abroad, or continue to receive remittances from household members working abroad.[94] Although the high interest rates remain, money for loans tends to be available year round in Jhapa,

---

93 Russell (2007) draws particular attention to this process of circular migration and the expansion of social networks across space by examining what he describes as the "micro-diasporic identities" of Yakkha villagers who move away from their cultural heartland to spend time in the Tarai. Following Clifford's (1992, 1997) call for greater attention to "routes" as well as "roots" in anthropological research, Russell provides a detailed description of a chance encounter with a Yakkha man born and raised in the Tarai to show how ethnic identity is situational and changes in relation to both social context and geographical location (Russell 2007: 378). Describing how migrants have been peripheralized in studies of ethnic groups, his article attempts to show how a "routes"-influenced approach provides a fuller understanding of the Yakkha by incorporating migration into the analysis.

94 A small number of households in Jhapa also continue to own large amounts of cardamom in Mamangkhe which provides them with considerable income. One household produced 14 *man* of cardamom in 2006, worth over 100k NPR at the time. Other households produce between 1 and 3 *man* on average each year. Members of households that own cardamom land in Mamangkhe usually visit the village a few times a year: typically once before the cardamom season begins—to help with clearing and planting tasks or delegate work to others—and during or after the harvest—to oversee the drying, carrying and selling processes.

whereas villagers can often spend months trying to raise necessary funds from within Mamangkhe.

The increased centrality of the dispersed village in Jhapa to the lives of villagers in Mamangkhe can be seen by tracing the change in economic strategies and cultural values associated with circular labour migration abroad (to the Gulf and Malaysia) in relation to seasonal labour migration to Sikkim. While in the past, young adults accompanied their parents to Sikkim over the eastern border, today their hopes and aspirations are oriented towards the Gulf and Malaysia via the dispersed village in Jhapa. Since living in Jhapa offers, to many villagers, a variety of advantages over living in Mamangkhe, villagers consider that participating in the productive process of circular labour migration abroad will facilitate permanently moving from the core to the dispersed village.

Two separate questions emerge from this last statement. First, what are these perceived advantages and how are they related to notions of economic and social transformation? Second, to what extent did labour migration abroad enable villagers who currently live in Jhapa to settle there in the first place?

Regarding the first question, villagers mentioned a number of advantages as well as disadvantages of living in Jhapa. The advantages included: ease of transport, availability and access to health services and education in English, and the reduced cost of market goods. Disadvantages included: the hot weather and the reduced quality of food.[95] What was not mentioned by villagers in Jhapa but frequently expressed by those in Mamangkhe was the reduced work load for those living in Jhapa. Not only do villagers in Mamangkhe consider the work migrants abroad carry out to be less strenuous than work in the village, but there is a widespread perception that living in Jhapa is physically less demanding than living in the village.[96] While the former perception

---

95 These figures were derived from the survey carried out in Jhapa.

96 Pettigrew (2000) describes how although life in the village is perceived by "urban villagers" as more difficult, the psychological stresses on town-dwellers are equally so: "town-dwellers face social, psychological, and cultural stresses which are not experienced in the village context". These include: "loss of 'culture', the often negatively experienced encounter with caste society, the ongoing pressures of 'keeping up' with neighbours, kin, etc. in an increasingly consumerist world" (2000: 22, *footnote 26*). This could be considered a somewhat romantizied view since rural villages clearly

is not necessarily the case, the latter is undoubtedly true—partly because of the lack of agricultural land and partly because families in Jhapa rely much more directly on remittances for their income. As one villager put it "Here [in Mamangkhe] we have to work hard, we have to carry food, our back hurts, we only eat boiled millet-meal [*kodo-ko dhiḍo*], we suffer [*dukha pāuncha*]. In Jhapa, people have fun, don't have to carry food, and always eat rice".[97] This association between a reduced work load and economic prosperity is strongly linked to notions many villagers have that Western tourists, who occasionally trek through the village, are on permanent holidays: that they never do any work at all.[98]

The advantages of living in Jhapa are therefore a combination of perceived economic and practical benefits, and cultural notions of an improved quality of life—the reduced demand for physical labour and increase of leisure time (for which many villagers use the English term "free time"). These are all strongly associated with notions of development, or *vikas*, and progression from being *garīb* to becoming *dhani*. Most of the households in Mamangkhe that are widely considered to be *dhani* own properties in Jhapa,[99] which has no doubt reinforced the association villagers in Mamangkhe make between economic prosperity and living in Jhapa.[100] With regard to the second question, just over half of the household heads currently living in Jhapa (52.8%) had been

---

have stresses and pressures of their own.

97 Interview with Buddha Raj carried out on 15/5/2008.

98 Not only was this idea constantly mentioned to me throughout fieldwork, but the category of work was strongly associated with physical exertion. My efforts to learn the Limbu language and interview villagers were not considered work unless, for example, they were tied to expressions of physical exertion and exhaustion from countless hours of walking.

99 Raj's household (Chhetri) owns property in Ilam. Most Limbu villagers who were planning to purchase property outside the village mentioned Jhapa as their ideal with the exception of one family, that was planning to buy property in Taplejung bazaar (Fungling), and another that wanted to move closer to Tharpu without leaving the Kabeli valley.

100 There are few material differences between the richest households in Jhapa and Mamangkhe. The availability of electricity in Jhapa means that a few households have purchased televisions and a few houses have telephones. Yet most aspects of the domestic economy remain the same: for example, all households cook with firewood in an outdoor kitchen.

working abroad immediately prior to settling in Jhapa.[101] Slightly less than half of them (41.7%) had been working on cardamom production in Mamangkhe.

Labour migration abroad played an important role in enabling villagers to settle in Jhapa, but much of this has been seasonal migration to Sikkim, which though foreign is so close and so culturally similar as hardly to count. Households that have been living in Jhapa the longest tend to have members who either worked in the army or in Sikkim.[102] The most recent arrivals tend to have made, or be in the process of trying to make their fortunes working in the Gulf or Malaysia. The differences in average ages show that there has been a substantial generational shift from army and cardamom-related labour mobility (in Sikkim) to labour migration in the Gulf and Malaysia. This shift is reflected even more deeply in Mamangkhe where villagers as young as 16 begin the visa application process to work abroad,[103] whereas villagers who continue to work in Sikkim tend to be over 40 years old, have worked there before, and continue to have links with friends and employers in Sikkim. It is likely that a majority of the households that settle in Jhapa in the future will have been involved in labour migration abroad. Cardamom production, though, will continue to have an impact on the economic condition of households and on the perpetuation and aggravation of economic inequality.

While it is clear that there are already economic inequalities in Jhapa, particularly noticeable in the strikingly different investments made in property, there seems to be considerable similarity in the economic strategies and social aspirations of households throughout the dispersed village. Almost all households, for example, have members who have been abroad, were abroad at the time of the survey, or plan to go abroad in the near future. Almost two-thirds (64%) of households send their children to private schools and over two-thirds (69%) of households have no significant agricultural land besides their small

---

101 This includes "abroad (not in Sikkim)", "Sikkim", and "army".

102 For example household 8806, which was among the first to settle in Jhapa in 1997, has a father-in-law (the household head's wife's father) who worked for the British army. The male head of household 8808 worked for the Indian army for 14 years and moved to Jhapa in 1998.

103 The oldest villager I came across who was planning to work in the Gulf was 37 years old.

kitchen garden. If households which are considered to be poorer have such similar living strategies to richer households, how are richer households differentiating themselves?

To a large extent, richer households are able to pay for more expensive work visas for jobs with higher-paid salaries. These households have better access to capital, either by saving or borrowing, and can invest in any technical or linguistic training needed for particular jobs. In the long term these economic differences will be increasingly accentuated as households with access to higher-paid jobs abroad buy larger properties, send their children to cities for higher education, perhaps migrate to another part of Nepal or abroad and ultimately perhaps become part of Nepal's "new middle-class" (Liechty 2002: 46). Generally speaking poorer households, with less access to capital, obtain less expensive and therefore less lucrative visas, and therefore often struggle to repay their debts and transform their economic fortunes. The dichotomy often presented to describe different migration strategies for different economic classes in Nepal is that the rich go to the Gulf, or south-east Asia, while the poor go to India (Thieme 2006: 1).

These differences will be explored in more detail in the section on international mobility below using a number of short case studies.

International mobility in Nepal

One of the earliest cases of foreign labour migration was before the Anglo-Gorkha War (1814-1816) when Nepalis travelled to Lahore to join the army of the Sikh ruler Ranjit Singh (Dahal 2000: 42; Seddon et al. 2002: 19).[104] The British began recruiting "Gurkhas" into the army of the East India Company immediately after the Anglo-Gorkha War (Caplan 1995: 19), and India continued to recruit them after independence from Britain in 1947. The history of foreign labour migration and remittances therefore stretches back almost 200 years. While large numbers of Nepalis were recruited into the British and Indian armies, an even larger number were migrating to India throughout the latter half of the 19th century in search of land and employment opportunities. The 1901 census of India carried out by the British Raj indicated that there were

---

104 Hence one of the Nepali terms for soldier is *lāhure*, and hence the term *lāhure* means "labour migrant" in contemporary usage.

200,000 Nepali speakers settled in India; most of them living in West Bengal, Sikkim and Assam (Seddon 1995: 368). By 1961 there were over one million Nepali and hill-language speakers in India (Hutt 1997). The eradication of malaria in the Nepali Tarai (plains) during the 1950s was followed by a large wave of both internal migration from the overpopulated hill areas to the plains and international migration from Indian districts just south of the border.[105] During the 1970s and 1980s, population pressure increased in both the hilly areas and the Tarai, providing a powerful incentive for Nepali emigration.

According to the national census, there were 400,000 Nepalis abroad in 1981 and 93% of these were in India. In 1991 the total number of migrants had increased to 660,000 but the percentage of Nepalis in India had fallen to 89% (Seddon et al. 2002: 23). This fall is explained by the increased number of Nepalis migrating beyond India, mostly to other parts of Asia such as Southeast Asia and the Gulf.

The Gulf, which opened up to Nepali migrant workers in the 1990s, had an estimated 40,000 Nepalis working there in 1997, a figure which it is estimated may have risen to 200,000 in 2001 (Seddon et al. 2002: 25). Estimates of the total numbers of Nepali migrants working abroad are conservative figures based on legal and official migrant numbers, but there are also large numbers of migrants working illegally. While there may be, for example, 250,000 migrants working in the public sector in India, there could be over three times that many migrants working in the private sector. This would mean that while officially there are said to be around 250,000 Nepalis working in India, in reality there may be well over 1 million migrants (ibid.).[106]

---

105 The Nepal-India border is extremely porous (many more informal crossing points than official policed ones) and Nepalis (usually) need no documentation to cross the border (Hausner 2007).

106 There were no cases of female migrants who had travelled abroad (with the exception of women travelling with their husbands to Sikkim). Dil Kumari, a widow, was in the process of applying for a visa (in April 2008) to work in beauty salon in Dubai: this has so far not materialized. Rumours abound regarding the dangers of working abroad, with particular focus on stories of sexual abuse by employers. There are numerous studies that show how Nepali women—up to 15,000 annually—are employed in the commercial sex industry in India (Human Rights Watch 1995, USDS 2009), particularly in Mumbai, as well as in Nepal (Seddon 1995). According to the Nepali newspaper Kantipur, there are currently around 12,000 women working in Israel, mostly as "caregivers" (Kantipur Report 7/7/2009).

The importance of these figures is that they bring to light the fundamental role migration, and more specifically the remittance economy, plays in the economic development of Nepal. It is estimated that while remittances only accounted for less than 3% of Nepal's GDP in 1995, they accounted for about 12% of GDP by 2004 (World Bank 2005). According to Seddon, the true figure could be anything from 18 to 25% of GDP (a total of 70 million NPR remitted) (Seddon et al. 2002: 36). These figures exceed the total amount of money derived from tourism, foreign aid and exports combined (Lokshin et al. 2007: 2). According to a World Bank study "almost 20% of the decline of poverty in Nepal between 1995 and 2004 can be attributed to increased work-related migration and remittance inflows" (Lokshin et al. 2007: 4). Despite this decline in poverty, the study also points out that "migration and remittances have only a marginal impact on income inequality in Nepal" (Lokshin et al. 2007: 26).

Data from the Nepal Living Standard Survey (NLSS), a nationally representative survey of households carried out in the periods 1995-1996 and 2003-2004, showed that the proportion of households receiving remittances increased from 23% in 1995 to 32% of all households in 2004. These remittances accounted for around 44% of mean household yearly expenditure in 2004. Remittances can reduce or reverse the impact of labour and capital loss caused by migration (Taylor 1999:.69), as well as enable households and individuals to overcome the constraints of credit and risk on their ability to engage in productive activities (Stark 1991). In other words, remittance money gives households access to credit by reducing debts and increasing the amount of cash available. In relation to migration, this credit allows households to cover the costs of more expensive visas and support other household members going abroad. Households which are unable to provide money for members to migrate remain as poor as before, while those who migrate but make no money or are unable to send remittances may remain severely indebted.[107]

Dil Kumari mentioned that if she didn't get the visa for Dubai, she would apply for a visa for Israel; she had already bought a Hebrew phrasebook in Kathmandu. Since no females have worked abroad, this chapter focuses solely on male international labour migration.

107 There are also situations where migrants pay for their visas but never leave the country, losing their money to incompetent or corrupt manpower offices. Others may be told to wait a few months before departure (a few

International mobility from Mamangkhe village
Trade-related mobility

The earliest form of long-distance mobility from the village which villagers have memories of is trade-related mobility. Travelling south-east towards Darjeeling, small groups of villagers used to carry items from the village and exchange them with goods which were locally unavailable. One of the oldest villagers, Ratna still remembers his first trip to Darjeeling in 1942 when he was 14 years old.[108] It took nine days from Mamangkhe to reach Darjeeling carrying loads of 40 kg to 60 kg. Travelling south to Angkop the small group of between four and five people would reach Phedi just below the Nepal-Sikkim border on the fourth day of travel, crossing the border at Lam Pokhari on the fifth day and travelling through Rimbik in Sikkim and Bijanbari to reach Darjeeling on the ninth day. They would trade village and hill goods such as butter, chickens, *chiraita*, and bring back metal for tool-making, nails, cloth, sugar, salt and spices. He made once-yearly trips from 1942 to 1961, by which point a road to Ilam made the journey shorter and market goods had become available in the village. Ratna mentioned that his father had undertaken this journey for many years before Ratna joined him in 1942 and that long-distance trade had taken place for as long as anyone could remember.

Although villagers used to travel through parts of West Sikkim on trips to Darjeeling, it was only around 1949 that two villagers, a Chhetri (Thapa) who lived in Sudap (Ward 8) and a Limbu from Yempang village, travelled to Sikkim with the intention of looking for work.[109] According

---

months can become a whole year) and accumulate large debts waiting to leave.

108 Data collected from an interview with Ratna carried out on the 8/6/2008.

109 Balikci (2008) recounts that "in the year 1938, a group of dozen Limbus from eastern Nepal, were granted permission by Sir Tashi Namgyal to settle and open fields within the Phodong Estate at Mangshila [in Sikkim]" working as labourers for the Tingchim Lhopos (the Bhutia or Sikkimese) and teaching them "how to plough and practise permanent irrigated agriculture" (Balikci 2008: 53). The migration of Nepali labourers had been encouraged by the British in Darjeeling as early as the 1870s and J.W. Edgar, the Deputy Commissioner of Darjeeling at the time, reported the presence of numerous Nepali migrants in south-west Sikkim, though few in other parts of the country and none in Gangtok (*ibid.*: 49-50, footnote 20).

to a number of informants, the Chhetri worked on cardamom plantations for six years and finally returned having earned 2,500 NPR. He used this money to buy a large amount of land in Sudap and in parts of Ward 7, including higher altitude grazing land. After a number of years he sold all his property to a Chhetri villager from Yempang and migrated to Jhapa. The experience of the Chhetri villager encouraged other villagers to follow his example and they also began to travel to Sikkim.

Army-related mobility

A few years before this, a total of seven Limbu villagers joined the British Army as Gurkha soldiers.[110] Of these seven villagers, three have died, two have migrated to Jhapa and Ilam, and only two still live in the village.[111] One of these villagers is Phul Bahadur (PB), who was born in 1928, the same year as Ratna Bahadur. A biographical sketch of his life provides an interesting perspective on the relationship between income, economic mobility, cardamom, and land ownership.

Phul Bahadur

Phul Bahadur, known in the village as Jordhara Babai,[112] was born in 1928. He joined a Gurkha regiment in the British Army in 1944, and fought for three years until India's independence from British rule in 1947. After independence he joined the Indian Army and retired in 1967. During his years in the army, PB sent money to his father in the village who regularly deposited it with Lakshmi Prasad Koraria (LP), a Chhetri

---

110 Caplan (1970: 115) indicates that 43.8% of all Limbu males over eighteen years of age in the Indreni settlement cluster had served or were serving in the army at the time of his fieldwork. This is considerably more than the number of villagers that were recruited in Mamamgkhe, perhaps in large part due to the considerable remoteness of the village from recruitment centres or towns, as compared to the settlements around Ilam bazaar. I could find no evidence for recruitment into the army prior to joining the British Army during the 1940s.

111 I was only able to carry out interviews with one of the two villagers, Phul, since the second villager, Lakshmi Prasad's father Ram Dal, was severely ill and not available for interviews.

112 The name Jordhara is a made up of two Nepali words: *jor*, meaning "a pair" and *dhārā* meaning "a spring of water". The nickname derives from the fact that Jordhara's house is located between two springs of water.

who lived in Ward 5.[113] This was the first shop in the village, and cloth, salt, metal for tools, as well as money-lending and depositing services were available. LP is remembered best for having set up the first school in Mamangkhe in 1958 by donating his own land in Ward 5 and setting up Class 1. As a shopkeeper, LP used to collect butter and *chiraita* in the village, then carry it down to Ilam for sale and trade.[114] PB's father, Satra Hang, had a reputation for being extremely miserly. He wouldn't eat meat, saying it was a waste of money, and his family was one of the few that did not sell off a single plot of land to Chhetri villagers. When PB retired from the army he had saved up enough money to buy land and property in three different parts of the village.

He bought the land and house of Chandra Muni Kharel's eldest son K.P. Kharel, also known as Jordhara (the nickname was passed on), in 1971 for 18,000 NPR, four years after returning from the army. He had saved up a total of 12,000 NPR from his army salary, and borrowed an additional 6,000 NPR from local merchants. In 1980, PB bought land in Tilling that his eldest son currently lives on. Finally, he bought land from Man Bahadur Gurung, which had formerly belonged to LP, in Ward 4 for his youngest son for 300,000 NPR in 1983: 150,000 NPR of his own money, most of which he had earned selling cardamom since his retirement from the army, and the other half borrowed from a Bhote who lived in Yamphudin.

Besides the three properties he was able to purchase since retiring, PB also managed to acquire additional forest for cardamom cultivation. He also recently (June 2008) agreed to pay for a large part of the debt his daughter-in-law had with a Gurung merchant who lives in Tharpu bazaar. He is considered by other villagers to be extremely wealthy. This is mainly because of the considerable amount of land he and his children own (a total of at least 11 *hal* of agricultural land) but also because of the large amounts of cardamom he produced before dividing the land between his children (an average of 200 kg per year on his plot, but approximately 640 kg including the land he bought and gave to his children as part of their inheritance).

Without going into the life histories of the other villagers who returned from the army, it should be sufficient to mention that with the

---

113 In what is now household 513.

114 *Chiraita* is no longer harvested and villagers say it was overharvested in the past and is much harder to find these days.

exception of one villager, who left the army after two years and therefore only received a half-pension, they were all able to return and purchase considerable amounts of land. With the exception of property (land and house) which belonged to Chhetri villagers who had already begun to migrate from the village, any other land available for purchase was usually somewhat marginal land; either overgrown, too steep to be agriculturally productive, or too high to be accessible. LP's father Ram Dal, for example, in addition to buying cardamom forest plots which today produce between 160 and 180 kg per year, purchased a large amount of land above the village which is too forested and steep to be used for agriculture and provides little more than firewood. As a result of the increase in demand for firewood, he is now able to exchange firewood for clothes with the village tailor and for *khetālā* labour with a number of villagers. Broadly speaking, money remitted and saved during and after army service allowed a number of households to purchase sizeable plots of land and cardamom forest. The families of ex-army villagers produce, on average,[115] 240 kg of cardamom per year (almost double the village-wide mean of 128 kg) and own, on average, 2.75 *hal* of land[116] (1.4 times more than the village-wide mean of 1.94 *hal*).

Sikkim

The vast majority of villagers did not join the army. Instead, from the early 1950s onwards, they migrated across the Nepal-Sikkim border in search of employment in Sikkim, usually in cardamom production but sometimes as shepherds, porters and pit-sawyers. As mentioned earlier, it was only when the first migrant returned from Sikkim around 1955, after six consecutive years abroad, that other villagers began to work there. Some worked seasonally, others worked for longer periods, and a few villagers settled permanently. Data from the survey shows that at least 114 male household heads (57%), of a total of 201 households, had worked in Sikkim at some point in the past. Of these 114 male household heads, 106 of them had worked on cardamom, three as shepherds

---

115 These figures are derived from the mean of predicted cardamom production in 2007 and actual cardamom produced in 2006.

116 This figure refers to land for millet and maize production only.

(*goṭhālā*), two as tailors, one as a work supervisor, one carried oranges, and one worked as a blacksmith.

In-depth interviews with villagers indicated considerable variation in the economic success of individuals who had worked in Sikkim. Some had been able to return with enough money to buy new property, cardamom fields and pay off debts, while others had barely made any money. Some villagers had become supervisors of work groups, or had been given complete responsibility for cardamom production in large tracts of forest. Others had worked during every stage of the cycle of cardamom production, from clearing and planting, to harvesting, drying, and carrying; all this while living in fairly poor conditions in temporary shelters the whole time. Generally, villagers who were more economically successful explained their success in terms of an ability to save money, rather than a difference in salaries. Again, a biographical sketch of one of the first villagers to travel to Sikkim, and a man who continues to work there to this day, will provide an ethnographic perspective on the relationship between mobility, Sikkim, and economic transformation.

Ran Hang

Ran Hang, known in the village as Mota[117] was born in Mamangkhe in 1938. His parents arranged his first marriage in 1956, but he and his wife did not get along well. He married a second woman in 1960, but his parents did not accept this so, after failing to get his first wife to leave, he decided to go to Sikkim with his second wife. He left the village in 1960 with his wife and found his way to Mangan in North Sikkim. He worked in the market for a few months until a Bhote (Bhutia) offered him the job of overseeing work on a large piece of land he owned. He continued to work for the same man for the next 49 years. Usually he would travel to Sikkim in August and return to Mamangkhe around December-January. He would stay in the village for one to two months, and return to Sikkim for another four months until June. After the first six months of work in 1960, he returned with his second wife to Mamangkhe and travelled back to Sikkim alone. While he was working in Sikkim for the second time, she ran away from the village with another man so he continued to live with his first wife. He says that

---

117 From the Nepali word *moṭo* meaning fat or corpulent.

although most of his work was focused in and around Mangan, he also worked in villages and areas north of Mangan: Ningla, Singlek, and Myang. Ran Hang's salary derived from a plot of cardamom forest which produced between six and seven *man* of cardamom per year, so he was expected to supervise the work of other employees as well as maintaining his own plot of cardamom.

When his first son was born in 1962 (from his first wife), Ran Hang separated from his father's house in Ward 4 and moved to a house in Ward 6 under a *bandhaki* arrangement. He bought a small plot of land just above the main path in Ward 4 in 1965 (later selling a portion to a close relative), another plot of land where his eldest son now lives in 1966, and he bought the house he now lives in from a Limbu for 7,000 NPR in 1971. He also bought rice paddy land around this time which produced between 2 *muri* and 2.5 *muri* of rice per year (between about 160 kg and 200 kg), but lost all of this in a landslide six years ago. In addition to all this, he was able to also purchase small plots of forested land in Ward 3 which he converted for cardamom production. The extension to his house and CGI roofing were added in 2001 as a result of a gift of 30,000 NPR from his boss in Sikkim.

It is in large part as a result of acquiring so much property that Ran Hang's household has been able to provide enough land for his children to live on separately (two of his sons have separated), as well as giving him access to credit for visa expenses and the consumption of market goods.

It is important to note that while Ran Hang was able to transform the economic condition of his household, probably the majority of households were only marginally transformed. Returning from Sikkim, other less successful migrants may have used their savings to reduce their debts slightly, to pay for their children's education, or, in case of eight household heads, to pay for a visa and chance their luck abroad. The survey data show that there was no statistically significant relationship between the value of household surpluses and whether household heads had worked in Sikkim; nor was there any significant relationship between the number of years villagers had spent in Sikkim and their household surplus (or total production).

The reduction in cardamom production in Sikkim in the early 2000s coincided with the beginning of long-distance migrations to the Gulf and Malaysia. At the time of the survey there were an estimated 25 villagers working in Sikkim, only four of whom were household heads. In the past, particularly during cardamom season, large numbers of villagers would travel in groups and household heads would bring their older children.[118]

For about 50 years then, from the 1950s to the end of the 1990s, Sikkim was the major destination for adult men seeking employment outside the village, and the most common form of work was cardamom-related. From the end of the 1990s onwards, labour migration to Gulf countries began with a few villagers initially and with mixed success rates. Particularly in the last five years, considerable numbers of villagers have begun to migrate to the Gulf and Malaysia. While there were only four household heads in Sikkim at the time of the survey, there were 17 household heads in Gulf countries and Malaysia.

International mobility (beyond Sikkim)

There are a total of 23 household heads who have worked further afield than Sikkim or other parts of India, in countries such as Saudi Arabia, Dubai and Qatar.[119] One of the first villagers to travel abroad was 22 years old when he left the village for the first time in 1998. He worked in Qatar as a construction worker for two years initially, returning to Qatar after a short break. He has been abroad continuously since then, sending remittances regularly, and returning for visits every two to three years. The countries beyond India that villagers have worked in include: Malaysia (8 household heads), Qatar (7), Saudi Arabia (5), Dubai (2) and Bahrain (1). In Malaysia, jobs were exclusively factory-based and ranged from the production of plastic tubing to bread. In the Gulf countries, most villagers worked on construction sites, although a few worked as security guards. Salaries in Malaysia tended to be the lowest of all, although visas were quickly and cheaply arranged.

---

118 The survey data are somewhat limited in that it does not show figures for mobility for all individuals in the sample. Had this been done, total figures would no doubt have been extremely high as they would have included villagers who were not household heads.

119 Bruslé (2008, 2009) provides an interesting insight into the experience of Nepali migrants in Gulf countries. Other perspectives include Marsden (2008) on Pakistani migrants in Dubai, Shah and Menon (1999) on migrants in Kuwait, and Zachariach et al. (2004) on Indian workers in the United Arab Emirates.

Considering the cost of work visas, as well as additional expenses incurred during the many journeys to manpower offices before departure, it seems somewhat surprising that so many young adults are able to generate the fairly large sums of money required. In contrast to travelling to work in Sikkim, for which very little money or organization is required, travel to the Gulf or Malaysia requires households to mobilize considerable amounts of capital. Visas with reliable agencies can cost anything from 80,000 NPR to well over 100,000 NPR depending on the type of work offered and average monthly salaries expected. The cheapest visas (and these are often available for less than 80,000 NPR) tend to be for manual work—building construction, production line work in a factory, etc.—which usually offers wages only marginally higher than the salary of a village primary school teacher. Slightly higher-paid work usually requires additional skills such as knowledge of English or other languages, computer literacy, possession of a driving licence, School Leaving Certificate (SLC) or higher, etc. These, with the exception of the SLC, are skills which few people have in the village. While there were a number of villagers, particularly in Jhapa, who were investing time and money in acquiring more of these skills to be able to apply for better-paid jobs (with even more expensive visas), the majority of villagers still travel abroad on very basic visas, working mostly in construction and factories for extremely low wages.

Seddon (2001) shows how differences in foreign labour opportunities between poorer households and wealthier households can contribute to widening economic and social inequality. He notes that poorer households generally obtain low-paid and insecure jobs abroad, while wealthier families are able to arrange jobs with better salaries and security. For poorer households, foreign labour remittances are used as a supplement to income from farm work and thus serve as part of a "survival strategy". More affluent households are able to use extra income as part of an "accumulation strategy" above and beyond their subsistence or survival needs (Seddon 2001: 140).

The success stories of a small number of villagers, those who for example started on low wages but over the years began to earn more, have helped to perpetuate the association villagers make between labour migration abroad and economic upward mobility. As Seddon points out, instances of "social climbing" tend to "encourage the more disadvantaged sections of rural society to see migration as a means to betterment" (2001: 142). The reality is somewhat different and just as the economic condition of households in both the core and dispersed village is heterogeneous, so are the fortunes of individuals who travel abroad. While there are success stories for some, many villagers experience considerable hardship abroad and often find after a number of years of work that either little has changed economically or they are worse off than before. They may end up earning considerably lower wages than they were originally told by their agency in Nepal, and be unable to pay back the debts incurred for their initial work visa. There is therefore a high degree of risk for households with members planning to travel abroad. Money is borrowed, land (almost always cardamom-producing land) is mortgaged to raise capital, and animals are sold. Yet despite the obvious economic risks associated with travel abroad, villagers rarely mention any concerns about this or their fears and worries about working so far from home. Villagers speak instead in a somewhat blasé manner about the vicissitudes others have faced and often shrug off any doubts with statements emphasizing the lack of economic opportunities in the village, and in Nepal, compared to those offered abroad.

This attitude of indifference towards the risks entailed in working abroad is also mentioned by Pettigrew (2000) in her study of Gurung migrants, who notes that "while day-to-day stories of hardship in foreign lands are actively concealed by returned migrants in an attempt to maintain prestige and also to spare worried relatives, an increasing number of tragic stories relate to mistreatment by employers, violence against women, or infringement of human rights" (2000: 20). While there are, as yet, few "tragic stories" discussed within the village, there are a number of rumours about violence against women which were mentioned by women in the village during conversations about labour migration abroad.[120]

Three separate case studies of recent migrants bring to light the difficulties households face raising capital to pay for visas and the results of successful or unsuccessful attempts to work abroad. These

---

120 There are no cases of women who have been involved in foreign (beyond Sikkim) labour migration, although one woman who planned to apply for a work visa in the United Arab Emirates in 2007 ultimately failed to obtain it. The Nepal government discourages women from going abroad to work, and there are few studies that have examined female migration in any detail (Adhikari 2009, Thieme 2006, Thieme and Müller-Böker 2009).

case studies also highlight the risks poorer households take considering the economic repercussions should migrants be unsuccessful abroad, and the motivations of migrants to travel abroad. The first case study examines the attempts made by two young adults to travel abroad together. The second focuses on the efforts of a non-Limbu villager to organize work visas for his two oldest sons. The last case study focuses on a young adult who recently migrated from Mamangkhe to Jhapa after returning from the United Arab Emirates.

Dhane and Rosan

This first case study is of two young male villagers who decided to apply for the same work visa abroad with the hope that they might travel and live together. Both Dhane and Rosan live in households with small production surpluses. In other words, although they have enough land to produce food without over-reliance on the market, it is not enough for self sufficiency and, additionally, they both have relatively large households (7 and 5 members respectively). Both Dhane and Rosan had finished secondary school in early 2007 and decided to try and apply for jobs as "security guards", known to be a higher-paid job which requires knowledge of English and a pass at SLC level in secondary school.

They travelled to Phungling in December 2007, just after the cardamom season, and used some of the money from selling cardamom to get their passports made. In January they travelled to Jhapa to visit a number of manpower offices in Birtamod and applied for jobs as security guards with a company known as "Group 4".[121] They returned to Jhapa again towards the end of February for their interviews. Rosan, who had memorized the question and answer sheet properly, passed the interview but Dhane failed it. Dhane managed to get into another interview session for a less respected security guard company and passed that one. This meant that they would end up going to different countries: Rosan to Qatar and Dhane to Dubai.[122] "Group 4" visa applications, unlike other work visas, are usually ready fairly soon after

---

121 This is most likely the company known as G4S plc, formerly known as Group 4 Securicor, the world's largest security services provider.

122 As of January 2009, Dhane's visa had not yet come through. His visa cost was 120,000 NPR and he had borrowed about half of this. He therefore now has to pay interest on about 60,000 NPR (an additional 16,000 NPR per year) without even having left the village.

a successful interview, and Rosan's father divided the total cost of the visa, which must be all paid up front, between himself and his economically more successful younger brother.

The total amount of money to be paid to the manpower agency in Birtamod was 134,000 NPR. This included flights, visa arrangements and administrative fees. This is an extraordinarily large amount of money for a household whose total yearly crop production in 2007 was worth approximately 34,400 NPR. In addition to the fee for the manpower agency, another 29,000 NPR were borrowed over the course of the year for the passport (5,500 NPR), travel costs, food, clothes, medical tests and a number of security guard interview training sessions. The final total amount of money borrowed by Rosan's household was therefore 163,000 NPR. It was agreed that Rosan's uncle would be responsible for raising 113,000 NPR either from villagers who owed him money or villagers who could lend money to him. All the money raised by Rosan's uncle would have a minimum interest rate of 30% per year. The remaining 50,000 NPR was given, at the lower interest rate of 24% per year, by Rosan's sister's husband who lives in Khewang.

Rosan's visa was processed quickly and he left the village in March of 2008 and flew to Qatar four days later. He phoned the village briefly three weeks later and commented to his father that his initial salary was going to be 800 Qatar Riyal (QAU) per month and not the original 900 QAU per month the agency had mentioned. If he is able to save 50% of his salary, it will take him at least two and a half years to pay back all the money he borrowed initially (with interest) and begin earning money. With only about 6 months left before the initial 3 year visa ends he can expect to earn little more than 60,000 NPR total.

The main reason Rosan decided to work abroad was to enable his household to pay back a number of local debts. The largest of these, a debt of 100,000 NPR with the local merchant Raj, meant that a large proportion of their cardamom-producing forest had been taken as *bandhaki*—land which produced between 80 and 120 kg of cardamom each year which Raj collected to pay for the interest on the 100,000 NPR. The plan was for Rosan to pay the principal back to Raj and his household's cardamom plots would return to them.

This case study draws specific attention to the tremendous burden of debt that households bear, and the risks, and further indebtedness, they are prepared to accept in an attempt to be relieved of their debt. It also shows how local debts are intimately connected with cardamom production, which is one of the few means by which households can make money in the village and ultimately, transform their economic and social condition. Labour migration abroad is the evident choice for villagers who want to earn substantially more than they can in the village, since even the lowest salaries abroad usually match those of school teachers in the village. Cardamom production either directly or indirectly supports this parallel economy by helping households pay for work visas, allowing cardamom-productive land to be considered as collateral for loans, giving cardamom-productive land value for *bandhaki* arrangements, and providing a high-value commodity which ultimately requires only periodic intensive labour input. Finally, the sale of cardamom increases the total availability of cash in the village economy, which is fundamental for households wishing to get loans to pay for visa fees and travel expenses.

Indra Bardewa's sons

The second case study is of a non-Limbu household with no cardamom production. Indra Bardewa belongs to the Damai caste and is one of two related tailors who earn a living mostly by sewing clothes both in Mamangkhe and in the settlement of Aitabare in Jhapa where Indra owns a small house. His household owns a small amount of land (roughly 1 *hal*), and as a result of the combination of low levels of agricultural production (total value of 16,800 NPR) and a large household size (11 members) has a deficit household surplus of -17,760 NPR. This figure does not reflect the actual economic condition of the household which is relatively well off largely as a result of the continuous demand for clothes and small amount of cardamom trading that Indra was involved with.

Indra's eldest son Nabin (20 years old) first travelled to Kathmandu in mid-2006. He had arranged with a manpower office in Birtamod that had told him the visa was ready and all that was left was to visit the central manpower office in Kathmandu and pay the visa fee of 85,000 NPR. What was supposed to be a few days of waiting turned into a few weeks, then many months of delay. Food and board was provided for free by the agency but the money borrowed to pay for the visa was already gaining interest (9,200 NPR per month). After approximately 10 months the visa application was cancelled (and original fee refunded) and Nabin returned to Mamangkhe. He remained there for another 8 months until his father was able to organize a cheaper work visa through another manpower in Birtamod. By this time, the original 85,000 NPR had become a debt of 133,000 NPR. At this point his second oldest son, Lakshmi (18 years old), decided he wanted to go abroad. Both Lakshmi and Nabin are married and both have a son. Their main motivation to go abroad was to make money for their immediate family (wife and son) and the household as a whole. Their longer term plan is to sell the property they own in Jhapa and buy another house with more land for the whole family to live in.

Indra was able to collect money from three families in Jhapa: a Limbu family originally from Mamangkhe who had permanently migrated, a Limbu family who lived in Jhapa and Mamangkhe, and a non-Limbu shop keeper. This additional money helped to pay for Lakshmi's visa (which was 85,000 NPR) and money returned from the failed visa was used to pay for Nabin's second visa—only 65,000 NPR this time. This time both their visas were processed fairly fast and by January 2008 they were both in Qatar: Nabin with a job as a cleaner, and Lakshmi working in housing construction. Nabin is earning around 14,000 NPR per month and Lakshmi is earning around 16,000 NPR per month. Indra calculated it would take them both a minimum of two years, perhaps even three, to pay back all the debt their household has accumulated over the years. Only then would there be any possibility of saving money to eventually purchase property in Jhapa.

This case study shows how Indra took advantage of non-kinship relations he had with a number of households in both Mamangkhe and Jhapa to raise money for the visa fees of his two sons. The advantage of borrowing money in Jhapa is that it can be borrowed within a relatively short space of time: money is always available in Jhapa, whereas there can be severe problems of cash scarcity in Mamangkhe at certain times of the year. The disadvantage of borrowing money in Jhapa is that households lend money at interest rates as high as 48% per year (four rupees per hundred per month). As with the first case study, this second case study demonstrates the size of debt that a household accumulates and the uncertainties it is prepared to live with. It also shows how villagers living in Mamangkhe rely on social networks which increasingly include the dispersed village in Jhapa to borrow money.

Khagendra

This final example is of a young Limbu villager who belongs to a relatively wealthy household. Khagendra was born in Mamangkhe in 1982, passed his SLC exams in 2000 and married a Limbu woman from Phidim in 2001. His father's household produced an average of 260 kg of cardamom per year (2006-2007) and had a surplus of 51,040 NPR in 2007 (a "medium surplus" producer in Table 15).

In 2003, Khagendra's uncle, who was working in United Arab Emirates (UAE) at the time, made arrangements (by "pulling") for Khagendra to join him in UAE. The visa was 80,000 NPR and a number of family members provided an interest-free loan to supplement household savings from cardamom production. His starting salary was 16,000 NPR per month, but this went up incrementally until he was earning around 30,000 NPR per month. He was able to pay back the cost of the visa within the first 6 months, and had saved around 300,000 NPR 18 months after that. He returned to Mamangkhe in 2007 and bought a small house along the main path through the settlement of Aitabare in Jhapa (directly opposite Indra's house).

Khagendra described the work he carried out in UAE, irrigation and oil pipe mechanics, as extremely tough. He was even posted to Somalia for 6 months by his company in UAE. Living conditions there were even poorer. He says he is contemplating studying Korean and applying for work in South Korea, which would be better paid and less physically demanding than his last job in UAE.

The relatively large amount of cardamom produced by Khagendra's natal household and close relatives in Mamangkhe meant that Khagendra was able to pay for the initial visa with household savings and interest-free loans. This in turn meant that he was able to repay the visa and begin earning money far quicker than most migrants. Khagendra's case provides an example of the circular nature of economic and social change: access to capital (interest-free loans as well as savings from cardamom) and social networks (kinship ties to individuals abroad who can help arrange visas) translated rapidly into economic success abroad (a high salary and secure long-term job), which in turn led to economic and social change at home: income from the first 18 months abroad was used to purchase a house, build a small tea shop for Khagendra's wife, buy a number of market goods (including a mobile phone and Korean language books), and pay for his son's education in an English medium private school.

Conclusion

In many ways little has changed in Nepal since Philippe Sagant carried out his fieldwork in the 1960s and early 1970s. The epigraph that begins this chapter mentions how households survive despite soldiers leaving the village for long periods of time. If the term "soldier" is replaced with the words "international labour migrant", much of the rest of the paragraph still rings true today. Subsistence agricultural activities that dominated and patterned rural life in the 1960s continue relatively unchanged to this day. Sagant mentions the scarcity of land and the small size of subdivided plots. This is still the case today despite considerable rural to urban migration. Additionally, the increased cost of land, particularly cardamom-producing land, as well as its unequal distribution throughout the village, makes it hard for households with little land to change their economic circumstances. The "notables, political leaders or moneylenders" who try to "increase their 'vast domains'" still exist today as a section or class within the village. There are two main differences though. First, the dominant sections of society today are above all large cardamom producers and successful labour migrants—the two usually go hand in hand. Second, instead of increasing the total amount of land they own in the village, contemporary equivalents of Sagant's "notables" and "moneylenders" are much more likely to purchase property in the dispersed village in Jhapa, finance the cost of visas for other household members, and pay for the cost of private schooling. Eastern Nepal is still saturated with "men hungry for land", but many of these men are also increasingly travelling abroad for work, and adopting many of the same cultural ideals as the newly urbanized or proletarianized populations of developing countries across the world.

The development of international migration has taken place in tandem with the growth of the dispersed village in Jhapa. This growth can be accounted for by a variety of factors. The earliest part of this growth was directly related to households making profits from cardamom production in Mamangkhe as well as savings from seasonal labour migration to Sikkim. The improvements of rural infrastructures between the core and dispersed village, which allowed villagers to travel further and more frequently than they could in the past, no doubt also played a significant role. The recent rise in the number of settlements in Jhapa is more directly tied to the growth of international migration as a productive process. The term "process" is particularly suitable for describing this most recent form of migration since it includes a number of preliminary—as well as subsequent—processes to beginning work abroad: travel expenses for initial enquiries at manpower offices; an extremely lengthy visa application process; obtaining capital—savings and loans—to pay for the often exorbitant visa processing fees; remitting part of the income back to the village to repay the loans; and finally returning, after a number of years abroad, with savings.

The increased number of settlements in Jhapa has had a series of interrelated effects. One of the most significant of these is the growth of Jhapa-based social networks which villagers in both Mamangkhe and Jhapa increasingly rely on for migration-related information and advice, as well as for capital in the form of loans. Although there are a number of wealthy households in Mamangkhe who have in the past, and to some extent continue to provide credit and loans, there are frequent problems of cash flow in the village which lead villagers to borrow money from wealthier households in Jhapa.

Another effect of the emergence of an "urban Mamangkhe" in Jhapa, and what Pettigrew (2000: 13) refers to as "urban villagers", is the gradual absorption of the ideals and aspirations of urban society—cultural notions of success, satisfaction, and leisure time—by both villagers living in Jhapa and Mamangkhe. These ideals and aspirations are partly expressed through consumption preferences and practises, physical activity (or lack of), and cultural practises. Villagers in Mamangkhe frequently commented on the emerging differences between themselves and those living in Jhapa. Several villagers described those who live in Jhapa to be physically lazier and weaker than those in Mamangkhe, citing both the lack of agricultural work and the availability of transport for carrying goods and travel as reasons for this.[123] Young adults who live in Jhapa and visit Mamangkhe are

---

123 Most of the conversations about the differences between villagers in Jhapa and Mamangkhe occurred during a village festival on the 17th and 18th of July, 2007. A large number of villagers from Jhapa had come up to

sometimes viewed with suspicion. Rumours among young adults in Mamangkhe describe how some young adults in Jhapa are involved in criminal activities—for example stealing motorcycles and selling them on.[124] Finally villagers commented that those who live in Jhapa usually don't speak the Limbu language and children don't learn it from their parents. This is considered to be a negative consequence of moving to Jhapa.

Notions of economic differentiation in Mamangkhe, and of what it means to be rich, are increasingly linked to elements of life in Jhapa and include the ability to: access social networks which, particularly for international migration, increasingly centre around Jhapa; purchase property and market goods; pay for an English-language education and computer tuition classes; use hospital treatment and medicines when needed; and finance expensive work visas which guarantee a comparatively high salary. Young adults in Mamangkhe have reoriented their ambitions towards Jhapa. The experiences of a small number of successful villagers—those who have been able to earn good incomes abroad and purchase property in Jhapa—have served to frame the understanding that younger villagers have of how it is possible to transform one's life. In this sense, the dispersed village in Jhapa, the social networks that revolve around Jhapa, and the increased mobility between Mamangkhe and Jhapa, have all led to the development of a particular model or pathway for socioeconomic transformation.

If migration is above all a "project of transformation", this project is structured to a large degree by the economic and cultural conditions that surround migrants. The emergence of Jhapa as a hub for international migration has come to serve a dual purpose: it increasingly provides financial support—loans to pay for visas—for migrants

Mamangkhe for occasion. I asked a dozen villagers, most of whom were friends who lived in Ward 4, what they thought the main differences were.

124 During the village festival mentioned above, one Jhapa resident, a 23-year-old Limbu, was stabbed in the leg by a local villager following a brawl after a football game. Although no one seemed aware of the exact circumstances which had led to the incident, the general feeling was that the Jhapa resident must have provoked the attack. A number of villagers commented that people from Jhapa were trouble-makers. They described many of these younger visitors using the term *phaṭāhā* meaning "prattler, babbler; one who ex- aggerates [sic]" (Turner 1931: 400), although the word also suggests untrustworthy behaviour and bad character.

planning to travel abroad; it also provides a template to many villagers for what is desirable, achievable, and legitimate change. For Sagant, the soldier returning to the village represented a threat which would end in confrontation. This confrontation has come to be represented by the increasing differences between the core village of Mamangkhe, and the dispersed village in Jhapa; between those villagers who emerge successfully from the process of international migration and those who are less successful.

This is not to say that only successful migrants live in Jhapa and unsuccessful migrants live in Mamangkhe: both wealthy and poor households exist in both settlements. Nonetheless, a strong case can be made that successful migrants will most likely move away from the core village, probably, but not exclusively, to Jhapa. Wealthier households are more strongly associated with Jhapa because they tend to have more relatives who have already moved away from the core village or are working abroad. It is also more likely that they have children who are already enrolled in English-language schools in Jhapa and they may already have bought rice paddy and property but not be permanently living in Jhapa.[125] In other words, although the dichotomy between Jhapa and Mamangkhe does not exactly match that of wealthy and poor households, there is a strong association between economic wealth and the ability to live in Jhapa. Economic differentiation between households is increasingly expressed as the different abilities households have of accessing or owning resources in Jhapa.

Despite the growing importance of Jhapa and international migration for socioeconomic change, Mamangkhe continues to play an essential part in the economic lives of villagers in both sites. The main reason for this is the continued relevance of cardamom production as a means of slightly improving economic conditions for smaller producers, and significantly changing the economic conditions of large producers. The ability of households to finance work visas is still largely dependent on cash available through cardamom production. There was some evidence that money saved by migrants was re-loaned, on returning to the village, to help finance other villager's visas. Typically, this money is used to pay back any outstanding debts, to pay for any purchases

---

125 There are at least 5 households in Mamangkhe that have bought rice paddy in Jhapa but do not yet own a house. They hire others to cultivate the rice on an *adhiyã* basis, and sell most of their own share of the produce.

(property, market goods), to finance a wedding, or to pay for a new work visa. Cardamom production is therefore the most significant source of capital within the village. The high price it commands in the market has provided large producers with the opportunity of investing their considerable earnings in lucrative visa arrangements abroad. Smaller producers, who cannot afford more expensive visas, face a greater risk that their (cheaper) visa arrangements turn out to be unfavourable, increasing their burden of debt and leading to loss of (usually cardamom-producing) land.

The previous chapter described how cardamom production in Mamangkhe acted and still acts as a wedge between already existing inequalities of land and resource distribution. It does this by prizing apart these inequalities, leading to yet greater socioeconomic differentiation. The productive process of international migration also plays a part in this differentiation but it relies on cardamom for its success. When the capital available to large cardamom producers is invested in lucrative work visas abroad, the impact of both productive processes working together is profound: wealthy households become even wealthier while smaller producers struggle to afford anything more than low wage visas and face the consequences of indebtedness.

Chapter 6
Ecological and Socioeconomic Change

Changes in land use, land ownership and food production

It is hard to pinpoint exact dates for the introduction of specific crops and agricultural practises to the village. Villagers generally talked of three periods of food production: forest-based food production with a focus on wild harvesting and hunting; millet and maize based food production in cleared forest areas (swidden agriculture) supplemented by wild foods; and the most recent period of wet rice cultivation combined with maize and millet production. There was no knowledge of the history of food crop introductions (with the exception of rice) although the stories surrounding the early history of the village all suggest a relatively permanent settlement pattern associated with the swidden production of maize and millet. It is unclear therefore at what point the Limbu transitioned from the first period of food production, based on hunting and gathering in the forests and a semi-nomadic lifestyle, to the second which relied more on staple crops, swidden agriculture and permanent sites of residence.

Such clear-cut transitions are not necessarily important to draw out, particularly since the mythologies and histories of the Limbu themselves do not deal with these ambiguities. What is clear from these stories is that there is still a strong sense of the ancestral Limbu, a human unlike those alive today. Living entirely on hunted meat, wild yams such as *tambhuŋ khe* (L.) (*Dioscorea bulbifera* Lin.), and fruits and berries such as *tiŋ'rekse* (L.) (*Rubus ellipticus* Smith), the ancestral Limbu had incredible strength (could carry boulders the size of a small house) and health (never experienced sickness). Contemporary villagers therefore conceive of a historical time when a Limbu community lived in the same settlement area as the current village and survived by hunting, gathering and fishing. More precise accounts refer to stories told to villagers by their grandparents and great-grandparents about what life had been like before rice became the staple food in the village. According to some this was still the case around the 1900s when there were only a few rice terraces in the village and hardly anyone even knew what rice tasted like. While there were still many villagers living in shelters, the first solid houses, such as those visible today, were built around the 1890s. Despite most villagers not yet growing rice, houses had become permanent sites of residence and the land around a house and closest to it informally belonged to the household (although, formally, all land belonged to the community and had not yet become a tradeable asset). This land was used for maize[126] and millet production, and the forest continued to serve as an important source of food, fuel, medicine, and building material.

Figure 37: Sorting and cleaning a harvest of edible tree lichen.

---

126 Regmi (1971: 17, footnote 21) notes that "cultivation of maize had become so common around the last decade of the eighteenth century that the area of dry lands was determined with reference to the quantity of maize seeds that would be required for its sowing. The crop was thus probable introduced in the hill regions of Nepal not later than the early eighteenth century and must have made a major impact on the economy of the region".

Figure 38: A basket load of wild mushrooms.

The main elements that stand out from villagers' accounts of the past relate to: a reduction in the consumption of wild foods (both hunted and gathered); a reduction in the health and strength of the Limbu as a result of this decreased consumption; the initial abundance of land and resources which decreased as the internal population increased and migrants settled; and the construction of more permanent houses based on stone, rammed-earth and wood.[127]

The most dramatic period of change in land use and food production began with the arrival of Nepali-speaking Bahun-Chhetri migrants. Most villagers mention Sirbelas Kharel as the first non-Limbu to arrive in the village from Khewang, settling in lower Ward 3 around 1895 and building the first rice terraces in the village shortly after arriving. At

---

127 Macfarlane notes that among the Gurung, traditional houses would have been made of wood, mud and thatch but that "such has been the change that not one of this type remains in Thak" (McFarlane 1976: 96). In the same section he writes that "Pignède also points out that large rectangular houses of stone and slate are replacing the smaller mud and thatch kind; the bigger houses become the symbol of success abroad" (ibid.) (c.f. Toffin 1981).

that time rice was produced only in settlements at lower elevations downriver and although families could buy and carry it up to the village, the high market price meant that most families continued to subsist on a maize-based diet. Local production of rice in the early 1900s increased availability and reduced the cost of rice, and many Limbu families began receiving rice in exchange for their labour. While wet-rice production in the early 1900s was new to the Limbu, many villagers mentioned that the Limbu had learnt about terracing years before the arrival of Bahun-Chhetri and were using it extensively for maize and millet production. Some villagers suggested that their ancestors might have learnt about this technology by traveling to areas where rice was already being grown. Again, no villager seemed to have any specific historical accounts, stories or myths associated with the transition from the earliest period of food production to the more sedentary agriculture of today.

The history of the Bahun-Chhetri arrival to the village is somewhat confused. While most villagers described Sirbelas Kharel as the first non-Limbu in the village, extremely detailed accounts by a current Chhetri resident of Mamangkhe, B.R. Bhattarai (see below) contradict this. He described how his ancestor R.K. Bhattarai, first visited the village in 1789, renting grazing land above the village settlement for over thirty years before finally "receiving" the land from a subba in 1825. This was an informal agreement between him and the subba who nominally controlled the land in the area. Eventually, he became the formal owner of the land through a *rājināmā* agreement in 1915.

It is interesting to note the justifications given by Limbu villagers today for why their ancestors accepted, and even encouraged, the arrival of these Bahun-Chhetri settlers. Allen (1997) mentions that the Thulung Rai (who also live in east Nepal) seem to have welcomed immigrants, who probably first arrived before the Gorkha conquest. Bahuns were invited to a place near the author's field site because of their astrological knowledge and literacy, although as he points out "it is difficult to imagine a Brahman immigration not preceded or accompanied by an immigration of Kāmīs to make the iron ploughshares that Brahmans need in order to grow rice, of Damais whom they need to make their clothes, and perhaps of Sārkīs to remove their dead cattle" (Allen 1997: 310). In the case of Mamangkhe village, one of the most cited reasons for encouraging the arrival of immigrants was the desire to "develop", *vikas*. The Chhetri were perceived as more knowledgeable about agriculture and allowing them to settle would "develop" the village. Villagers also mention that as the Chhetri spoke Nepali, which was the language of the state, knowledge of Nepali would also be useful for the Limbu. Villagers describe how they hardly spoke a word of Nepali before the Chhetri arrived and that it was a Chhetri who set up the first school in the village in the 1950s.

The second reason cited by villagers was the abundance of land. Chhetri settlers initially moved onto unused land either above the main settlement area, as was the case with the Bhattarai family, or below it, as was the case with the Kharel family. A number of villagers explained that because there was so much unused forest, there was no problem in allowing access to some of it for a few migrant families, particularly since they would employ Limbu villagers to clear the forest and work on the land. This provides an insight into the active role Limbu villagers played in allowing non-Limbu settlers onto their land. Finally, and somewhat in contradiction to the second reason, villagers explained how it was the subba who gave land away, often for negligible sums of money or in exchange for a few rolls of cloth and some millet. These latter statements portray villagers as relatively powerless and the subba as a sort of local-level monarch.

The arrival of the Bahun-Chhetri led the way to increased intensification of land use around more permanent house structures in several settlement clusters throughout the village. There is evidence in villagers' historical accounts that terracing technology had been used by the Limbu for some time before Bahun-Chhetri migrants arrived, but these migrants brought with them the technologies of wet-rice cultivation which required considerable labour to construct and maintain. The cultivation of wet-rice, which is more suited to lower altitudes, required large tracts of forest to be cleared and transformed into terraces below the main settlement area and close to the Kabeli River. The increase of labour opportunities in and around the main settlement areas of the village, as well as the increased dependence on sedentary agriculture, meant a decrease in both swidden agriculture and hunting and gathering in the forest.

There is, of course, a strong relationship between residential mobility (or lack of it) and the agricultural form adopted by a community. Villagers' historical accounts of life in the village emphasize the permanence of sites of residence. In other words, villagers mention how ancestors as far back as six or seven generations ago within the same sub-clan, lived in a house on the same spot as the current one. This means that for at least six or seven generations—though perhaps more—villagers must have mostly cultivated land either around or close to their houses; land which therefore informally belonged to each household. Most of the land immediately around the main settlement areas in each ward, and particularly the oldest wards such as Ward 4, would have been intensively cultivated. The Bahun-Chhetri did not initially encroach on this land because they first settled on the fringes of the village. They then cleared large tracts of forest around their houses for rice and maize cultivation, thus increasing the total amount of agricultural land in the village. Although no figures were collected on total land cleared by Sirbelas Kharel and his descendants in Ward 3, the general impression held by Limbu villagers is that it was a tremendous amount which required many years of considerable labour input. The forested land that the first Kharel family and their descendants settled in Ward 3, is now occupied by over twenty households.

So far this section on changes in land use and food production in Mamangkhe has dealt with three periods or phases of food production: from the nomadic ancestors who first settled in the village and lived by hunting and gathering food to the introduction of wet-rice production by one of the earliest Chhetri settlers. Interviews with villagers brought out four themes: the long history of settlement in the area and the close relationship between houses and their surrounding land; the almost mythical nature of the ancestral Limbu who lived by hunting and gathering; the presence of terracing technology before the arrival of Chhetri settlers; and the involvement of Limbu villagers in encouraging or accepting the arrival of these settlers who cleared large tracts of forest for agriculture in marginal land above and below the main settlement area.

With regard to the history of Chhetri settlement in the area, villagers tended to emphasize the arrival of the Kharel family in Ward 3 and only a few seemed aware that the Bhattarai family in Ward 2 had arrived almost one hundred years before this. Perhaps this is related to the fact that the Kharel family, which eventually extended across ten households, had such a transformative impact on the landscape and local economy. It might also be related to the symbolic importance rice has among the Brahman-Chhetris (Daryn 2006, Poffenberger 1980).[128] As a staple crop, rice also plays an important role in Brahman-Chhetri ritual and social life, elements of which have also been absorbed into Limbu ritual and social practises. Although the Bhattarai family arrived well before the Kharel, they focused their productive activities on rearing cattle and producing butter and cheese: activities which required less labour from the Limbu than rice cultivation. According to B.R. Bhattarai, they first began to cultivate rice around 1944. The Kharel had started rice cultivation almost fifty years before this and the task of clearing large tracts of forest and building terraces on the steep slopes had been largely carried out by the Limbu.

The arrival of the Kharel, and earlier settlement of the Bhattarai, marked the beginning of non-Limbu migration into the village. From around 1940 onwards a large number of Bahun-Chhetri families, as well as Dalit, Kāmī, Sārkī, and Gurung families moved to the village. Some of them settled on marginal land on the periphery of the main settlement areas, in the same way as the Kharel and Bhattarai had done before them. Others were able to settle on land within the main settlement area, living among the Limbu on land previously farmed by Limbu villagers. Land was still formally kipat and as such could not be formally owned by non-Limbu settlers, but negotiations were carried out between settlers and the previous "owners" of the land, and informal agreements were signed by both parties legitimating the transfer of land from Limbu to non-Limbu hands.

Limbu villagers describe these Bahun-Chhetri settlers as both cunning and industrious. Their economic success derived from both their ability to take advantage of Limbu villagers and their hard work. Limbu villagers recount how the Chhetri were clever because they did not waste their money on alcohol and meat. Some mentioned how they took advantage of Limbu illiteracy by modifying the figures in ledgers

---

128 Daryn (2006: 186) describes how "high-caste Nepalese in general and Thamgharian Brāhmaṇs in particular, as well as their Newāri *jyāpu* (farmers) counterparts, share what may be called "a culture of rice." By this I mean that for them rice is not only the staple quantitatively but also qualitatively, that is, in terms of its central meaning and significance for personal, ritual, and social life". Poffenberger (1980: 76) writes how "As Hindus from the west moved into the hills of Nepal. They spread the concept of paddy cultivation. Along with the material technology of paddy cultivation, values regarding the high status associated with the consumption of rice were also diffused among the tribal groups".

related to the debt incurred by Limbu villagers.[129] Others described how the pots for measuring units of weight (for trading, selling or giving grain in lieu of cash) were always smaller in Chhetri households allowing them to save some of their grain production. Villagers' stories also described Chhetri settlers as extremely hard-working. Just as stories abound of the mythical Limbu, a number of villagers described how, for example, one of the first Chhetri villagers was strong enough to carry a full grown buffalo from one field to another.

This slightly contradictory perception of the historical (and present-day) Bahun-Chhetri, as both sly and hard-working, points perhaps to the contemporary suspicion villagers have of economically successful fellow-villagers. While there is a widespread belief that hard work (including labour migration abroad) has its economic rewards, there is an underlying suspicion about the means by which people become *dhani* and perhaps an unarticulated fear of the long-term repercussions of economic success on the village. This in turn relates to the fairly explicit relationship between economic success and migration from the village to Jhapa: it is clear to most villagers that the majority of those who are economically successful—villagers who went from being *garīb* to *dhani*—usually do not return to the village but settle elsewhere. This specific pattern of migration related to economic success, was first demonstrated by the Bahun-Chhetri only a few generations after arriving in the village.

The history of non-Limbu settlement in the village is covered in more detail elsewhere. As mentioned earlier, from 1940 onwards roughly eleven different castes or sub-castes migrated and settled in the village. A few of these families left the village soon after arriving and a number of them (particularly the Dalit and Gurung) still remain in the village today. The majority of these families began to leave the village from the late 1960s onwards. By the late 1980s only a handful of Chhetri households remained from a total of almost thirty a few decades before. The majority of Chhetri had departed before cardamom cultivation had become widespread (Ratna B. only started selling

---

129 Caplan (1970: 63-64) also mentions this: "Another ruse was employed in land-pledging transactions whereby the creditor would provide a small loan and after obtaining the signature—or, more likely, the thumbprint—of the kipat-owner, would then add 'a few zeros' to the amount, thus making it impossible for the kipat-owner ever to raise the required amount to repay the loan and resume his lands."

cuttings in 1974) and before the cadastral survey was carried out in the village in 1986. There might in fact be a relationship between the village "pre-survey" carried out in 1966 and the departure of Chhetri families. Perhaps it was this early attempt by the state to formalize land ownership in the area which encouraged Chhetri settlers to leave. This could only be a partial explanation since there would have to have been villagers willing and able to buy the land from the Limbu. In fact, in all probability, it was the income from working in Sikkim's cardamom economy (from around 1956 onwards) that allowed newly rich Limbu villagers either to buy land or pay back debts they had incurred—thereby reclaiming their land.

Another factor which probably influenced the migration of Bahun-Chhetri households from Mamangkhe, was the "intervention of technology that controlled malaria and turned the Tarai into a new frontier for human occupance" (Gurung 1989: 21). The movement of Nepal's hill villagers to the lowland Tarai had been taking place ever since the Rana regime had tried to solve the increasing problem of population pressure in the hills of Nepal by providing land entitlements to Bahun-Chhetri villagers in the Tarai. The panchayat regime also encouraged migration from the hills for political reasons, hoping to make the Tarai less "Indian". It was only during the 1960s and 1970s that a programme of malaria eradication made more parts of the Tarai accessible for Nepali migrants from the hills. The timing of the malaria eradication programme suggests that it probably played an important role in encouraging Bahun-Chhetri villagers to begin migrating in the late 1960s.[130]

While it is inappropriate with so few historical data to speculate too much on the causes for Chhetri departure from the village, there are two points which are worth returning to. First of all, whatever caused or motivated so many Chhetri settlers to migrate, Limbu villagers today emphasize the element of economic success in their portrayal of

---

130 Campbell (2004: 153) mentions how many of Nepal's hill villagers who migrated to the Tarai "competed with commercial logging and biodiversity protected areas for access to forest margins in a more desperate struggle for land than has generally been apparent in the hills". Ghimire (1992) writes about government attempts to protect land (particularly forest) in the Tarai from being settled by landless and propertyless migrants who in some cases are evicted from their homes despite having settled on land years before.

Chhetri history in the village. For villagers today, it was economic success above all else that allowed the Chhetri to leave the village. Secondly, the fact that cardamom cultivation emerged after the departure of so many Chhetri families underlines the close relationship Limbu villagers have with cardamom cultivation. While Chhetri villagers became wealthy by increasing the productivity of land, trading goods, and lending money, Limbu villagers (those with access to surplus land) became wealthy (and continue to do so) by producing and selling cardamom.

As cardamom cultivation became more widespread, land previously used for maize and millet production was converted to cardamom forest.[131] Since maize and millet continued to be the most important staple crops for the Limbu, some of the rice terraces built by the Chhetri who had departed were used for maize and millet production and total rice production in the village fell (see "*Raj Kumar Gautam*" below). The rapid growth of cardamom cultivation throughout the village led to yet another shift in the perception of the value of land. Whereas prior to the arrival of the Chhetri, marginal land (dangerous, steep, rocky, sandy, and infertile land) had been considered largely useless, the Chhetri showed how even this land could be rendered productive. The ecological qualities and economic value of cardamom led villagers to consider using almost any type of land as viable for planting cardamom: the rocky banks of streams that divide settlements into wards; the boundaries between terraces; extremely steep slopes in forested areas; and water-logged sections of forest.

One of the most important characteristics of cardamom is the fact that it requires relatively little labour input for most of the year. Except for the harvest season, the tasks of planting and clearing cardamom forests can be carried out at almost any time throughout the summer from May to August. This flexibility means that even families with a large amount of cardamom can continue to work on their subsistence crops (although typically those with large cardamom plots are able to afford hiring villagers to work for them). It also means that cardamom

---

131 Terraced and un-terraced slopes previously cultivated with maize and millet, usually on land closest to the main settlement areas, are recognizable by the presence of relatively young alder trees (often no more than twenty years old according to villagers) planted by villagers to provide shade on previously cleared land.

can be cultivated at any distance from a villager's house since it doesn't require the sorts of inputs and regular attention that subsistence agriculture requires (ploughing, fertilizing, and repeated weeding). These three elements of labour flexibility, distance, and market value have meant that a very large proportion of the land within the administrative boundary of the village is cultivated with cardamom. With the exception of community-owned land used for firewood and fodder, cardamom plants are constantly visible in the forest when one walks from one side of the village to the other at almost any elevation below the uppermost houses in the settlement area.

The history of land use in the village is a history of the gradual increase in the use of a land market and the means by which certain villagers were able to accumulate more land than others. The early history of the village, as told by villagers themselves, emphasizes the importance of access to the forest as a resource for all, and ancestral (sub-clan) ownership of land surrounding permanent sites of residence. Villagers explained how, until the early 1900s, it was the subba who gave permission to families within sub-clans to clear forest and move from one plot to another around the main settlement area. The arrival of non-Limbu migrants who were willing to pay for land led to the weakening of the kipat system of land ownership. From the 1920s through to the early 1960s, non-Limbu settlers and particularly the Bahun-Chhetri castes, increased their control over land and the economy by employing the Limbu to extend and intensify agricultural production and by lending money and food to increasingly indebted villagers. The pre-survey of 1966 served as the final warning before land became fully commoditized and the kipat system completely replaced by the private ownership of land. According to several Limbu villagers interviewed, after 1966 the cleverest villagers were those who started to buy as much land as they could having understood that the final survey (the *nāpi*) was shortly to come. They bought other people's land, including land from departing Bahun-Chhetri families, so that when the *nāpi* took place in the mid 1980s, they had more land than others. It was the *nāpi* which identified the exact boundaries of all the plots of land in the village. Forested land which lay above the settlement area became government land administered by the community as a whole (*sārvajanik*).[132] All other forested land, be it below the village settlement area, or land leading up towards the village of Yamphudin, had been privatized by individuals during the late 1960s around the time of the pre-survey.[133] This was the final stage of a process of land privatization

---

132 Harper and Tarnowski (2007: 35-42) outline the history of community forestry in Nepal from the 1950s through the 1990s. Each decade provided a new approach to forest management, usually prompted by donor agencies' demands. The Forest Nationalization Act in 1957 (slightly refined with the Forest Preservation Act of 1967) placed all forest in Nepal under control of the Forest Department. According to an FAO/World Bank report (1979) "after nationalization of the forest, the people considered that the state was taking away their rights in the forests and lost their sense of responsibility; they did not feel there was any necessity to conserve the forests...The effect of the Nationalization Act was to accelerate forest degradation". Dahal (1994: 17-18) points out that although a number of scholars argue that large forest tracts were felled immediately after the enforcement of the Act, evidence shows that large scale deforestation only occurred after 1960. It was only in the 1970s that international concern with environmental protection and community forestry led to new legislation being passed in 1978 which, in theory, handed over government forest land to local level (*gaun panchayat*) control. Yet it was not until the Decentralization Act of 1982 that villagers were given the legal right to control the management of their forests. It is hard to trace the outlines of this history of community forestry at the village (Mamangkhe) level. For one thing, the relative isolation of the village and historical conditions meant that much of the legislation regarding land (agricultural or forested) prior to the formal dissolution of the kipat system of land ownership would have had little impact in the area.

133 This matches with the historical accounts provided by Dahal (1994), Bajracharya (1983), and Gilmour and Fisher (1991), among others, which describe how the original Forests Nationalization Act (1957) ignored traditional communal rules of forest management, fomented distrust towards government, and encouraged the acceleration of forest clearing by villagers keen to establish their individual rights over previously communally-managed land. Daniggelis (1997) describes the cadastral survey, which took place in 1994 in the upper Arun valley region, as a direct cause of increased deforestation (Daniggelis 1997: 212-13). Villagers felt threatened by the survey which they imagined would require them to pay higher taxes to the government and restrict their access to forest resources. To this day, the Rai villagers are wary of the National Park (Makalu-Barun National Park and Conservation Area established in 1992) and "outside control" of land and resources, as it has regulated their swidden cultivation practices and limited their access to *chiraita*, which they rely on as an important cash crop (Daniggelis 1997: 207-9). The Sherpa in the same region view the National Park (and therefore the restrictions it has imposed) more positively as they have benefited more from increased tourism by providing accommodation and working as porters and guides.

which had begun well over 100 years before with the arrival of the Bhattarai family and, subsequently, the Kharel family.

As with the economically successful Bahun-Chhetri, villagers describe how certain Limbu were *calākh* (clever, artful) in understanding early on the advantage of buying land during the 1960s and 1970s from both departing Chhetri families and Limbu villagers.[134] Villagers therefore do not seem to ascribe contemporary differences in land ownership to aspects of kinship such as sub-clan affiliation or belonging to a subba lineage. From the way villagers talk about the period leading up to the *nāpi*, it seems clear that the accumulation of land and the emergence of cardamom cultivation coincided in such a way as to redistribute the fortunes of certain villagers to the detriment of others. Prior to this period the distribution of land seems to have favoured the Bahun-Chhetri, Sārkī, and Gurung castes as well as the various subba families in the village who represented each sub-clan. The emergence of a section of Limbu society with access to capital—saved from army salaries and pensions, work in Sikkim, and trade—paired with increased state intervention aimed at commoditizing all land in the village, worked to the advantage of certain Limbu who were clever enough to invest their capital in land. These were the Limbu who had realized that the era of an abundance of land was over and that its increasing scarcity would also mean a rise in the value (and cost) of land in the future.

Such political conflicts between local and State level land and resource management have been noted in other parts of Nepal, particularly where National Parks and conservation areas have been developed (Campbell 2003, Mehta and Kellert 1998, Ramble and Chapagain 1990). The absence of a national park or conservation area (the Kachenjunga Conservation Area, established in 1997, is a two-day walk uphill from the village and is not considered part of the village's resource base) and a long history of political autonomy in the region, have contributed to the relative lack of local/State political conflict in relation to access to forest resources and forest management.

134 Although Pfaff-Czarnecka (2008) refers largely to the period of post-1990 democratic reforms, her words are equally applicable in this particular context—the transition from the kipat system to one private ownership through State legitimation: "Nepal conforms to a widespread pattern of transitional situations all over the world, in which reforms have been undertaken, but have not been successfully implemented. Very often, formal rules and regulations are not realized or institutionalized, and, rather than lose their former prerogatives, resourceful strongmen manage to gain ground within the new system" (2008: 74).

If the history of land use and land ownership was dictated above all else by the arrival of the Bahun-Chhetri and the *nāpi* of 1986, one might be misled into thinking that little has changed since then. Whereas access to land may have varied between Limbu families throughout the period leading up to the *nāpi*, it was the cadastral survey which not only cemented the already unequal distribution of land (by documenting exact figures for land ownership) but legitimated this inequality for Limbu villagers. It did this by almost perversely leading villagers to believe that those who had not successfully increased their total land holding in the lead-up to the survey had not been as *calākh* as those who had. In part, this may have something to do with the legacy of economic success left behind by various non-Limbu settlers who migrated from the village only a few generations after arriving.

It is therefore worth examining more closely the life histories of two influential non-Limbu migrants. The first of these, mentioned earlier, is B.R. Bhattarai, whose ancestors were arguably the first non-Limbu migrants to settle in the village in the late 1800s. Although a few Bhattarai households still remain in the village, the majority of the descendants of R.K. Bhattarai migrated to other parts of Nepal and India. B.R. Bhattarai's life history draws attention to the enterprising nature of non-Limbu settlers and the means by which they became wealthy before the economic boost provided by army recruitments, work in Sikkim and the introduction of cardamom cultivation. With regard to cardamom cultivation, although B.R. Bhattarai's household does produce a large amount of cardamom (between 400 and 600 kg per year), his son confirmed that his family had accumulated wealth (particularly in terms of land and livestock) well before this.

The second life history is of a Jaisi,[135] Raj Gautam, who arrived in the village a few years after the *nāpi*. This life history will help to outline the contemporary relationship between wealth, land use, money-lending or debt, and cardamom cultivation. In particular, by detailing the relationship between debt and land ownership, a relationship which spans well over 100 years of village history, this section will explain the

---

135 Turner (1931: 207) describes them as "a low caste of Brāhmans (said to be the offspring of a Brāhman with a Brāhman widow)". Fürer-Haimendorf (1966: 19) describes them as "the offspring of unions of Upadhya and Kumai men with Brahman widows or the descendants of such offspring". Although technically a Brahmin caste, the Jaisi in the village describe themselves as Chhetri and are considered Chhetri by other villagers.

process by which inequality continues to be severely exacerbated today. It is this process of increased inequality which is resulting in the emergence of economic differentiation or class.

Babi Ram Bhattarai

The life history of the first Chhetri family to arrive in Mamangkhe provides an important perspective on non-Limbu migration to the area, and an understanding of the reasons why non-Limbus families were so economically successful. Combining this early history of the Chhetri with the research presented of Ratna Bahadur's life history in Chapter 4, a fuller picture emerges of the extent to which Chhetri families were able to penetrate even the most remote villages in east Nepal. At their peak, there were 28 Chhetri households in the village (wards 1 to 7) around the early 20th century, and there are now only seven. When speaking with villagers about the history of Mamangkhe, they would frequently mention how they felt surrounded by Chhetri households during the period before the Chhetri started migrating south around 40 years ago.[136] Villagers usually use the term *Chhetri* to refer to all non-Limbu settlers, occasionally switching to the broader term *parbate* or *parbatiyā*, although this still would not include the Gurung who settled in the village around the same time as Nepali-speaking groups.

Most of the large, more modern-looking houses that are located along the main path through wards 4 and 5 were built by Chhetri families some 50 years ago. One of the families still living in Mamangkhe is of the Sivakoti clan, although most of the members of the household live in Jhapa. The Gautam family, of the Jaisi caste (discussed below), arrived more recently to teach and open a shop. This family has since become one of the wealthiest in the village. The five remaining households, who all live in wards 1 and 2, all share a common ancestor: Ram Krishna Bhattarai. One of the youngest descendants of Ram Krishna is Mohan, the only villager to have a bachelor degree. He teaches English at the village school in Ward 5. His father is Babi Ram Bhattarai and Ram Krishna is Babi Ram's great-great-great-grandfather.

---

136 Two villagers went so far as to describe the village of 50 years ago as a "Chhetri village", which is inconceivable today in a village that hosts the Limbu museum, teaches the Limbu language at school, and is known far and wide as a village where even the children still speak the Limbu language.

Ram Krishna is said to have arrived in Mamangkhe around 1825 from Tellok, the VDC half-a-day's walk south-west towards Tharpu,[137] and built a small house on the site of Babi Ram's current house in upper Ward 1. He had first come to raise buffalo and cows in the *got* above the current settlement area in 1789. At this time, he grazed livestock (buffalo, cows, and goats) on land by paying a small fee to the local subba, and only formally received land in 1825. Ram Krishna was therefore the first Chhetri to move to the area. He had seven sons. Rogi Bir was the *jantare* son (sixth-born) and Rogi Bir also had seven sons. Bala Bir, the *sāīlā* son (third-born) was Babi Ram's grandfather. Bala Bir had two sons, Man Bahadur (*jeṭhā*), who moved to Tellok, and Dal Bahadur (*kānchā*), who was Babi Ram's father. Dal Bahadur had five sons: Karka Bahadur (*jeṭhā*) went to live in Hampang; Ganga Ram (*māīlā*) still lives in Mamangkhe; Man Bahadur (*sāīlā*) went to live in Manipur, India (although his children all migrated to Jhapa); Jagari Ram (*kāīlā*) also moved to Hampang; Babi Ram (*antare*); and Dal Modran (*kānchā*) who lives in Taplejung bazaar.[138]

When Ram Krishna initially moved to Mamangkhe, he worked on land taken as *bandhaki*. It was only in 1915 that Babi Ram's grandfather, Bala Bir, was able to buy the land as *rājināmā*. He is said to have bought this land from the subba for 200 NPR, the equivalent of about 2 *kaḍor* NPR today: in other words, an enormous and somewhat unrealistic sum of money.[139] Dal Bahadur, Ram Krishna's great-grandson and Babi Ram's father, was one of the first villagers to cultivate rice paddy in terraces in upper Ward 1, starting work on terracing in 1944. The whole area was

---

137 Much of the data on Babi Ram's ancestors and history comes from an extended, semi-structured interview carried out with Babi Ram on the 30/5/2008.

138 There are two other Bhattarai families in Mamangkhe and they live in wards 8 and 9. They are both related by being descendants of Ram Krishna. The "Ponpe Bhattarai" who live in Ponpe across the Khaksewa River from Mamangkhe, descended from Rogi Bir's youngest brother Indra Bahadur (Ram Krishna's *kānchā* son). Another family that lives in Sudap, Ward 8, is descended from Rogi Bir's antare son. Rogi Bir's *māīlā* son Ganga Ram had five sons: the eldest died, the second works abroad, the third lives in a *got*, the fourth works in Mamangkhe, and the youngest, *kānchā*, lives in Ponpe.

139 Several villagers commented that no one really knew for certain what the original amount had been.

terraced for wet rice cultivation.[140] Over the last 40 years, with the departure of many Chhetri families, only maize, millet and potatoes have been cultivated on the terraces, with small amounts of cardamom grown adjacent to the rivulets that cut the hillside into sections and provide boundary markers between wards. The whole area surrounding the house that Babi Ram and Mohan occupy today was inhabited solely by Chhetri families although, more recently, three Gurung families also live in separate households. The Limbu lived much lower down, in what are now wards 4, 5 and 7 (Pauwa). Above them, in wards 1 and 2, and below them, in Tekadin (Ward 3) were the Chhetri and later Gurung households, herding cattle and cultivating rice in terraces.

Babi Ram was born in Mamangkhe in 1942, and married a woman from Khewang, across the valley, at the age of 11. They have a total of nine children, all but one of whom have left the village and live mostly in Jhapa and Kathmandu. They are considered by most villagers to be extremely wealthy, mostly as a result of cardamom production, relatively large maize and millet production, and income from renting out grazing land to herders. Survey data shows that they produced 10 *muri* of millet (approximately 800 kg), and 1,000 *jhutta* of maize (roughly equivalent to 10 *muri*). They have one of the highest surplus figures (94,720 NPR) of the whole village, partly as a result of having only three household members. They still own rice fields below their house, but these have been left uncultivated as there is a general shortage of labour, both within the household and in upper Ward 1. Babi Ram mentioned that most of the work for their food crops and cardamom is carried out by *khetālā* who come up from lower wards 1 and 2. As no members of the family consume millet beer, and only occasionally consume millet bread, there is a substantial surplus of millet, and farm labour is often paid for with millet, equivalent to 100 or 50 NPR for a day's work (men and women respectively).

Babi Ram's household has produced an annual average of 493 ⅓ kg of cardamom over the last three years and has also inherited a substantial amount of non-agricultural land for both firewood and fodder. Rogi Bir had been able to buy this land in upper Ward 1 for very little money as it was considered to be of little use by the Limbu at the time. In 1973,

---

140 Seeing the Chhetri working in the water-logged terraces, the Limbu are supposed to have said "why are the Chhetri playing like buffalo on the land!?".

Babi Ram planted the cardamom cuttings that Ratna B. had sold him in forested areas with good water availability. He is now one of the largest producers of cardamom in the village and has been able to buy one *bighā* of land in Charpane, Jhapa. His eldest son and daughter live there and he says he plans to build a 5,000,000 NPR house which will take 10 to 12 years to complete. In addition to the land he inherited from his father, he also bought, in 1973, grazing land above the settlement area from Sirbela's son, Chandra Modi. He now rents this to other families for grazing their cattle and earns some 4,000 to 5,000 NPR per year from this.

This short life history of Babi Ram provides an insight into the larger history of high-caste Hindu migrations in east Nepal. Although specific details, such as dates and payments, may not be precise, one can begin to gain a general sense of how non-Limbu populations were able to survive and eventually to flourish in remote and unfamiliar environments. Ram Krishna, in particular, first rented unused grazing land from a subba over 180 years ago, and thus established links with villagers which eventually led to his being able to informally claim unused land (upper Ward 1 was uninhabited until the Chhetri arrived). He was able to make unused land agriculturally productive and combine this with cattle herding, producing butter, and being one of the first to plant cardamom cuttings sold by Ratna B. As a result, Ram Krishna and his descendants were not only able to survive but became economically successful enough to be able to leave the village altogether, with many migrating to Kathmandu and cities in the plains. This is broadly the pattern most of the other Chhetri families have followed, and is the pattern which strongly marks contemporary life in Mamangkhe.

Raj Kumar Gautam

Raj Kumar Gautam is a more contemporary version of Ram Krishna. Considered by many to be one of the wealthiest villagers, he became one of the pivotal figures in my research when it became clear how many people owed him sizeable sums of money. He is an important political figure who orchestrated the installation of the first electric micro-hydro station (1 kilowatt) in 1996. Throughout fieldwork, he played an important informal role in village meetings and proposals related to the VDC budget, and his shop by the primary school in Ward 5 was one of the centres of village gossip, news and discussions. His wealth and access to cash through contacts with merchants and cardamom buyers make him an important source of credit for families hoping to raise capital to go abroad or pay back debts. His wealth in particular, combined with his reputation as a money-lender, also makes him a controversial figure, and one that arouses strong emotions among many villagers. Perhaps surprisingly, given that he was born and brought up in Limbu-speaking areas and that it would be an advantage to his business interests, he does not speak Limbu although he understands a few common phrases.

Having grown up in a relatively poor household, Raj inherited only a small plot of land from his father and moved to Mamangkhe to begin teaching. Raj was born in 1954 in Khewang and met his wife in the same village.[141] He studied up to Class 10 and passed the SLC. He married in 1976 when he was 22 years old. He inherited 6,000 NPR worth of rice paddy (which produced 400 kg of rice) and no house. He and his wife lived in rented houses between 1977 and 1981, paying *bandhaki* every time they moved. Raj became a school teacher in Khewang initially and started a small shop business in one of the rented houses in 1978 selling cloth and biscuits. Eventually, he was earning enough money to buy more land with a small house in 1981, for 20,000 NPR on which he produced between 15 and 16 *muri* of maize each year. He continued with the shop, expanding it a little to provide more basic food goods, and sold the land he had inherited for 17,000 NPR in 1989, almost three times the value since he inherited it in 1977. Two years later, in 1991, he bought a section of cardamom forest for 60,000 NPR and built a bigger house for the expanding family. He moved to Mamangkhe that same year in a house below the school for two years before acquiring the house they currently live in for 20,000 NPR under a *bandhaki* agreement. He started buying local cardamom in 1993 and together with the 400 to 600 kg produced on his land in Khewang, sold it initially to merchants in Gopetar, Pachthar district, and later to merchants in Birtamod, Jhapa.

According to Raj, this period, around early 1990s, was a period of rapid growth in cardamom production. New areas of forest were cleared for cultivation but, more significantly, rice paddy terraces in lower

---

141 Most of the data on Raj emerged from three in-depth semi-structured interviews carried out on three separate days: 9/3/2008, 24/5/2008, and 2/6/2008. Data from the survey is also used.

parts of the village were planted with cardamom, and the local cost of rice started to increase. In the year Raj moved to Mamangkhe, he bought 480 kg of local rice (*dhān* or unhusked rice), supplementing this slightly with rice bought in Gopetar. The price of rice in 1994 was around 800 NPR for a *muri* (80 kg sack). Between 1998 and 1999, the production of rice had fallen so dramatically that there was none available for purchase locally and the cost of rice in Gopetar had increased to 1200 NPR per *muri*. Raj had to buy his rice from other villages, and increasingly from the plains and from India.

Raj mentioned that up to 2004, people were starting to spend increasing amounts of money on market goods at his shop. They had more disposable income as a result of both income from local cardamom production and earnings from seasonal work in Sikkim. In addition, since the completion of the road extension from Ilam to Gopetar,[142] merchants and shops were moving closer to the village, more goods were becoming available, and families started spending more money at Raj's shop. Raj began to extend credit to villagers who sold their cardamom to him. He would note down their purchases throughout the year and the account would be balanced by the value of cardamom sold to him by villagers during the harvest season. A number of factors seem to have coincided around this period.

First, more and more families were buying their rice from Gopetar, and those who couldn't carry it themselves were paying between 80% and 100% more per kg for the cost of paying a porter. Second, although there was more money available in the village, much of it was being spent on market goods, as the quantity and range of goods increased. Finally, in the last few years before 2003 there was a slight decrease in cardamom production in parts of the village, as first-generation plants started to age and became less productive. While people were still borrowing money on credit from Raj by buying goods from his shop, some families were spending more money than they would be able to pay back with their cardamom.

This all came to a head in 2004 when Raj started to take villagers' land under a *bandhaki* arrangement. He took part of one villager's (SP) cardamom-producing land under a *bandhaki* arrangement, worth a total of 130,000 NPR. SP owed Raj around 100,000 NPR having borrowed small

---

142 Work on this had been completed by around 1992, though only the section from Ilam to Phidim has been pitched to this day.

amounts of money to buy rice and a larger amount for the marriage of one of his sons around two years before. Finding himself unable to repay even the interest on the debt, he gave Raj cardamom land which produced 120 to 160 kg of cardamom annually.[143] Under their *bandhaki* arrangement, which runs to this day, the cardamom produced each year only pays the interest on the debt, leaving the original amount owed unchanged.[144]

The most recent *bandhaki* Raj has arranged is with a villager, Kumar, who started borrowing money in 2004 to pay back debts he had with merchants in Tharpu at that time. Together with this, Kumar was producing an average of 20,000 NPR worth of cardamom per year, but consuming 50,000 NPR worth of goods per year from Raj's shop. He was unable to pay back a debt of 80,000 NPR to Raj for five years until very recently when, in May 2008, he gave a portion of his cardamom-producing land to Raj for 80,000 NPR. This is land that produces an average of 120 kg of cardamom per year. Raj harvests the cardamom on Kumar's land to pay the interest on the money he first lent him, and when Kumar is eventually able to raise 80,000 NPR, he can "buy" the land back, though legally it has never left his hands.

The above are just two examples of *bandhaki* mortgages of cardamom land which resulted from a series of intersecting economic and ecological changes that came about during the early 1990s. As a result of the growth of cardamom production in the village, rice paddy was displaced to make room either for cardamom, or, in some cases, for maize and millet crops if cardamom had been planted on terraces traditionally reserved for these. Local rice, which had been relatively abundant up to around 1993, became the rarity it is today. Of the 201 houses surveyed in 2007, only 41 produced rice and these produced an average of only 248 kg per household per year. When the average household consumes approximately 81.4 kg per month, this is barely

---

143 Under this arrangement, Raj hired *khetālā* to work on the land and produce the cardamom, which he received as payment for the interest on the original loan.

144 As Sagant (1983: 198) notes, in an article about money lending among the Limbu, "plots are mortgaged in order to secure a loan of grain because of a poor harvest, a landslide, or a return to the village after a disappointing and unprofitable migration. This practice of giving up a piece of land in order to procure enough to eat is paradoxical, for it means putting a mortgage on the future as well."

enough to last 3 months. Unfortunately, no data are available for rice production 15 years ago, but many villagers described a severe reduction in rice production over the last few decades. Babi Ram's father, for example, was one of the first to cultivate rice in Ward 1, and now much of his land is either cultivated with maize and millet or left fallow.

Cardamom cultivation was increasing but fluctuations in productivity combined with dying first-generation transplants in the years leading up to 2004 meant that the total amount of cardamom produced in the village may have declined. There is no precise data on cardamom production during this period but Raj, the largest buyer of cardamom throughout this period, points out that there was a drop in the productivity of cardamom while the market price continued to rise.

This ties closely with the difficulty faced by villagers to repay the debts they were incurring with Raj and others in the village. Increased consumption of market goods as the previously remote village became more integrated with the market, and the increased cost of basic foods like rice which had to be brought in, led in turn to increased debts. Figure 39 shows these relationships as a flow chart.

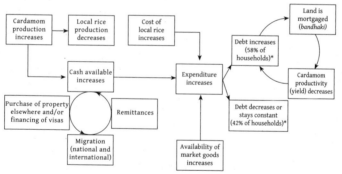

* Based on data from surplus and deficit production, although the figures for debts increasing and decreasing are only approximate.

Figure 39: Model representing the relationships between rice and cardamom production, increased expenditure, and indebtedness

Another significant change in the village was the decline of seasonal migration to Sikkim, and the increase of international longer-term migration to the Gulf states and Malaysia. While this subject is covered in more detail in Chapter 5, it is relevant here because Raj lent money to some of the first villagers to travel abroad (beyond India) in 1998. According to Raj, the main bulk of international migration, excluding travel to India, began in 1999. In 1998, Raj started lending money to villagers for their work visa fees. Generally, he would support two villagers each year, with an interest rate of 2 or 2.5 per 100 NPR per month, exactly the same as today. For each of these, as with any other sizeable loan of usually above 10,000 NPR, a *tamasuk* is written up and the papers are signed with at least two or usually three witnesses present. Copies are kept by both parties. The total amount lent, the interest rate per month, the period of the loan, and specifications of the land to be taken as collateral if the loan cannot be repaid are all spelled out in the document. Before agreeing on the specific plot of land, Raj visits the land suggested by the *asāmi* (debtor) to determine the productivity of the cardamom, they agree on a certain plot, and the specific plot number is noted as it is recorded in documents at the land ownership offices in Taplejung bazaar.

Since 1999, of all the loans that Raj has made, only one family has had so much difficulty in repaying the loan that Raj has resorted to taking the plot of land indicated in their *tamasuk*. This is not to say that most villagers have been economically successful. The fortunes of migrants from the village have always been extremely mixed.[145] In the case of the family mentioned above, much of the money earned abroad by Sukhlal (the fourth son) was spent within the household on education, buying roofing sheets, and Sukhlal's marriage celebrations. The initial loan was 80,000 NPR for a visa to work in Malaysia for three years. The total left unpaid after returning from Malaysia was 114,000 NPR, equivalent to the initial visa fee plus an accumulated interest of 34,000 NPR. Raj took a plot of cardamom forest which produced between 3 and 200 kg of cardamom per year, roughly 30,000 NPR worth of produce. In 2006, a close family member, Phul, paid back the total debt owed by Sukhlal to Raj, equivalent to the original *bandhaki*, and took possession of the cardamom plot for himself. Phul and Sukhlal's father share a close ancestor, Sattra Hang, and are therefore both of the same sub-clan, the Mangar Mabo. Although Phul earns money from the cardamom

---

145　One of the first migrants to travel to a Gulf state (in this case, Saudi Arabia), had managed to pay his way there with money he had earned in Sikkim and borrowed from relatives. He returned after two years having spent all his money gambling on his way home.

and Sukhlal's family still gets nothing, the principal that keeping ancestral land within the family rather than splitting it between non-related families has been maintained.

This is an interesting example of intra-clan support, though still within a model of only partial cooperation. With the help of Phul, the land stays within the extended family or sub-clan, but the total debt continues and eventually Sukhlal will have to pay Phul the same amount he would have had to give to Raj. Families do support each other but they do not give money or valuable land away for nothing.

Since 2003, Raj still owns land taken under a *bandhaki* agreement from six families. Two of these six families were mentioned above, Sukhlal and Kumar, and the other four have slightly smaller debts. Raj managed to sell 720 kg of cardamom in 2006, and 280 kg in 2007 from the cardamom land of these six families. Thus, over the last five years, he made a profit of over 150,000 NPR simply from the interest on debts incurred by six families.

The loans extended to villagers by Raj go beyond these six *bandhaki*. Raj mentioned that aside from *bandhaki* arrangements, he had lent more than 100,000 NPR to at least a further five households each. One villager, Sing Bahadur, has 100,000 NPR debt, which means that every year the interest on the debt alone is 30,000 NPR (at 2.5 per 100 NPR per month). Last year (2007), he produced 680 kg of cardamom, which paid off all the debt his household had incurred during the year from buying goods through Raj, plus the yearly interest on the original debt. The year before this, his household only produced 280 kg, which paid for the interest but only partly covered that year's debt. This example gives a good sense of the volatile relationship between cardamom production and debt. While a good harvest will help families pay back debts and cover the cost of food for the coming year, a bad harvest can force families into a difficult cycle of debt (see Figure 39) from which, particularly because of the high interest rates, it becomes increasingly hard to extricate themselves.

It is not only the very large debts, of over 100,000 NPR, that squeeze households economically. A substantial number of households owe smaller amounts of money to Raj, and the high interest rates mean that delaying payments becomes expensive. Raj said that between 25 and 30 households owed him over 10,000 NPR from expenses in the shop and smaller loans, and roughly 50 to 60 individuals had debts of over 1,000 NPR. Raj mentioned that anything over 1,000 NPR would eventually, after a few months of not being repaid, become loans with interest. In other words, if a household has been buying goods from his shop and their bill tops 1,000 NPR, they will automatically be charged interest on this after a somewhat arbitrary period of "a few months". This is equivalent to 100 per 1,000 NPR every four months, or one day's wage.

While this account shows how an indebted villager can find it hard to get out of debt, the other side of the story relates to how Raj finds it hard to collect long-standing debts from villagers. Although he is able to collect the equivalent of the interest on debts from cardamom production, sometimes collecting more if production increases and sometimes less, he admits that it would be extremely hard to collect the original amount, or principal, owed from all villagers. This would amount to a personal fortune of an estimated 1,000,000 NPR. This tension between the money-lending figure of Raj and his debtors is undoubtedly one of the main sources of the largely suppressed antagonism that exists between Raj (and his family) and other villagers. Having said this, a number of points need further elaboration including: the nature of this suppression; and the underlying reasons for this antagonism.

It was clear from living in the village that any signs of explicit antagonism, that is, highly public displays of (negative) emotion, are frowned upon by villagers.[146] There is plenty of gossiping and bickering in private, and a number of couples in the village have a reputation for frequent (very loud and public) arguing, but people rarely get into heated (potentially volatile) arguments with each other, and when they do it is clear from those watching the argument that it is considered inappropriate behaviour. It was not uncommon that a villager would

---

146 Desjarlais (1992) writes about how among the Yolmo "villagers usually strive to achieve a smooth personal façade when interacting with others" (1992: 76) and that "anger, in particular, is rarely expressed openly in Yolmo society, for it can greatly disrupt the smooth flow of social life" (1992: 115). Hardman (2000) focuses specifically on emotions among the Lohorung Rai and shows how there are particular norms about the expression of emotions such as anger: "anger is not considered to be something that must always be suppressed, nor something to be expressed in whatever way one feels like...anger has its place and its rules" (2000: 242). McHugh (1989, 2001) has written about emotions and personhood among the Gurung, describing how "the Gurung assumption that human relationships are fragile underlies a style of interpersonal interaction in which one is constantly assured and reassured of the responsiveness of others through greetings, gifts, and offers of food" (1989: 78).

confess to me how much they disliked another villager, explaining that they were mean, untrustworthy, and borrowed things without returning them, only to be sitting next to them joking and laughing a few hours later. Since this sort of contradiction occurred frequently, what I initially perceived as inconsistency of opinion, or even hypocrisy, can probably best be described as a social ability (or even prescription) to put aside one's negative opinion in the effort of maintaining functioning social relations.

In relation to Raj, a number of villagers expressed, in private conversations with me, strong feelings of antipathy towards him. Comments were made about his wealth and the numerous *bandhaki* he possessed, the general feeling being that he had acquired his wealth by cheating local villagers (the Limbu) of theirs. Yet no villager was ever able to provide me with specific examples of foul play when asked to do so, and research into many of the larger debts accumulated by villagers towards Raj, as well as his current *bandhaki* arrangements, also revealed nothing to justify the accusations. This privately expressed antipathy has much deeper historical and cultural roots than simply being a reflection of the economically skewed relationship between Raj and other villagers. It links directly to the complex subject of inter-ethnic relations in Nepal and the historically unequal opportunities afforded to the politically and economically dominant high caste Hindus throughout Nepal (particularly Brahmin and Chhetri) which has resulted in widespread resentment and hostility towards these groups by ethnic minorities (Cox 1990).

Raj's view of the villagers, particularly the Limbu, is that they spend too much money on celebrations (funerals and weddings), on alcohol, and on goods in his shop or elsewhere, as well as lacking any sense of long term planning or money saving. His relationship with other villagers tends to be mediated by matters of business (and occasionally politics), and he rarely meets other villagers for purely social reasons.

Raj mentioned that he thought he would be able to collect some of the larger debts from families with larger cardamom production in the next few years, as long as he tightened credit available to them from the shop. This would apply to perhaps three or four of the oldest *bandhaki* he possesses. The rest, he said, would probably never pay their debts back. Despite problems collecting debts, he has managed to buy, as *bandhaki*, some property in Ilam bazaar worth 240,000 NPR some years ago which he uses as a stopover on his business journeys to Jhapa. His long-term plan is to move to Ilam with his family and open a shop there.

This account of the characteristics of Raj's credit and money-lending activities in the village economy shows not only the extent to which villagers rely on credit, but the difficulties they face emerging from the vicious cycle of debt because of both high interest rates and the fluctuation of cardamom production. With almost 100 individuals indebted to Raj in varying degrees, it is not hard to imagine how certain families, following a similar economic strategy to that carried out by Raj—money-lending combined with land accumulation and market trade—were able to arrive in the village over 200 years ago, amass a fortune and migrate to other regions of Nepal. The main difference between them and the villagers today is the production of cardamom and international labour migration. These two factors have enabled a larger proportion of villagers to become more prosperous. They have also increased the amount of debt households are willing and able to sustain, and increased the risk of landlessness and impoverishment should families be unable to settle their debts. Ultimately though, households with little land, and little or no cardamom production, continue to find it extremely difficult to make ends meet.

Dhan Kumar[147]

The following case study serves as an example of the difficulties faced by families with access to few resources. Despite belonging to the same lineage as the subba who exercised authority over what is today Ward 4,[148] this particular family inherited only a negligible portion of what was formerly an extremely large amount of land.[149] This in turn

---

147 The data for this case study was mostly collected on two extended interviews with Dhane on 28/05/08 and 01/06/08.

148 Dhane's father was Ser Bahadur, whose father was Bhirka Bahadur—Bhagi Dhoj's eldest son. Bhirka B., Bhagi D. and Bhagi D.'s father Makkhar Doj were all *subba* representing the Mangar-Mabo sub-clan. Ser Bahadur's eldest brother Rim Lal was the Mangar-Mabo *subba* when the Land Reform Act of 1964 formally abolished the subba system.

149 A large amount of land which was administered by the *subba* Rim Lal, was sold in 1984 (just before the cadastral survey) to a Chhetri villager from

highlights the Limbu perspective on history: that the *calākh* villagers were those who bought land prior to the cadastral survey of 1986 and were then able to profit from cardamom production.

Dhan Kumar (Dhane) was born in 1981 in a house at the top of Ward 4. The extremely steep and rocky land surrounding both his own house and the ancestral house above it is the source of his family's nickname "Pakha".[150] When both his father and elder brother died, he was forced, as the oldest remaining male in the household, to stop attending school (having passed Class 8),[151] get married, and start earning money. He married a Lungdoyu Mabo woman from Pauwa (Ward 7) in 1999 and they have two young children. The maize and millet his household produces lasts roughly 5 to 6 months and after this they depend entirely on purchased rice.[152] He earns most of the money the family needs by carrying rice and goods from Tharpu for other villagers. He usually makes the trip to Tharpu four to five times every month of the year. With the fixed rate of 10 NPR per kg he is able to earn about 400 NPR for two days of work,[153] considerably more than the village wage of 100 NPR per day, but also significantly more exhausting. His household consumes about 45 kg of rice every month which costs about 1,200 NPR. Table 20

Khewang for 3000 NPR and a few sacks of millet—far less than its true value (according to one informant he had actually paid 5,000 NPR, about 50,000 of today's money after having a "mind-crack"—he used the English word). A legal case was started by Rim Lal's brothers who disapproved of this sale and considered it illegitimate because they had had no say in the deal. They fought the case in the district courts for three years and won the land back in 1987. This land was divided into seven sections and Dhan's father received one such portion, albeit one of the smallest ones. Dhane therefore inherited one-third of this portion, which is the land he now grows cardamom. Rim Lal's family never received any of this land.

150 Steep hillsides are described as *pākhā* in Nepali. The adjective *pākhā-pākhero* for example means "Precipitous hillside on which nothing can be grown" (Turner 1931: 372).

151 At that time, the main school in the village only had 8 classes. To continue studying villagers had to travel to schools in other villages, an expense many families are still often unable to bear.

152 Dhane's household has a deficit per capita of 540 NPR. The total value of everything produced by the household was 10,800 NPR, well below the village average of 27,850 NPR.

153 He usually carries a 50 kg sack of rice and up to 5 kg of additional purchases, but spends between 100 and 150 NPR on food during the journey which significantly reduces his earnings.

outlines the estimated total expenditure per month for Dhane's household:

Item	Cost per month (NPR)
Rice	1,200
Salt	100
Cooking oil	150
Spices	30
Meat	250
Total	**1,730**

Table 20: Dhane's estimated monthly expenditure

In addition to these expenses, Dhane estimated that he required a total yearly expenditure of at least 2,000 NPR for clothes and 500 NPR for his son's school equipment. Thus, with a total estimated monthly cost of around 2,000 NPR it would take at least five portering trips to earn this amount of money, excluding a further two trips to bring rice for his household and for his mother. This means at least 14 days per month spent portering goods to the village, not including the necessary day of rest after returning from a portering trip. Dhane supplements his income from portering with an average of five days' (per month) work as a *khetālā*. Although the demand for portering varies throughout the year, it reaches a peak during the cardamom harvest season when large producers hire villagers to carry their cardamom to market for sale. During the last cardamom harvest, Dhane carried cardamom approximately 13 times, earning a total of 6,000 NPR. This money all went towards reducing the debt of 55,000 NPR he has with a local Limbu villager, much of which was inherited from his parents' household. When he split from his parents' household after marriage, he took with him two-thirds of the total family debt.[154] This original family debt is due in part to money Dhane's father borrowed to buy more agricultural land, and in part to unpaid bills at the village shop. He had earned almost 18,000 NPR two years ago by transporting CGI roofing (600 NPR per trip), which reduced his total debt to 25,000 NPR as of May 2008.

In the past, Dhane's household produced only about 40 kg of cardamom per year. On a good year, with prices between 200 and 250

---

154 The total debt had been divided between the three sons, but because one of them died and the other son was only 5 years old at the time Dhane married, he inherited the largest portion of debt.

NPR per kg, even such a small quantity would usually be enough to pay for a whole year's rice consumption. Unfortunately much of the household's crop died a few years ago. Having replanted as much as he could on the small amount of suitable land he has available to him, he hopes to start producing about 40 kg, or perhaps a little more, by 2009.

Dhane mentioned that if he didn't have such a burden of debt (the original loan as well as yearly interest on the principal), he would be able to start saving money with the prospect of providing more food and clothes for his family, supporting his children through school and ultimately financing a work visa to travel abroad. He explained how the impact of cardamom has been positive for those who have land to plant it on and for those who benefit from the demand for porters during harvest season. The downside, he continued, is that rice paddy has been replaced with cardamom in many parts of the village, which has both reduced the demand for *khetālā* labour and increased the cost of rice. He described how rice was 12 NPR per kg in Tharpu ten years ago and was now 28 NPR per kg or 29-30 NPR if bought on credit, which many villagers do. He observed that although wages have also gone up in the last decade, they have not kept up with the cost of goods. This assertion can be examined in a little more detail by comparing, over the same time period, the changes in local wage rates and the cost of rice.

According to a number of villagers, wages for most *khetālā* work for men (certain tasks such as sawing or chopping wood and stone laying are paid more) went up in 2004 to the current rate of 100 NPR (half this amount for women and children). The village rate had been 50 NPR in the period 1992 to 2004, and 30 NPR in the years before 1992. It was unclear when the village as a whole had first agreed to have consistent daily wages in all wards of the village. Dhane was referring to 1998 when the cost of rice was 12 NPR per kg. It has since increased by over 130% to around 28 NPR (May 2008). In 1998, daily wages were only 50 NPR, and although they doubled to 100 NPR in 2004, this rise does not match the rise in the cost of rice. With today's daily wages villagers can buy 3.6 kg of rice whereas they could buy 4.2 kg ten years ago.

This increase in the cost of goods in the village, paired with a decrease in the demand for labour (as mentioned above by Dhane), and an increase in the consumption of market goods (as mentioned by Raj above), has pushed many families into debts which burden them for years if not generations (see Figure 39 above). Cardamom cultivation provides certain families not only with an important income—with which they can, for example, cover the cost of rice consumption for a year—but also gives them the possibility of borrowing money through *bandhaki* arrangements with families who have access to cash. By increasing the value of forested land, cardamom cultivation has given the possibility to families with sizeable cardamom plots to access loans for travel abroad or for investing in land outside the village.

This case study has provided a brief insight into the economic struggle faced by a single household with little access to resources and a large inherited debt. While there are very few landless households in the village, there are a considerable number of households like Dhane's with no cardamom, little access to capital (for example by mortgaging land), and few means of providing an income other than portering, pit-sawing work, and the occasional periods of locally available work on road or bridge construction.[155] A large proportion of these households are situated in wards 1, 2, and 7, which have the lowest average surplus production figures[156] and—with the exception of land owned by one Gurung and two Chhetri households in Ward 1—the lowest average land ownership figures.

A closer look at the composition of households and historical reasons for the economic difficulties they face reveals an extremely varied picture. It also brings out some of the limitations of relying solely on economic indicators like "surplus production" or "land ownership" to describe economic variation. One household (#725) is made up of an unmarried 16-year old Limbu girl and her younger brother. Their father died two years ago and their mother now lives with another man in the village but provides little economic support to her children. They produce a small amount of food on 1 *hal*, maintain a small number of livestock, regularly work as *khetālā* and receive some support from neighbouring households. Another household (#736) is inhabited by an unmarried 32-year old Limbu woman who takes care of her younger brother's (*māila*) son. Her two sisters have married and live in other villagers, and two of her four brothers are abroad, while the other two

---

155 During the survey, 11 respondents mentioned that they had worked on bridge and road construction in the last year.

156 Data for average surplus production (NPR) by Ward: (1) -566; (2) -1295; (3) 7680; (4) 18991; (5) 9936; (6) 10903; (7) -3331.

live in the village. She receives some financial help from her *māila* brother, which helps to pay for rice and other market goods (she has no cardamom). The 1 *hal* of land she owns produces enough food (millet and corn) to last 2-3 months of the year. A final example is household #201, inhabited by a young married Limbu couple with three children. They have 1 *hal* of unproductive land, and an *adhiyã* arrangement on some additional agricultural land that belongs to a Gurung. It is the *adhiyã* land that enables them to produce the small amount of food they grow. They have lost access to their cardamom through debts incurred by the father (hence their production deficit of -9360 NPR). The husband worked in Sikkim for three years as a teenager, but today earns most of his money portering and working on the road construction project in Tellok VDC.

These three households are extremely poor by village standards, but have access to land, financial or at least social support from neighbours, and the ability to work for others should the need arise, either as *khetālā* or *parma*, or as wage labourers outside the village.

These examples show how even households considered to be among the poorest in the village are able to subsist on a small plot of land—occasionally undertaking paidwork, and receiving the support of relatives—despite having a deficit of production. Yet the qualitative difference between these households and those with access to more regular and substantial sources of income—whether through labour migration and remittances, or from cardamom cultivation—is considerable. While many poorer households, particularly those with no cardamom, are able to subsist, whether by incurring increasing debts or living a fairly hand to mouth existence, there are growing opportunities for wealthier households to transform their socioeconomic circumstances through increased education, labour migration, and by acquiring land and property.

Chandraman Bahadur

The final case study in this chapter focuses on a relatively wealthy Limbu villager, Chandraman Bahadur (Chandra), who inherited a considerable amount of agricultural land and cardamom forest from his father, Tej Bahadur.[157] Much of this land, and that of his two brothers,

---

157   Chandra's household had a surplus income per capita of 8,773 NPR in 2007,

was obtained by his father in the years before and immediately after the *nāpi*. Somewhat unusually, Tej made his fortune while never leaving the village. He never worked in Sikkim or travelled further afield, never held a government job of any kind or any prestigious position in the village—although his father was the Mangar-Mabo *subba*, as the sixth son in a large family Tej inherited only a small plot of land when he married. This case study serves to underline the important role that land ownership plays in the economic history and fortunes of households. It also emphasizes that the association the Limbu make between economic success and cleverness or cunning does not only extend towards Chhetri and other non-Limbu settlers, but also includes Limbu villagers. This inclusion encourages the persistence of a certain kind of mythology in the village which has a strong impact on the aspirations many villagers have for their own futures. This mythology includes the idea that economic success leads necessarily to geographical and social mobility. As many villagers pointed out: just as many Chhetri settlers departed from the village after a few generations, so too the Limbu have begun to follow this pattern.

Chandra was born in the village in 1966. He married a woman from Pedang in 1985 and lived with her in his family house, located below the main path in Ward 4, until 1993. The land they currently live on, just above the main path in Ward 4, was originally made up of two plots owned by two different families. A smaller part of it, estimated as 1 *hal* of land, was bought by Chandra's father in 1986 for 10,000 NPR. It was sold by Dhane's father Ser Bahadur who used this money to buy the larger, but steeper, plot of land above this one from a Chhetri who in turn migrated to Jhapa. The larger plot of land, on which both the main house and the shop and lodge were built, was bought for 100,000 NPR in 1994 from a Limbu villager, with money lent to Chandra (with no interest) by his father. Chandra had separated from his parents' household the year before and spent a year living in a small house on the smaller plot. Chandra and his wife built what later became a shop and lodge in 1995 with their own money (earned from their share of the family's cardamom production) and the larger house which they live in today was built in 1997 for another 100,000 NPR with his father's money.

---

well above the village average of 1,725 NPR. The value of all household production in 2007 was 87,200 NPR.

Besides the land which Chandra's household lives on and cultivates,[158] Tej bought additional land in several parts of the village. When asked how his father became wealthy despite never working outside the village, Chandra replied that it was by saving money: he didn't waste his money on clothes and he was extremely stingy (*kanjus*). When Tej married and split from his parents' household in 1963, he inherited about half a *hal* of land for maize and millet on which he was able to produce only 7 *jhutta* of maize and a few kg of millet. He focused his productive activities initially on increasing the number of pigs and buffalo and eventually on maintaining a large herd of goats. During an interview about his father's life history,[159] Chandra began to draw a diagram on the ground with his finger (see Figure 40 below). He described how there were different economic activities which his father was involved with and that he had been able to make and save money from each of them.

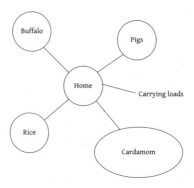

Figure 40: Diagram drawn by Chandra during an interview to depict the relationship between various economic activities carried out by his father Tej

It is interesting to note that the circles for all the activities were the same size, except for cardamom where he had drawn a particularly large circle to emphasize the relative importance this had on the whole

---

158   According to survey data they own 4 *hal* of terraces near the house, which produces 13 *man* of millet and 1300 *jhutta* of maize, and rice terraces which produce a total of 3 *man* of unthreshed rice.

159   This interview took place on 4/6/2008.

household economy. Carrying loads was a minor activity which had been more important when Tej was younger. Perhaps for this reason he had not bothered to circle it. Rice was considered an economic activity because, for a period, the family had produced a surplus of rice which they had sold locally. Maize and millet were only used for subsistence, which explains their absence in the diagram.

In 1965 Tej bought his first plot of land. This was rice paddy in lower Ward 5 sold to him by a Limbu villager. In 1977 he planted cardamom (and alder trees for shade) on a large proportion of this land, and first harvested cardamom in 1980. His next purchase of land was in 1978. This was 3 *hal* of land close to the ancestral home in Ward 4, sold to him by a Damai family who moved closer to the school in Ward 5. The third purchase of land was the 1 *hal* bought for Chandra mentioned above. The following year Tej obtained a portion of the land which Rim Lal had illegitimately sold to a Chhetri from Khewang (see footnote 148). Finally, he bought about 3 *hal* of land in Ward 5 for his youngest son in 1994. All the cardamom plots owned by Tej[160] produced 1,000 kg of cardamom in 2006 and were predicted to produce 720 kg in 2007. With market prices hovering around 10,000 NPR per 40 kg, this would have meant total earnings of around 250,000 NPR in 2006 and 180,000 NPR in 2007. Much of this money is used to pay back a number of debts incurred by Tej for buying land and building houses for his sons.

Chandra still has an outstanding debt of just over 100,000 NPR with an interest rate of 12% per year, considerably lower than the more usual 24 to 30% per year. He plans to pay back all this debt in 2009 and from then on continue to save money to buy land somewhere close to the district capital of Fungling. Although most villagers who leave the village tend to move south where land is actually cheaper than in Fungling, his family prefers the cooler weather in Taplejung and doesn't want to move far from the village. Chandra mentioned that he would open up a small hotel and restaurant with his wife, send his children to private school, and continue to farm on land around the house. They would not sell their land and property in the village, partly because it is unlikely anyone would buy it, and would continue to cultivate cardamom.

---

160 Ownership of the family's cardamom plots were split between the three brothers in 2008.

This case study shows the important economic role cardamom production played and continues to play within a household economy. While other economic activities predominated in the past—army employment, working in Sikkim, raising animals in the village, etc.—the rise of cardamom cultivation since the mid-1970s had a profound impact on the ability households had to raise capital. During the period leading up to—and directly after—the *nāpi*, households with capital usually raised from working in Sikkim or in foreign armies, were able to purchase land from villagers who in turn migrated from the village usually to more urban areas in the plains. Somewhat atypically, Tej was able to raise money and purchase land without ever leaving the village, enabling him to benefit from the introduction of cardamom production during the late 1970s onwards.

Conclusion

The study of change—be it ecological, economic, social or political—is an inseparable part of any anthropological research project. The activities and behaviour of individuals, communities, and institutions, are constantly modified, adjusted, and negotiated through interaction with factors both internal and external to the community or social group. When studying change, an anthropologist necessarily becomes a historian, documenting the gradual or sudden shifts that occurred within human societies. Yet "change" is not an isolated category:

> The student of change...can no more study 'social' change in general than he can study 'society' in general. His data are specific social and cultural institutions, and he has to study the modification of these through time, in the context of other co-existing social, cultural and sometimes, ecological factors (Beattie 1964: 241).

One of the challenges in attempting such a study is the length of time an anthropologist is able to remain continuously in the field. In his 1959 re-study of the Tikopia, Firth (1959: 22) noted that:

> Such a comparison as I have made in Tikopia is strictly speaking, no more than an estimate of similarities and differences at two separate periods of time. It is a *dual-synchronic*, not a strictly *diachronic* study. To interpret it in terms of social change, as trends and not simple differences, would involve assumptions about regularities in the

interim period—or at least assumptions that any kinks in the movement could be disregarded as insignificant.

His study of economic and social change is derived from a comparison between social, economic and political life in 1929 and 1952. Some aspects of society had not changed: respect for the institution of chieftainship had continued; as had patterns of marriage which favoured localized choice. Economic changes had been considerable, not only in terms of the increased circulation of market goods such as mirrors, razors, beads, and perfumed soap, but also in changes in production processes: the simple intensification of agriculture and fishing was not enough to meet the demands of a rising population (Firth 1959: 112). Craft work had decreased and labour migration had increased, with roughly 40% of all working males absent from the island during the middle of 1952. Incomes and the total amount of money available in Tikopia may have increased but so too had the material demands of Tikopia inhabitants. This combination led to many Tikopia "still further away than before from the possibilities of attaining their desired standard of living" (ibid: 125).

Mair points out that in seeking to explain the direction of change—and this is particularly the case in relation to the impact of the global market and the monetization (and bureaucratization) of economic life in agricultural communities—"most of us make assumptions derived from 'naïve introspection': that most men aspire to some level of material wealth and comfort, that all care for the esteem of their fellows, that many compete for power or prestige" (Mair 1969: 5). Certainly at first glance Mair's notion about the aspirations of "men" seems to hold true. Yet changes do not take place simply because of individual aspirations, or through a larger-scale assembling of these individual level aspirations. Social changes can be imposed from outside, they can be the result of conflict, or the result of ecological limitations (population size). In fact, it would be an enormous task to list all the possible causes and types of change which can take place in society. While some have tried to categorize different kinds of social change, [161] it seems more

---

161 Firth (1959: 246-247) proposes three types of social change: the first provided for in the social structure; the second, more radical, as a change in the character of the social system itself; and the third, an "organizational change", related to "changes in ways of doing things, which themselves continue to be done, and in the extent and range of particular complexes

helpful to accept Beattie's comment that a study of social change would be no different to a study of society in general; that the two are inseparable. This should not be interpreted to mean that since a study of society as a whole is an impossible task, no study of change should take place at all. Rather, any study of change must be contextualized within a study of particular elements of society.

In the case of this book, the principal element within society chosen for the study of change has been the *change in distribution of resources*. This distribution has changed largely in response to *changes in the productive processes* within the village. The subsistence-based productive system which is so widespread in the village today, emerged as semi-nomadic Limbu communities transitioned from relying on hunting and gathering with swidden agriculture, to become sedentary agriculturalists. The extent to which this new productive system overlapped or was influenced by the arrival of Hindu migrants from the west is uncertain. What is certain is that their arrival, and the increased population pressure which followed, encouraged and hastened the adoption of technologies appropriate for intensifying land use, the best example being the development of wet rice cultivation. This intensification of land use led to land becoming a limited and contested resource. The change in distribution of land as a resource was the result of the accumulation of land by non-Limbu migrants, particularly Chhetri, to the detriment of Limbu inhabitants. The life history of Raj served to highlight a more contemporary version of this story of land and resource accumulation through dispossession.

It is hard to speculate about the changes in distribution of resources after the arrival of non-Limbu migrants because of a lack of clear data related to land and resource distribution prior to their arrival. Clearly, land was used less intensively and population densities were far smaller than they were to become with sedentary agriculture, as noted by Allen (1997: 306) among the Thulung Rai. This would likely have meant that use of resources was largely balanced throughout the population and allocated according to household needs. Land became a limited resource, and therefore unequally distributed, largely as a result of the expanded population resulting from the arrival of migrants as well as the decline in mortality figures.

---

of social relationships, which remain formally unaltered".

Increased pressure on land from population growth—as well as the increasing fragmentation of agricultural land, decreased availability or vicinity of forest and fodder, and other ecological changes which resulted from this growth—was only one among many of the changes which were taking place. Reduced availability of land (and therefore reduced food production) combined with the increased demand for market goods led to villagers increasingly migrating in search of labour opportunities elsewhere. Infrastructural developments led to increased mobility across larger distances. The money economy began to dominate economic exchanges and the introduction of cardamom as a cash crop led to the village becoming directly connected to the international market. All these events played a role in the development of new patterns of resource distribution.[162]

The transition from subsistence food production to a productive process that included cardamom cultivation led to another important change in the distribution of resources, as well as a redefinition or revaluation of land. The high prices that cardamom commanded in the market led to cardamom-producing land becoming an extremely valuable resource. The arrival of non-Limbu settlers had led to the revaluation of marginal forest land which Bahun-Chhetri migrants had converted into productive land. The arrival of cardamom led to an increase in the value of all forested and cardamom-productive land. As was described above, the "cleverest" villagers were those who claimed or bought as much land as they could in the period leading up to the *nāpi* in 1986. They were then able to profit from the expansion of cardamom production during the 1990s.

For the productive processes mentioned so far—both subsistence food production and modern-day cardamom cash crop production—land has always been the central resource. Migration was the first productive process not to be directly tied to the land. Yet despite migrants working seasonally in Sikkim or for longer periods of time further afield, they still rely indirectly on land in two ways. First, for many migrants, and particularly for international labour migrants, land can be mortgaged or pledged to gain access to credit or loans. Second, many migrants invest their remittances and savings in land, a

---

162 These patterns of change were widespread throughout Nepal and similar processes are documented by Hitchcock (1966), Caplan (1970), Fisher (1990).

pattern which continues to this day—although in the past, land would be purchased within the village, while today it is typically purchased elsewhere.

The history of the changes in productive process is a history of the gradual integration of new productive processes into the economic system of the village. Subsistence agricultural production incorporated cash crop cardamom production. The successful addition of international labour migration as the third productive process was partly a result of the success of cardamom production. Cardamom production led to an increase of cash within the village economy and an increase in the value of cardamom productive land (which could now be easily mortgaged by households considering sending a member to work abroad). Each of these productive processes has played a part in changing the distribution of resources (particularly land and capital) between households across the village.

In the past, before the introduction of cardamom as a cash crop, economic differentiation ran primarily along ethnic lines. Differences existed also among the Limbu, resulting from army-related labour or political power for example, but these differences were not as marked as those between the Limbu and Chhetri who had settled since the 1800s. The shift from solely subsistence production to subsistence with cash crop production allowed a certain proportion of the Limbu population to become wealthier. This in turn meant that ethnic or caste-based economic differentiation became superseded by a class-based differentiation which resulted largely from the unequal access to cardamom-productive land. Economic differentiation in the past—a result of the predominance of subsistence production and later cardamom production—was correlated with land ownership in the village much more directly than it is today. Since the growth of international labour migration over the last decade, economic differentiation has become more linked with differences of mobility— the ability to migrate and kinds of migration which can be undertaken— and access to resources elsewhere (in Jhapa for example) than perhaps it has in the past.

A certain proportion of the households in the village have been able to benefit from all three of the major productive processes: subsistence food production, cash crop cardamom production and international labour migration. This has given them a significant economic advantage over households that are only involved in subsistence food production, or international migration and subsistence food production. The gap between the poorest households in the village, those with significant deficits of food production and little or no land, and the wealthiest, those who own property elsewhere and pay for an English-language education for their children, is much more significant today than it was when economic differentiation was based solely within subsistence food production.

Incomes and the total amount of money available within the village may have increased for a substantial proportion of households, but their material demands have also increased: the ready availability (and increased cost) of market goods, the increased dependence on commercial rice (due to a reduction in local production and availability), and the changes in social aspirations of the younger generation (due to the experience of working abroad and influence of urban and global consumer cultures), have all contributed to this.[163] Firth's observation about villagers in Tikopia applies just as well to the villagers of Mamangkhe who, despite the increased wealth of some villagers, are perhaps "still further away than before from the possibilities of attaining their desired standard of living" (Firth 1959: 125).

---

163 In the words of Sahlins (1972): "it was not until culture neared the heights of its material achievements that it erected a shrine to the Unattainable: *Infinite Needs.*"

Conclusions

The principal conclusion to be drawn from this book is that the history of the village of Mamangkhe, and indeed other villages in Nepal, can be seen as a history of changing productive processes—the increased incorporation within a monetized capitalist economy—and the impact these have had on both the emergence of economic differentiation or class, and the development of socioeconomic and ecological change. The introduction of each productive process—from the intensification of agriculture following the arrival of Chhetri settlers, to the rapid development of a cash crop economy—had a different effect on the distribution of resources and wealth within the village.

The intensification of land use, including the introduction of wet rice cultivation, which followed the arrival of the earliest Chhetri migrants, had one principal effect: the unequal distribution of land and, consequently, also of wealth. By both nominally "buying" kipat land from the Limbu and clearing marginal land, many of these early Chhetri migrants came to own disproportionately large tracts of land. Access to Limbu labour, which could be paid for in kind with surplus food production, and the increasing encroachment by Chhetri villagers onto Limbu owned kipat land (often a result of unpaid debts), led to many Chhetri villagers eventually selling all their land to Limbu villagers who could afford to buy it and migrating en masse to other parts of Nepal from the 1950s onwards.[1]

The introduction of cardamom benefited not only large and small producers, but also non-producers who could sell their labour as porters or *khetālā*. However, the economic differences between households

---

1   Whelpton (2005: 83, 161-2) mentions that following an ethnic revolt by the Limbu population against Parbatiya settlers in Mechi zone in 1950-1, many Brahmin families moved temporarily to the Tarai. Most of these returned once order had been restored, but it is possible that these events played a part in encouraging Chhetris in the middle hills to sell up and move out.

which may have existed in the past (in terms of levels of subsistence production) were exacerbated by the introduction of cardamom. It is at this point that one can begin to describe an emerging process of rural class formation. Before cardamom, economic differences were both much less extreme—since less profit can be made from surplus subsistence-crop production—and tied much more directly to ethnic differences: the Chhetri controlled proportionately more land and could sell their surplus crop production or trade it in exchange for goods and labour.

The development of cardamom as a high-value cash crop had a number of effects. First, it provided both Limbu and Chhetri villagers with cardamom productive land—usually uncultivated forest land— access to cash and the market economy. Since many Limbu villagers owned forested land which could be cultivated with cardamom, the earlier economic differentiation along ethnic lines (rich Chhetri villagers and poor Limbu villagers) became increasingly economic differentiation along production lines (rich large cardamom producers and poor small or no cardamom producers). Second, cardamom production led to the revaluation of forested land. Such areas had previously offered little more than firewood and fodder but now became a lucrative source of income. This meant that cardamom-producing land could be mortgaged in exchange for loans and the repayment of debts. This resulted not only in households taking on larger loans than they would have in the past, but encouraged households with increasing access to capital to consider investing in land and property elsewhere. Third, the increased cash availability in Mamangkhe, as a result of cardamom but also of cardamom-related work in Sikkim, led directly to the development of the dispersed or extended village in Jhapa which is, in turn, tied to the development of the third productive process: international labour migration.

This more recent process shares a long history with seasonal labour migration to Sikkim and other parts of India that began in the early 1950s. Beginning in the late 1990s, villagers from Mamangkhe began to travel for work to a number of Gulf countries and Malaysia, with, perhaps, the most profound effect on the village economy and society. In economic terms, successful labour migrants have been able to repay debts, purchase property in Jhapa and support a new set of economic demands: paying for private English-medium education and supporting the costs associated with an increased dependence on market goods. In terms of social changes, international migration, paired with the profits from cardamom production, has led to the emergence of a dispersed village in Jhapa, a kind of urban or peri-urban Mamangkhe. This dispersed village has become both a hub for the social networks that villagers increasingly rely on for migration abroad and, for many villagers, a symbol of the opportunities offered by economic wealth and success.

These three productive processes have all ultimately been based on land ownership. In the case of subsistence agriculture, Chhetri settlers were able to accumulate land and produce surpluses which allowed them eventually to migrate from the village to settlements in urban Nepal. In the case of cardamom, ownership of land allowed for cardamom production but also led to the mortgaging of land to repay debts or gain access to capital through loans. In the case of migration, households often relied on loans derived from mortgaged land to finance visas to work abroad. Income saved from both cardamom and migration has resulted in increasing numbers of households purchasing land in Jhapa or elsewhere, thereby repeating the pattern of migration which had been started by Chhetri villagers fifty years earlier.

However, while many have benefited from each productive process, there remain villagers who struggle to make ends meet. Some of these are heavily indebted and have lost access to much of their productive land. Others, with little or no land of their own, have survived for several generations by working as *khetālā* for other households. Not all the non-Limbu migrants who arrived in Mamangkhe over one hundred years ago were able to become wealthy enough to emigrate. Even among the Limbu, there exist those who own considerable portions of land and produce large surpluses of food, as well as those who have large deficits of food production and have to rely heavily on seasonal work and access to credit with shopkeepers.

The second conclusion in this book concerns the integration of the village and its inhabitants with national and global processes. One of the key guiding theoretical positions in this book has been that of anthropological political economy and its "attempt to place anthropological subjects at the intersection of local and global histories" (Roseberry 1988: 179). This book has attempted to present both sides of an historical picture to show how individuals and groups, although shaped to some extent by economic and political systems beyond their control, also play an active role in creating and engaging with these systems. Historically, Chhetri migrants were encouraged by the Gorkha state to settle in the east as a means of extending political and cultural control over unconsolidated territory. Their arrival in the village and the introduction of new agricultural technologies and practises can be portrayed as a purely externally imposed historical event. Yet stories abound within the village of how the first Chhetri villager was invited to the village in an attempt to "develop" it. Cardamom, which has had such a profound impact on the local economy and has directly linked the village to an international cardamom market, was introduced by a villager in the late 1960s at a time when the closest market for the crop was six days' walk away. In other words, while Mamangkhe is still a geographically remote village in north-east Nepal that may have become increasingly integrated into the national and international socioeconomic system, this has not taken place without the active involvement of the local population.

The repercussions of this involvement have been numerous. The increased availability of market goods, the experiences that international migrants have of other cultures, and the increased familiarity that villagers have of an urban-based consumer lifestyle, have led to a shift in cultural and social values towards emphasizing income and wealth, consumption, education, and accumulation. The emergence of Jhapa as the launch-pad for life as an international labour migrant provides a concrete model for change which villagers increasingly include in their own "projects of transformation".

A number of subsidiary conclusions emerge from the book. The first is that the erosion of kipat land, through privatization and land appropriation, began far earlier than previously described (Caplan 1970, Forbes 1996, 1999). Research showed that the first Chhetri to arrive in Mamangkhe visited the area as early as 1789, acquiring nominal ownership of a plot of land above the main settlement area in 1825. Another Chhetri family arrived around 1895, taking possession of a huge area of land below the main settlement area in Ward 4. The gradual enrichment of Chhetri households at the expense of Limbu villagers resulted in large part from this early commoditization of kipat land.

Another—and somewhat more significant—point which emerges from this research is that despite the significant processes of economic and social change taking place in the contemporary village, there are still strong signs of Limbu cultural resilience and even activism. On a national or at least regional scale, a considerable number of ethnic activist groups have emerged since the 1990s and continue to make headline news with their large scale *bandh* (general strikes). In the recent elections for a constituent assembly (2008), the Federal Limbuwan Autonomous State Council, together with a number of other ethnically based political groups, formed an umbrella organization and won two seats in parliament.

At a more local level, villagers continue to perform rituals and rely on shamans—of which there are over two dozen in the village—to regain and maintain their health. The Limbu language is still widely spoken by adults and a considerable number of children, and many young adults consider it a source of pride rather than shame to be fluent. The village has also independently organized to teach the Limbu language within the school system, making it one of the few schools in the area to do so. There is also a strong sense of appreciation for the village environment which became particularly clear during journeys to Jhapa or elsewhere with younger villagers. Positive factors concerning their environment which villagers frequently mention, include: the quality of the food and water; familiarity with everyone in the area; a feeling of safety; and the cooler climate (compared to the plains). There also emerged, during the course of the research, an impression that many Limbu villagers would prefer to stay in their village but feel drawn towards the plains because of their perceptions of what living in Jhapa would mean in their lives: no need to carry food supplies; easy access to good education and health services; and less dependence on subsistence food production. Villagers frequently commented that they believed things would change dramatically when the road currently under construction (and scheduled to take at least 10 more years) finally reaches the village. Its completion would encourage people to stay in the village, provide better prices for their cardamom, and reduce the cost of market goods.[2]

---

2   If the conclusions from the study on the *Impact of Road Development* (Blaikie et al. 1976) are anything to go by, the arrival of a road in Mamangkhe might not have such a rosy effect as imagined by villagers: "The introduction of roads...would not deliver the benefits of increased agricultural production, increased commercialization, and trade as forecast...The roads would have effects, but these would essentially serve to deepen dependency and underdevelopment rather than alleviate it" (Blaikie et al 2002: 1256).

It may also lead to greater impoverishment for those who live by portering.

Mamangkhe village today is marked by a continued reliance on cash crop cardamom production and an increased involvement of younger Limbu villagers in international labour migration. It is also marked, in large part as a result of these two activities, by increased economic differentiation between households in the village. While, many households have benefited from the effects of the increased integration of the village in the national and international market, a certain proportion of households are becoming burdened by debt, are losing agricultural land through mortgages, are increasingly having to purchase their food from the market as a supplement to their subsistence production, and are dependent on wage labour within the village or on extremely low-paid work abroad. While distinct classes with distinct roles in production have yet to emerge from this—in large part because all households are involved in some form of agricultural work (be it subsistence and/or cash crop production)—it seems likely that in the near future, the degree of economic and social differentiation in the village will become increasingly marked. In this respect, this book has examined rural class formation in its early stages, suggesting that the productive processes taking place today are leading to the formation of distinctly different economic and social classes, although they have yet to be fully constituted.

This book has attempted to provide an innovative ethnography of Nepal by combining the strengths of older ethnographies and Marxist-influenced sociological works, with the descriptive detail of more contemporary accounts of villages and cultural phenomena in Nepal. Early ethnographies, such as the works of Macfarlane (1976), Pignède (1966), and Sagant (1976), were based on long-term fieldwork, an in-depth familiarity with a particular culture and language, and described and analysed a wide range of economic and cultural activities. With the exception of Macfarlane's (2001) more recent and fairly brief contribution, these older ethnographies tended to pay little attention to the processes of change and transformation which affect societies. The neo-Marxist works of Seddon, Blaikie, and Cameron (1979, 1980, 2002) were important contributions to the study of rural economics, class formation, and peripheral capitalist (under-)development in Nepal. Yet although their extensive use of surveys has influenced this research project, their research could be accused of both a considerable lack of cultural specificity, and of being directed by a somewhat crude (anachronistic) use of neo-Marxist frameworks to understand Nepali society and economy. A more recent study by Liechty (2003), offered a new angle on economic and cultural change by examining consumer behaviour in Kathmandu. However, it failed to consider the importance of production and the interconnection between production and consumption. While a number of ethnographies have emerged which examine important cultural changes taking place in contemporary Nepali society, such as the work of Ahearn (2001), they usually fail to take into account the significance of economic activity in these changes. The contribution of this study has been to underpin the ethnographic and historical account of social and economic change with a detailed account of the economics that underlie these changes.

Appendix 1
Glossary

Nepali words are transcribed with diacritics following the spelling provided by Turner's *A Comparative and Etymological Dictionary of the Nepali language* (1931). A number of frequently used Nepali words such as *kipaṭ* were written without diacritics in the text as they are commonly used in the literature on Nepal. With the exception of ethnic/caste group terms and political parties, all Nepali words are italicized. Limbu words, marked "(L.)", are transcribed following the spelling provided in Chemjong's *Limbu-Nepali-English Dictionary* (2002) and Michailovsky's *Limbu-English Dictionary* (2002), although the Kabeli valley dialect occasionally diverges significantly from these two dictionaries. Many Nepali words, especially nouns, are used in Limbu as loan words.

adhiyã̃	sharecropping system under which the owner of land and labourer each receive half of the crop
alaĩchi	cardamom
alaĩchi bagān	cardamom plantation
alaĩchi phā̃dnu	clearing the undergrowth in cardamom forests
aṅkus	hook
antare	fifth-born son
arenji lɛːŋma (L)	clearing the undergrowth in cardamom forests
asāmi	debtor
baiśākh	first month of the Nepali calendar (mid-April to mid-May)
bajār	a market town or shopping area in a village
band	a strike or blockade
bandhaki	land or house mortgaged until repayment of debt
bāri	unirrigated agricultural land

bhāgne	to escape
bhatti	furnace or kiln; in the village context, cardamom drying sheds
bighā	unit of land roughly equivalent to about 5/8 of an acre
birtā	land grants given conditionally to individuals within the nobility, upper castes or religious groups
calākh	clever, artful
Chhetri (or Kṣatriya)	Parbatiya warrior caste
Chettra (or Kṣetra)	an administrative unit consiting of a number of VDCs
chiraita	a high-altitude medicinal plant (*Swertia chirata*) particularly used for the treatment of fevers; only rarely gathered by villagers in Mamangkhe today
churi	small knife used to trim and pick cardamom
Dalit	Politically correct term for "untouchable" lower castes
Damai	Parbatiya tailor caste
ḍā̃ḍā	ridge or outcropping rock
dānā	grain or fruit
dhān	unhusked rice
dhani	rich
dharni	a unit of measurement roughly equivalent to 2.4 kg
ḍhiḍo	polenta, usually made from millet or maize flour
Gaine	Parbatiya "minstrel" caste traditionally considered itinerant singers, *sarangi* (fiddle) performers and fishermen
garīb	poor
gā-vi-sa adhyakṣa	chairman of the Village Development Committee (VDC)
goṭ	cattle shed
goṭhālā	shepherds
Gurung	ethnic group in Nepal primarily found in midwestern hills
guṭhi	tax-free land grants given to a community for religious or social purposes
hal	literally, *hal* means a pair of bullocks and *dui hal bāri* refers to land that would take two days with one pair of bulls to plough
jāgir	land grants given as remuneration to government employees and functionaries, now used for any salaried employment

jāgirdārs	owners of *jāgir* land grants
Jaisi	low status Brahman said to be the offspring of a Brahman man and Brahman widow
jan āndolan	People's Movement in 1990
jantare	sixth-born son
jeṭhā	first-born son
jhutta	a unit of measurement used for maize, one jhutta is equivalent to a bundle of 8-10 maize cobs
jhãkri	a nepalese healer
jilla	district
kaḍor	a monetary unit equal to 10 million rupees, usually anglicized as 'crore'
kaĩlā	fourth-born son
Kāmī	Parbatiya blacksmith caste
kānchā	youngest son
kanjus	stingy, miserly
khājā	snack or small meal
khaṭṭhā	unit of land roughly equivalent to 338 square metres
khet	land which is watered and grows such crops as rice paddy.
khetālā	farm labourer who is hired
kholā	river
kipaṭ	communal land-ownership system common to the Limbu and other ethnic groups prior to the Land Reform Act of 1964
kipaṭiya	holders of kipat land
Kirānti (or Kirāti)	generic term for a variety of ethnic groups and their languages, including Limbu, Rai, Sunuwar, and Yakkha, identified with the Kirātas (mountaineers) of Sanskrit literature
kṛṣ vikās śākhā	agriculture development offices
lav bihāh	love marriage
Limbu	ethnic group primarily inhabiting the far eastern hills of Nepal
Limbuwān Mukti Morca	Limbuwan Liberation Front
Mabo	the most common Limbu clan name in Mamangkhe
Magar	ethnic group in Nepal primarily found in western hills
māila	second-born son

māliṅgo	a type of *Arundinaria* spp. bamboo
mālpot kāryālaya	land registry offices
man	a measure of weight equal to about 40 kg
maṭān	smaller secondary house usually used as a kitchen and eating area with the upper floor used for grain and fodder storage
mundhum (L.)	collection of Limbu myths and scriptures related to origin and chanted during rituals
muri	a measure of weight equal to about 80 kg
nala	tube or sprout
nāpi	survey of land
NPR	Nepal rupee; 100 NPR = 0.8 GBP (as of December 2009)
paisā	money
pakho	hilly or steep land
parma	unpaid reciprocated labour arrangement
parbate	commonly used term for the Nepali language and, by extension, Nepali-language speakers, i.e. high and low-caste Hindus
Parbatiyā	literally a hillman, used in the same way as *parbate* to refer to high and low-caste Hindus
pāthi	a unit of measurement roughly equivalent to 4 kg
phatca pekma (L.)	to elope
phedangma (L.)	Limbu priest or shaman
pūjā	religious rite or ceremony
QAR	Qatari Riyal; 100 QAR = 16.8 GBP (as of December 2009)
raikar	leasehold land, land held on rent
rāji-nāmā	a deed of resignation of rights or title used when the ownership of land formally changes hands
raksi	any distilled alcohol
ṛṇ	debt
rog	sickness, disease
ropani	a measure of land used in land registration documents in Nepal; roughly equal to around 508 square metres
sacīb	secretary
sadasya	member
sāhū	merchant, money-lender
sāīlā	third-born son

sāpaṭi	a loan of cash or goods
sarkārī karmachārī	government worker
Sārkī	Parbatiya cobbler caste
sārvajanik kām	community or voluntary work
sāṭāsāṭ	exchange of goods
sɛtluppa (L.)	a hasty marriage performed with little ceremony
siŋse (L.)	wild edible plants; used by a few Limbu villagers as the Limbu term for cardamom
SLC	School Leaving Certificate, equivalent to passing Class 10
subbā	Limbu village headman recognized by the State of Nepal
tamasuk	a written agreement related to debt between two parties with at least two witnesses
tānnu	to pull; used to describe the process by which migrants already abroad "pull" relatives to join them, bypassing migration agencies, reducing both the uncertainties of visa arrangements and the total cost to the migrant
thɔk yāllik (L.)	Limbu term for *parma*, unpaid reciprocated labour arrangement
thari	head of a clan or *thar*
ṭhekā	paid contract work or task-based work
thɛtlɔŋ (L.)	a loan of cash or goods
tusā	plant shoots
uttis	alder tree
UML	Communist Party of Nepal (United Marxist-Leninist)
VDC	Village Development Committee (*gāū vikās samiti* or *gā-vi-sa* in Nepali)
vikas	development
yaksa (L.)	a temporary shelter
yakthuŋ pa:n (L.)	the Limbu language
Yakthuŋba (L.)	Limbu name for themselves
yāllik (L.)	Limbu term for *khetālā*, hired farm labourer

Appendix 2
Chronology of Limbu and village history

1774   Limbuwan-Gorkha war ends with treaty recognizing Limbu rights to maintain kipat system and political autonomy

1786   Annexation of Further Kirant complete and the war in Limbuwan ends

1789   First presence of Chhetris in Mamangkhe with Ram Krishna Bhattarai renting grazing land above the village settlement

1816   Gorkha war with East India Company ends and the Sugauli Treaty defines the national borders of Nepal

1825   Ram Krishna Bhattarai (Chhetri) builds a house on land in upper Ward 1 of village formally marking the beginning of non-Limbu settlement in the village

1893   Estimated date of construction of the first permanent house in the village which still stands today

1896   Sirbelas Kharel (Chhetri) first settles in Mamangkhe, arriving from Khewang village

1949   First migrant travels to Sikkim; returns in 1955

1964   Land Reform Act formally abolishes kipat system of land tenure

1966   Pre-survey carried out in Mamangkhe to begin process of formally documenting land ownership

1969   Cardamom is first planted in Mamangkhe by Ratna Bahadur

1986   Cadastral survey is carried out in Mamangkhe between the 26th and 29th of May

1998   First international migrant departs for work in Qatar

Appendix 3
Mamangkhe Survey Questions

Section one. Demographic information
a. Male or female?
b. What is your full name?
c. What is your nick-name?
d. What is your clan name (within the Mabo-Limbu)?
e. What is your age?
f. Are you married?
g. At what age did you marry?
h. Did you have a "stolen"/"wooed" or arranged marriage?
i. Where is your wife's home?
j. What is your wife's clan name? (within Limbu if Limbu, or ethnic group name)
k. How many children do you have?
l. What are the names of your children?
m. Do they all live in this house nowadays?
n. If not, where do they live nowadays?
o. How many people (usually/nowadays) live in this household in total?
p. What is your father's name?
q. What is your grandfather's name?
r. What is you great-grandfather's name?

Section two. Education and language use.
a. Did/do you go to school?
b. Until what class did you study (are you studying in)?
c. Can you read and write in Nepali?
d. Do any of your children study in private schools?

e. What language do you speak most day to day?
f. What language to you speak most to your children?
g. What language do/did you speak most with your parents?
h. What language do your children usually speak to you?

Section three. Economics.

a. What work do you do to earn money?
b. How many bulls do you have (including recently born and young)?
c. How many cows do you have?
d. How many buffalo do you have?
e. How many pigs do you have?
f. How many goats do you have?
g. How many chickens do you have (only adult chicken)?
h. Do you have rice fields?
i. How much rice did you harvest last year?
j. How much millet did you harvest last year?
k. How much corn did you harvest last year?
l. How much wheat did you harvest last year?
m. How much barley did you harvest last year?
n. Did you sell any of your crop sold?
o. If so, approximately how much last year?
p. How many fields did you plant with millet and/or corn this year?
q. Do you work adhiyã on someone else's land?
r. How many fields do you do adhiyã on?

Section four. Cardamom.

a. How much cardamom do you think you will harvest this year?
b. How much cardamom did you harvest last year?
c. How much cardamom did you harvest the year before that (two years ago)?
d. How much cardamom did you harvest three years ago?
e. How much cardamom did you harvest four years ago?
f. When did you start growing cardamom?
g. Did your father have cardamom fields?
h. When did your father start planting cardamom?
i. How much did/does he usually harvest?

Section five. Consumption.

a. How much rice do you (in household) eat in a month (estimate)?
b. How many buffalos were killed last year?
c. How many pigs were killed last year?
d. How many goats were killed last year?
e. How many buffalos were killed this year?
f. How many pigs were killed this year?
g. How many goats were killed this year?
h. In the last two weeks, how many times have you eaten meat?
i. In the last two weeks, how many times have you eaten fish?
j. What is the most expensive thing you bought last year?
k. How much was it?
l. If someone gave you 100 rupees what would you do with it?
m. If someone gave you 1000 rupees what would you do with it?
n. If someone gave you 100,000 (1 lakh) rupees what would you do with it?

Section six. Conspicuous consumption.

a. Do you have a radio?
b. Do you have a pressure cooker?
c. Do you have a jāto?
d. Do you have a dhiki?
e. Do you have an okli?
f. What roof-type?
g. How many buildings are there in the household?
h. How many floors does the house have?
i. Estimate size of main building.

Section seven. Travel.

a. Have you travelled outside the district (Taplejung) in the last year?
b. Where did you travel?
c. Have you ever worked abroad (including Sikkim)?
d. Where did you travel?
e. When did you travel?
f. How frequently did you travel?
g. What work did you do?
h. How long were you abroad for?

Section eight. Health.

a. Have you been in ill in the last 2 weeks?
b. Have you been ill in the last month?
c. What illness have you had (in last 2 weeks or last month)?
d. What was the first thing you did to cure yourself?
e. What was the second thing you did to cure yourself?
f. Has anyone in the family been ill in the last two weeks?
g. Who in your family was ill?
h. For what illness?
i. What was the first thing you did to cure them?
j. What was the second thing you did to cure them?
k. When was the last time someone in your family visited the health post in Paua?
l. Have you or any family members ever visited a hospital (Taplejung bazaar or elsewhere)?
m. Do you ever use medicinal plants?
n. When was the last time you used medicinal plants?

Section nine. Ritual practice.

a. Do you perform pujas in your household?
b. Which pujas did you have last year?

Appendix 4
Jhapa survey questions

a. Male or female?
b. What is your full name?
c. What is you nick-name?
d. What are your relations (with Mamangkhe)?
e. Were you born in Mamangkhe?
f. Are you married?
g. At what age did you marry?
h. How many children do you have?
i. How many people usually live in this household in total?
j. When did you move here (how many years ago)?
k. Do you live in your own house?
l. If yes, how much did you buy it for?
m. What work did you do before buying house (how did you buy house)?
n. How often do you visit Mamangkhe?
o. Do you have cardamom in Mamangkhe?
p. What do you produce in Jhapa?
q. Do children go to private or Nepali schools?
r. What are the pros and cons of living in Jhapa?

Bibliography

Acharya, M., 1983. *Women and the Subsistence Sector: Economic Participation and Household Decision Making in Nepal*, Washington, D.C: World Bank.

Acharya, M. & Bennett, L., 1981. *The Rural Women of Nepal: An Aggragate Analysis and Summary of Eight Village Studies*, Kathmandu, Nepal: Centre for Economic Development and Administration, Tribhuvan University.

Adam, L., 1936. The Social Organization and Customary Law of the Nepalese Tribes. *American Anthropologist*, 38(4), 533-547.

Adhikari, J. & Bohle, H., 1999. *Food Crisis in Nepal: How Mountain Farmers Cope*, New Delhi: Adroit Publications.

Adhikari, R. 2009. The "dream-trap": Brokering, "study abroad" and nurse migration from Nepal to the UK. *European Bulletin of Himalayan Research* 35-36: 122-23.

Ahearn, L.M., 2001. *Invitations to Love: Literacy, Love Letters, and Social Change in Nepal*, Ann Arbor: University of Michigan Press.

Ahearn, L.M., 2003. Writing Desire in Nepali Love Letters. *Language & Communication*, 23(2), 107-122.

Allen, N. 1972. The vertical dimension in Thulung classification. *Journal of the Anthropological Society of Oxford* 3(2): 81-94.

Allen, N.J., 1997. Hinduization: The Experie nce of the Thulung Rai. In D. N. Gellner, J. Pfaff-Czarnecka, & J. Whelpton, eds. *Nationalism and Ethnicity in a Hindu Kingdom: The Politics of Culture in Contemporary Nepal*. Amsterdam: Harwood Academic, pp. 303-323.

Angbohang, K.S., 1978. *Gaunjee Thar*, HanRajang, Taplejung: Khadgendra Singh Angbohang.

Asad, T., 1987. Are There Histories of Peoples without Europe? *Comparative Studies in Society and History*, 29(3), 594-607.

Aubriot, O. 2009. International and national migrations from a village in Western Nepal: Changes and impact on local life. *European Bulletin of Himalayan Research* 35-36: 43-61.

Bailey, F.G., 1957. *Caste and the Economic Frontier: A Village in Highland Orissa*, Manchester: Manchester University Press.

Bajracharya, D., 1983. Deforestation in the Food/Fuel Context: Historical and Political Perspectives from Nepal. *Mountain Research and Development*, 3(3), 227-240.

Balikci, A. 2008. *Lamas, Shamans and Ancestors: Village Religion in Sikkim*. Leiden: Brill.

Banister, J. & Thapa, S., 1981. *The population dynamics of Nepal. Papers of the East-West Population Instisute No.78*, Honolulu: East-West Population Institute.

Barnouw, V., 1955. Eastern Nepalese Marriage Customs and Kinship Organization. *Southwestern Journal of Anthropology*, 11(1), 15-30.

Basch, L.G., Schiller, N.G. & Szanton Blanc, C. eds., 1994. *Nations Unbound: Transnational Projects, Postcolonial*, Amsterdam: Gordon and Breach.

Basnet, S., 2002. *Large Cardamom Farming and Marketing in Nepal: A Case Study of Soyung VDC in Ilam District, Nepal*. M.A. Thesis. Tribhuvan University.

Beattie, J., 1964. *Other Cultures: Aims, Methods and Achievements in Social Anthropology*, London: Cohen & West.

Bell, C.A., 1903. The Religion of the Khambus. *Journal of Asiatic Society of Bengal*, 72(3), 28-29.

Béteille, A., 1965. *Caste, Class, and Power: Changing Patterns of Stratification*, Berkeley: University of California Press.

Bickel, B. 1997. Spatial operations in deixis, cognition, and culture: where to orient oneself in Belhare. In J. Nuyts & E. Pederson (eds) *Language and Conceptualization*, 46-86. Cambridge: Cambridge University Press.

Bickel, B. 1999. Cultural formalism and spatial language in Belhara. In B. Bickel & M. Gaenszle (eds) *Himalayan Space: Cultural Horizons and Practices*, 75-104. Zurich: Museum of Ethnography.

Bista, D.B., 1972. *People of Nepal* 2nd ed., Kathmandu: Ratna Pustak Bhandar.

Biswas, P., 1934. A Short Note on the Limbus of the Darjeeling. *Indian Culture*, 1, 481-82.

Blaikie, P., Cameron, J., Feldman, D.J.P., Fournier, A., Seddon, D., 1976. *The Effects of Roads in West-Central Nepal*, Norwich: Overseas Development Group.

Blaikie, P.., Cameron, J. & Seddon, D., 1980. *Nepal in Crisis: Growth and Stagnation at the Periphery*, Oxford: Clarendon Press.

Blaikie, P., Cameron, J. & Seddon, D., 2002. Understanding 20 Years of Change in West-Central Nepal: Continuity and Change in Lives and Ideas. *World Development*, 30(7), 1255-1270.

Brower, B. 2003. The Organization of Transhumance in the Nepal Himalayas. In A. Rao & M. J. Casimir (eds) *Nomadism in South Asia*, Delhi: Oxford University Press.

Brush, S. 1976. Cultural Adaptations to Mountain Ecosystems: An Introduction. *Human Ecology* 4(2): 125-133.

Brush, S. 1977. *Mountain, Field, and Family: The Economy and Human Ecology of an Andean Valley*. Philadelphia: University of Pennsylvania Press.

Bruslé, T. 2008. The Nepali-Qatari migrant world. *Himal Southasian*. Available at: http://www.himalmag.com/read.php?id=2167 [Accessed May 26, 2010].

Bruslé, T. 2009. Who's in a labour camp? A socio-economic analysis of Nepalese migrants in Qatar. *European Bulletin of Himalayan Research* 35-36: 154-170.

Burghart, R., 1984. The Formation of the Concept of Nation-State in Nepal. *Journal of Asian Studies*, 44(1), 101-125.

Burris, V., 1987. The Neo-Marxist Synthesis of Marx and Weber on Class. In N. Wiley, ed. *The Marx-Weber Debate*. Newbury Park: Sage.

Cameron, M.M., 1998. *On the Edge of the Auspicious: Gender and Caste in Nepal*, Urbana: University of Illinois Press.

Campbell, A., 1840. Notes on the Limboos, and Other Hill Tribes Hitherto Undescribed. *Journal of the Asiatic Society of Bengal*, 9, 595-615.

Campbell, A., 1855. Notes on the Limboo Language, with an Alphabet. *Journal of the Asiatic Society of Bengal*, 24, 202-203.

Campbell, B. 1994. Forms of Cooperation in a Tamang Community of Nepal. In M. Allen (ed.) *Anthropology of Nepal: peoples, problems and processes*, 3-18. Kathmandu: Mandala.

Campbell, B., 2003. Resisting the Environmentalist State. In D. N. Gellner, ed. *Resistance and the State: Nepalese Experiences*. New Delhi: Social Science Press.

Campbell, B., 2004. Indigenous Views on the Terms of Participation in the Development of Biodiversity Conservation in Nepal. In A. Bicker, P. Sillitoe, & J. Pottier, eds. *Investigating Local Knowledge: New Directions, New Approaches*. Aldershot: Ashgate.

Caplan, L., 1967. Some Political Consequences of State Land Policy in East Nepal. *Man*, 2(1), 107-114.

Caplan, L., 1970. *Land and Social Change in East Nepal: A Study of Hindu-Tribal*, London: Routledge & Kegan Paul.

Caplan, L., 1972. The Multiplication of Social Ties: The Strategy of Credit Transactions in East Nepal. *Economic Development & Cultural Change*, 20(4), 691.

Caplan, L., 1990. Tribes in the ethnography of Nepal: Some Comments on a Debate. *Contribution to Nepalese Studies*, 17(2).

Caplan, L., 1991. From Tribe to Peasant? The Limbus and the Nepalese State. *Journal of Peasant Studies*, 18(2), 305-321.

Caplan, L., 1995. *Warrior Gentlemen: "Gurkhas" in the Western*, Providence, RI: Berghahn Books.

Caplan, L., 2000. *Land and Social Change in East Nepal: A Study of Hindu-Tribal Relations*, Lalitpur, Nepal: Himal Books.

Castles, S. & Delgado Wise, R., 2008. *Migration and Development: Perspectives from the South*, Geneva: International Organization for Migration.

Castles, S. & Miller, M.J., 2003. *The Age of Migration* 3rd ed., Basingstoke: Palgrave Macmillan.

CBS, 2006. Climate: Annual Rainfall in Various Stations 2001 to 2004. Government of Nepal, Central Bureau of Statistics. Available at: http://bit.ly/r8LK9G [Accessed October 7, 2009].

CBS, 2007. Population Profile of Nepal. Government of Nepal, Central Bureau of Statistics. Available at: http://bit.ly/CBS2007 [Accessed October 7, 2009].

Chakravarty-Kaul, M. 1998. Transhumance and customary pastoral rights in Himachal Pradesh: Claiming the high pastures for Gaddis. *Mountain Research and Development* 18(1): 5–17.

Chatterji, S.K., 1974. *Kirata Jana Krti. - The Indo-Mongoloids: Their Contribution to the History and Culture of India*, Calcutta: Asiatic Society.

Chemjong, I.S., 2002. *Limbu-Nepali-Angreji Shabdakos* 2nd ed., Kathmandu: Nepal Academy.

Chemjong, I.S., 2003(1967). *History and Culture of the Kirat People* 4th ed., Kathmandu: Kirat Yakthung Chumlung.

Chhetri, R.B., 2007. Changing Environments, Society, and Culture: Case studies of some Dalits and Kumals in Pokhara valley. In H. Ishii, D. N. Gellner, & K. Nawa, eds. *Nepalis Inside and Outside Nepal*. Social dynamics in northern South Asia. New Delhi: Manohar.

Clarke, G.E. 1980. *The Temple and Kinship among a Buddhist People of the Himalaya*. D.Phil thesis. University of Oxford.

Clifford, J., 1997. *Routes: Travel and Translation in the Late Twentieth Century*, Cambridge, Mass: Harvard University Press.

Clifford, J., 1992. Traveling Cultures. In *Cultural Studies*. New York: Routledge.

Coquery-Vidrovitch, C., 1978. Research on an African mode of production. In D. Seddon, ed. *Relations of production: Marxist approaches to economic anthropology*. London: Frank Cass, pp. 261-288.

Cox, T., 1990. Land Rights and Ethnic Conflict in Nepal. *Economic and Political Weekly*, 25(24/25), 1318-1320.

Cox, T., 1994. The current socioeconomic status of untouchables in Nepal. *Occasional Papers in Sociology and Anthropology*, 4, 90-109.

Crane, J.G. & Angrosino, M.V., 1974. *Field Projects in Anthropology: A Student Handbook.*, New Jersey: General Learning Press.

da Rovato, G., 1790. An Account of the Kingdom of Nepal. *Asiatick Researches*, 2, 307-22.

Dahal, D., 1994. *A Review of Forest User Groups: Case Studies from Eastern Nepal*, Kathmandu, Nepal: ICIMOD.

Dahal, D., 1996. The Fallout of Deviant Anthropology. *Himal Southasian*, 9(3), 50-51.

Dahal, R., 2000. Nepal's Remittance Bonanza. *Himal*, (13/2), 42-43.

Daniggelis, E. 1997. *Hidden Wealth: The Survival Strategy of Foraging Farmers.* Kathmandu: Mandala Book Point.

Daryn, G., 2006. *Encompassing a Fractal World: The Energetic Female Core in Myth and Everyday Life: A Few Lessons Drawn From the Nepalese Himalaya*, Lanham, Md: Lexington Books.

Deere, C.D. & De Janvry, A., 1979. A Conceptual Framework for the Empirical Analysis of Peasants. *American Journal of Agricultural Economics*, 61(4), 601-611.

Desjarlais, R.R., 1992. *Body and Emotion: The Aesthetics of Illness and Healing in the Nepal Himalayas*, Philadelphia: University of Pennsylvania Press.

van Driem, G., 1987. A Grammar of Limbu. *New York: Mouton.*

van Driem, G., 1997. A New Analysis of the Limbu Verb. In D. Bradley ed. *Papers in Southeast Asian Linguistics No. 14: Tibeto-Burman Languages of the Himalayas*, 157–173.

van Driem, G., 2001. *Languages of the Himalayas: An Ethnolinguistic Handbook of the Greater Himalayan Region*, Leiden: Brill.

van Driem, G., 1999. The Limbu Verb Revisited. In Y.P. Yadava & W.W. Glover, eds. *Topics in Nepalese Linguistics*. Kathmandu: Royal Nepal Academy, pp. 209-30.

Dumont, L., 1970. *Homo Hierarchicus: An Essay on the Caste System*, Chicago: University of Chicago Press.

FAO/World Bank, 1979. Draft Report of the Nepal Community Forestry Development Project Preparatory Mission. , (16/79).

Firth, R., 1959. *Social Change in Tikopia: Re-Study of a Polynesian Community*, London: Allen & Unwin.

Fisher, J.F., 1990. *Sherpas: Reflections on Change in Himalayan Nepal*, Berkeley: University of California Press.

Forbes, A., 1996. The Discourse and Practice of Kipat. *Kailash*, 18, 39-80.

Forbes, A.A., 1999. Mapping Power: Disputing Claims to Kipat Lands in Northeastern Nepal. *American Ethnologist*, 26(1), 114-138.

Foster-Carter, A., 1978. The Modes of Production Debate. *New Left Review*, 107, 47-77.

Frank, A.G., 1967. *Capitalism and Underdevelopment in Latin America: Historical Studies of Chile and Brazil*, New York: Monthly Review Press.

Fricke, T.E., 1993. *Himalayan Households: Tamang Demography and Domestic*, Delhi: Book Faith India.

Fürer-Haimendorf, C.V., 1964. *The Sherpas of Nepal: Buddhist Highlanders*, London: John Murray.

Fürer-Haimendorf, C.V., 1966. *Caste and Kin in Nepal, India and Ceylon: Anthropological Studies in Hindu-Buddhist Contact Zones*, London: Asia Publishing House.

Gaenszle, M., 2000. *Origins and Migrations: Kinship, Mythology and Ethnic Identity among the Mewahang Rai of East Nepal*, Kathmandu: Mandala Book Point.

Gaenszle, M., 2002. Countering the Great Traditions: Remakings of the Kirānti Past. In A. Harneit-Sievers, ed. *A Place in the World: New Local Historiographies from Africa*. African social studies series. Leiden: Brill, p. 384.

Gellner, D.N., 2004. Mark Liechty: Suitably Modern: Making Middle-Class Culture in a New Consumer Society [Book Review]. *Bulletin of the School of Oriental and African Studies*, 67(01), 101-102.

Gellner, D.N., Pfaff-Czarnecka, J. & Whelpton, J. eds., 1997. *Nationalism and Ethnicity in a Hindu Kingdom: The Politics of Culture in Contemporary Nepal*, Amsterdam: Harwood Academic.

George, C., MunanKāmī, R. & Bijl, B., 2007. *Sector Study on Large Cardamom*. Available at: http://bit.ly/oY6wXk: Asia Trust Fund. [Accessed January 10, 2009]

Gewertz, D.B. & Errington, F.K., 1999. *Emerging Class in Papua New Guinea: The Telling of Difference*, New York: Cambridge University Press.

Ghimire, K.B., 1992. *Forest or Farm?: The Politics of Poverty and Land Hunger in Nepal*, Delhi: Oxford University Press.

Giddens, A., 1981. *A Contemporary Critique of Historical Materialism*, London: Macmillan.

Gilmour, D. & Fisher, R., 1991. *Villagers, Forest and Foresters: The Philosophy, Process and Practice of Community Forestry in Nepal*, Kathmandu, Nepal: Sahayogi Press.

Glick Schiller, N., 2004. Transnationality. In D. Nugent & J. Vincent, eds. *A Companion to the Anthropology of Politics*. Malden, MA: Blackwell.

Glick Schiller, N., Basch, L., & Blanc-Szanton, C. eds., 1992. *Towards a Transnational Perspective on Migration: Race, Class, Ethnicity, and Nationalism Reconsidered*, New York: New York Academy of Sciences.

Godelier, Maurice, C., 1978. The Object and Method of Economic Anthropology. In D. Seddon, ed. *Relations of Production: Marxist Approaches to Economic Anthropology*. London: Frank Cass, pp. 49-126.

Graner, E. 2009. Leaving Hills and Plains: Migration and Remittances in Nepal. *European Bulletin of Himalayan Research* 35-36: 24-42.

Gregory, C.A. & Altman, J.C., 1989. *Observing the Economy*, London: Routledge.

Guneratne, A. 1996. The Tax-Man Cometh: The impact of revenue collection on subsistence strategies in Chitwan Tharu Society. *Studies in Nepali History & Society* 1.1: 5-35.

Gurung, H., 1989. Ecological Change. In K. P. Malla, ed. *Nepal: Perspectives on Continuity and Change*. Kirtipur, Nepal: Centre for Nepal and Asian Studies.

Gutkind, P.C.W., Wallerstein, I.M. & Williams, G., 1976. *The Political Economy of Contemporary Africa*, Beverly Hills: Sage.

Hachhethu, K., 2006. *Political Parties of Nepal*, Lalitpur, Nepal: Social Science Baha.

Hamilton, F., 1819. *An Account of the Kingdom of Nepal and of the Territories*, Edinburgh: Printed for Archibald Constable and Company.

Hardman, C., 2000. *Other Worlds: Notions of Self and Emotion among the Lohorung Rai,* Oxford: Berg.

Harper, I. & Tarnowski, C., 2007. A Heterotopia of Resistance: Health, Community Forestry, and Challenges to State Centralization in Nepal. In D. N. Gellner, ed. *Resistance and the State: Nepalese Experiences.* Oxford: Berghahn Books.

Hausner, S.L., 2007. Border Towns in the Tarai: Sites of Migration. *Occasional Papers in Sociology and Anthropology*, 10, 107-123.

Hitchcock, J.T., 1966. *The Magars of Banyan Hill*, New York: Holt, Rinehart and Winston.

Hodgson, B.H., 1858. On the Kirānti Tribe of the Central Himalaya. *Journal of Asiatic Society of Bengal*, 27.

Hodgson, B.H., 2001(1880). *Miscellaneous Essays Relating to Indian Subjects*, London: Trübner & Co.

Höfer, A., 1976. A Settlement and Smithy of the Backsmiths (Kāmī) in Nepal. *Kailash*, 4(4), 349-396.

Höfer, A., 1979. *The Caste Hierarchy and the State in Nepal: A Study of The*, Innsbruck: Universitätsverlag Wagner.

Holmberg, D., 2007. Outcastes in an "Egalitarian" Society: Tamang/ Blacksmith Relations from Tamang Perspective. *Occasional Papers in Sociology and Anthropology*, 10, 124-140.

Holmberg, D., Pettigrew, J. & Tamang, M.S., 2009. *Views from the Field: Anthropological Perspectives on the Constituent Assembly Elections. Baha Occasional Paper II*, Kathmandu, Nepal: Social Science Baha.

Hooker, J.D., 1854. *Himalayan Journals, or, Notes of a Naturalist in Bengal, The*, London: John Murray.

Humphrey, C. 1985. Barter and economic disintegration. *Man* 20(1): 48– 72.

Hutt, M., 1997. Being Nepali without Nepal: Reflections on a South Asian Diaspora. In D. N. Gellner, J. Pfaff-Czarnecka, & J. Whelpton, eds. *Nationalism and Ethnicity in a Hindu Kingdom: The Politics of Culture in Contemporary Nepal.* Amsterdam: Harwood Academic, pp. 101-144.

Human Rights Watch, 1995. *Rape for Profit: Trafficking of Nepali Girls and Women to India's Brothels*, Available at: http://bit.ly/93a73f [Accessed October 1, 2009].

Ishii, H., 1995. Caste and Kinship in a Newar Village. In D. N. Gellner & D. Quigley, eds. *Contested Hierarchies: A Collaborative Ethnography of Caste among the Newars of the Kathmandu Valley, Nepal*. Oxford: Clarendon Press, pp. 109-157.

Jones, R.L., 1973. *Kinship and Marriage among the Limbu of Eastern Nepal: a Study in Marriage Stability*. University of Wisconsin.

Jones, R.L., 1974. Religious Symbolism in Limbu Death by Violence. *Omega*, 5(3), 252-66.

Jones, R.L., 1976a. Limbu Spirit Possession and Shamanism. In J. Hitchcock & R. L. Jones, eds. *Spirit Possession in the Nepal Himalayas*. Warminster: Aris & Phillips, pp. 29-55.

Jones, R.L., 1976b. Sanskritization in Eastern Nepal. *Ethnology*, 15(1), 63-75.

Jones, R.L. & Jones, S.K., 1976. *The Himalayan Woman: A Study of Limbu Women in Marriage And divorce*, Palo Alto, Calif: Mayfield Pub. Co.

Kantipur Report, 7/7/2009. Alam to visit Korea, Israel to sort out labour issues. Available at: http://bit.ly/p3gDaS [Accessed July 20, 2009].

Kapadia, K., 1995. *Siva and Her Sisters: Gender, Caste, and Class in Rural South India*, Boulder: Westview Press.

Karibasappa, G.S., Dhiman, K.R., Biswas, A.K., Rai, R.N., 1987. Variability Association among Quantitative Characters and Path Analysis in Large Cardamom. *Indian Journal of Agricultural Sciences*, 57(12), 884-888.

Kirat Yakthung Chumlung (KYC) website; http://chumlung.org.np/index.php; District Agricultural Development Office document (2003-4).

Kirkpatrick, W. & W. Bulmer and Co, 1811. *An Account of the Kingdom of Nepaul*, London: William Miller Albemarle-Street; W. Bulmer and Co.

Konow, S., 1909. Tibeto-Burman Family. In G. Grierson, ed. *Linguistic Survey of India. Vol. 111.* Calcutta: India.

Leacock, E.B., 1954. *The Montagnais "Hunting Territory" and the Fur Trade*, Menasha, Wis.: American Anthropological Association.

Lenin, V.I., 1971. *Selected works [of] V. I. Lenin*, New York: International Publishers.

Lévi, S., 1905. *Le Népal: Étude Historique D'un Royaume Hindou*, Paris: E. Leroux.

Levine, N.E., 1987. Caste, State, and Ethnic Boundaries in Nepal. *The Journal of Asian Studies*, 46(1), 71-88.

Levine, S., 2007. Parental Wisdom vs. Youthful Romance: Getting Married in Two Nepali Communities. In H. Ishii, D. N. Gellner, & K. Nawa, eds. *Nepalis Inside and Outside Nepal*. New Delhi: Manohar, pp. 223-253.

Lewis, W.A., 1954. Economic Development with Unlimited Supplies of Labour. *Manchester School of Economic and Social Studies*, 22, 139-91.

Liechty, M., 2003. *Suitably Modern: Making Middle-Class Culture in a New Consumer Society*, Princeton, N.J: Princeton University Press.

Limbu, K., 1996. *Large Cardamom Farming and Marketing in Nepal: A Case Study of Morahang VDC in Tehrathum district, Nepal*. M.A. Thesis. Tribhuvan University.

Lokshin, M., Bontch-Osmolovski, M. & Glinskaya, E., 2007. Work-Related Migration and Poverty Reduction in Nepal. Available at: http://bit.ly/oYQ6cA [Accessed March 4, 2009].

Macfarlane, A., 1976. *Resources and Population: A Study of the Gurungs of Nepal*, Cambridge: Cambridge University Press.

Macfarlane, A., 2001. Sliding Down Hill: Some reflections on thirty years of change in a Himalayan village. *EBHR*, 20-21, 105-122.

Macfarlane, A., 2003. *Resources and Population: A Study of the Gurungs of Nepal* 2nd ed., Kathmandu: Ratna Pustak Bhandar.

Magubane, B., 1979. *The Political Economy of Race and Class in South Africa*, New York: Monthly Review Press.

Mair, L.P., 1969. *Anthropology and Social Change*, London: Athlone Press.

Malinowski, B., 1922. *Argonauts of the Western Pacific: An Account of Native Enterprise and Adventure in the Archipelagoes of Melanesian New Guinea*, London: George Routledge & Sons.

Manandhar, N.P., 2002. *Plants and People of Nepal*, Portland, OR: Timber Press.

Mande, S., Kumar, A. & Kishore, V.V.N., 1999. A Study of Large-Cardamom Curing Chambers in Sikkim. *Biomass and Bioenergy*, 16(6), 463-473.

March, K.S., 2002. *"If Each Comes Halfway": Meeting Tamang Women in Nepal*, Ithaca: Cornell University Press.

Marcus, G.E., & Fischer, M.M.J., 1986. *Anthropology as Cultural Critique: An Experimental Moment in the Human Sciences*, Chicago: University of Chicago Press.

Marsden, M. 2008. Lords of a Dubai labour camp: Pakistani migrants in the Gulf. *IIAS Newsletter* 49: 5-6.

Marx, K., 1970[1859]. *A Contribution to The Critique of Political Economy*, New York: International Publishers.

Massey, D.S., Arango, J., Hugo, G., Koucaouci, A., Pellegrino, A., Taylor, J.E., 1998. *Worlds in Motion: Understanding International Migration at the End of the Millennium*, Oxford: Clarendon Press.

Mayer, E. 1985. Production Zones. In S. Masuda, I. Shimada, & C. Morris (eds) *Andean Ecology and Civilization*, Tokyo: University of Tokyo Press.

McHugh, E.L., 1989. Concepts of the Person among the Gurungs of Nepal. *American Ethnologist*, 16(1), 75-86.

McHugh, E.L., 2001. *Love and Honor in the Himalayas: Coming to Know Another Culture*, Philadelphia: University of Pennsylvania Press.

Mehta, J.N., & Kellert, S.R. 1998. Local Attitudes toward Community-Based Conservation Policy and Programmes in Nepal: A Case Study in the Makalu-Barun Conservation Area. *Environmental Conservation* 25(04): 320-333.

Meillassoux, C., 1972. From Reproduction to Production. *Economy and society*, 1(1), 93-105.

Messerschmidt, D.A., 1976. *The Gurungs of Nepal: Conflict and Change in a Village*, Warminster: Aris & Phillips.

Michailovsky, B., 1986. Structure Syllabique et Variation Combinatoire: Voisement et Gémination en Limbu. *Cahiers de linguistique asie-orientale*, 15, 193–204.

Michailovsky, B., 1993. Catégories Verbales et Intransitivité Duale en Limbu. *Actances*, 7, 241-58.

Michailovsky, B., 1999. Tibeto-Burman Dental Suffixes: Evidence from Limbu (Nepal). In Yadava & Glover, eds. *Topics in Nepalese Linguistics*. Kathmandu: Royal Nepal Academy, pp. 478-94.

Michailovsky, B., 2002. *Limbu-English Dictionary of the Mewa Khola Dialect With English-Limbu index*, Kathmandu: Mandala Book Point.

Mikesell, S. 1988. Commodity penetration and subjection of labour to merchant capital in a Newar town in west-central Nepal. *Contributions to Nepalese Studies* 15: 19-24.

Momba, J.C. 1989. The State, Rural Class Formation and Peasant Political Participation in Zambia: The Case of Southern Province. *African Affairs* 88(352): 331-357.

Morris, J., 1933. *Gurkhas*, Delhi: Manager of Publications.

Mumford, S., 1989. *Himalayan Dialogue: Tibetan Lamas and Gurung Shamans in Nepal*, Madison: University of Wisconsin Press.

Murra, J.V. 1972. El Control Vertical de un Máximo de Pisos Ecológicos en la Economía de las Sociedades Andinas. In J. V. Murra (ed.) *Inigo Ortiz de Zuniga, Visita de la Provincia de León de Huanuco en 1562* , vol. 2, 429-476. Huanuco, Peru: Universidad Nacional Hermilio Valdizan.

Murra, J.V. 1985. 'El Archipielago Vertical' Revisited. In S. Masuda, I. Shimada, & C. Morris (eds) *Andean Ecology and Civilization*, 3-13. Tokyo: University of Tokyo Press.

Nair, K.P.P., 2006. The Agronomy and Economy of Cardamom (Elettaria Cardamomum M.): the "Queen of Spices". *Advances in Agronomy: Volume 91*.

Nash, J.C., 1993. *We Eat the Mines and the Mines Eat Us: Dependency and exploitation in Bolivian tin mines*, New York: Columbia University Press.

Natraj, V.K., 2003. Caste and 'Modernity'. *Economic and Political Weekly*, 38(51/52), 5406-5408.

Northey, W.B., 1937. *The Land of the Gurkhas; or, The Himalayan Kingdom of Nepal*, Cambridge: W. Heffer & sons, ltd.

Northey, W.B. & Morris, J., 1928. *The Gurkhas; Their Manners, Customs and Country*, London: John Lane.

O'Brien, R.C., 1979. *The Political Economy of Underdevelopment: Dependence in Senegal*, London: Sage Publications.

Ong, A., 1987. *Spirits of Resistance and Capitalist Discipline: Factory Women in Malaysia*, Albany: State University of New York Press.

Ortner, S.B., 1984. Theory in Anthropology since the Sixties. *Comparative Studies in Society and History*, 26(1), 126-166.

Ortner, S.B., 1989. *High Religion: A Cultural and Political History of Sherpa Buddhism*, Princeton: Princeton University Press.

Osella, F. & Gardner, K., 2004. *Migration, Modernity and Social Transformation in South Asia*, New Delhi: Sage.

Osella, F. & Osella, C., 2000. Migration, Money and Masculinity in Kerala. *The Journal of the Royal Anthropological Institute*, 6(1), 117-133.

Pandian, M., 2002. One Step Outside Modernity: Caste, Identity Politics and Public Sphere.

Parajuli, B.K., 2007. Occupational Change among the Gaines of Pokhara City. In H. Ishii, D. N. Gellner, & K. Nawa, eds. *Nepalis Inside and Outside Nepal*. Social dynamics in northern South Asia. New Delhi: Manohar.

Parkin, F., 1979. *Marxism and Class Theory: A Bourgeois Critique*, London: Tavistock.

Parry, J.P., 1979. *Caste and Kinship in Kangra*, London: Routledge & Kegan Paul.

Petras, E.M., The Global Labor Market in the Modern World Economy. In M. M. Kritz, C. B. Keely, & S. M. Tomasi, eds. *Global Trends in Migration: Theory and Research on International Population Movements*. Staten Island, NY: Center for Migration Studies.

Pettigrew, J., 2000. 'Gurkhas' in the Town: Migration, Language, and Healing. *European Bulletin of Himalayan Research*, 19, 7-39.

Pfaff-Czarnecka, J., 2008. Distributional Coalitions in Nepal: An Essay on Democratization, Capture, and (Lack of) Confidence. In D. N. Gellner & K. Hachhethu, eds. *Local Democracy in South Asia: Microprocesses of Democratization in Nepal and its Neighbours*. Governance. New Delhi: SAGE Publications.

Pignède, B., 1966. *Les Gurungs: Une Population Himalayenne Du Népal*, Paris: Mouton.

Poffenberger, M., 1980. *Patterns of Change in the Nepal Himalaya*, Delhi: Macmillan.

Portes, A. & Walton, J., 1981. *Labor, Class, and the International System*, New York: Academic Press.

Pradhan, K., 1991. *The Gorkha Conquests: The Process and Consequences of the Unification of Nepal, with Particular Reference to Eastern Nepal*, Calcutta: Oxford University Press.

Prindle, P.H. 1983. *Tinglatar: Socio-Economic Relationships of a Brahmin Village* 1st ed. Kathmandu: Ratna Pustak Bhandar.

Quigley, D., 1996. Change and Continuity: Studies in the Nepalese Culture of The Kathmandu Valley. In S. Lienhard, ed. Social Mobility and Social Fragmentation in the Newar Caste System. Alessandria: Edizioni dell'Orso, pp. 69-84.

Ramble, C., & Chapagain, C. 1990. Preliminary Notes on the Cultural Dimension of Conservation. Makalu Barun Conservation Project.

Rao, V.G., Mande, S. & Kishore, V.V.N., 2001. Study of Drying Characteristics of Large-Cardamom. *Biomass and Bioenergy*, 20(1), 37-43.

Ravindran, P.N. & Madhusoodanan, K.J., 2002. *Cardamom: The Genus Elettaria*, Taylor and Francis.

Regmi, D.R., 1980. Regmi Research Series. In *Series 12, December 1980.* http://bit.ly/digitalhimalaya : Digital Himalaya.

Regmi, M.C., 1965. *Land Tenure and Taxation in Nepal. Vol 3. The Jagir, Rakam and, Kipat tenure.*, Berkeley: Institute of International Studies, University of California.

Regmi, M.C., 1971. *A Study in Nepali Economic History, 1768-1846*, New Delhi: Manjusri Publishing House.

Regmi, M.C., 1976. *Landownership in Nepal*, Berkeley : University of California Press

Regmi, M.C., 1978. *Land Tenure and Taxation in Nepal* 2nd ed., Kathmandu: Ratna Pustak Bhandar.

Rey, P., 1973. *Les Alliances de Classes. Sur L'articulation des Modes de Production. Suivi du materialisme historique et luttes de classes.*, Paris: Maspero.

Risley, H.H., 1894. *The Gazetteer of Sikhim*, Calcutta: Printed at the Bengal Secretariat Press.

Rohini, S., 2002. Whither Subaltern Studies? *Economic and Political Weekly*, 37(29), 3076-3077.

Rönnow, K., 1936. Kirata: A Study on some Ancient Indian Tribes'. *Le Monde Oriental*, 30, 90-170.

Roseberry, W., 1988. Political Economy. *Annual Reviews in Anthropology*, 17(1), 161-185.

Rosser, C., 1966. Social Mobility in the Newar Caste System. In C. V. Fürer-Haimendorf, ed. *Caste and Kin in Nepal, India and Ceylon: Anthropological Studies in Hindu-Buddhist Contact Zones*. London: Asia Publishing House, p. 364.

Russell, A., 2007. Writing Traveling Cultures: Travel and Ethnography amongst the Yakkha of East Nepal. *Ethnos*, 72(3), 361.

Sagant, P., 1969a. Tāmpunmā, Divinité Limbu de la Forêt. *Objects et Mondes*, 4, 107-127.

Sagant, P., 1969b. Les Marchés en Pays Limbu. *L'Ethnographie*, 88-118.

Sagant, P., 1970. Mariage par Enlèvement Chez les Limbu (Népal). *Cahiers Internationaux de Sociologie*, 48, 71-98.

Sagant, P., 1973. Prêtes Limbu et Catégories Domestiques. *Kailash*, 1, 51-75.

Sagant, P., 1976a. Becoming a Limbu Priest - Ethnographic notes. In J. Hitchcock & R. L. Jones, eds. *Spirit Possession in the Nepal Himalayas*. Warminster: Aris & Phillips.

Sagant, P., 1976b. D'un Village Himalayen vers 1970. *Critique*, 1186-1191.

Sagant, P., 1976c. *Le Paysan Limbu: Sa Maison Et Ses Champs*, Paris: Mouton.

Sagant, P., 1976d. Les Limbu, Population du Népal Oriental. *L'Ethnographie, Nouvelle Série*, 72, 146-173.

Sagant, P., 1978a. Les Pouvoirs des Chefs Limbu au Népal Oriental. *L'Homme*, 18(1-2), 69-107.

Sagant, P., 1978b. Quand le Gurkha Revient de Guerre. *L'Ethnographie*, 120(77-78), 155-184.

Sagant, P., 1980. Usuriers et Chefs de Clan - Ethnographie de la Dette en Népal Oriental. *Purusārtha*, 4, 227-277.

Sagant, P., 1981. La Tête Haute. Maison, Rituel et Politique au Népal Oriental. In G. Toffin, ed. *L'Homme et la Maison dans L'Himalaya*. Paris: CNRS.

Sagant, P., 1982. L'Hindouisation des Limbu. - "Tout Limbu était Roi, Autrefois". In D. Macdonald, ed. *Les Royaumes de L'Himalaya*. Paris: Imprimerie Nationale.

Sagant, P., 1983. Moneylenders and Clan Headmen. In C. Malamoud, ed. *Debts and Debtors*. New Delhi: Vikas Pub. House.

Sagant, P., 1985. With Head Held High. The House, Ritual and Politics in East Nepal. *Kailash*, 12(3-4), 161-221.

Sagant, P., 1987. La Cure du Chamane et L'interprétation des Laics. *L'Ethnographie*, 83(100-101), 247-273.

Sagant, P., 1996. *The Dozing Shaman: The Limbus of Eastern Nepal*, Delhi: Oxford University Press.

Sahlins, M.D., 1972. *Stone Age Economics*, Chicago: Aldine-Atherton.

Sassen, S., 1988. *The Mobility of Labor and Capital: A Study in International investment and labor flow*, Cambridge: Cambridge University Press.

Schneider, J., and Schneider, P.T., 1976. *Culture and Political Economy in Western Sicily*, New York: Academic Press.

Schrader, H. 1988. *Trading Patterns in the Nepal Himalayas*. Saarbrücken: Breitenbach.

Seddon, D., 1995. Migration: Nepal and India. In R. Cohen, ed. *The Cambridge Survey of World Migration*. Cambridge: Cambridge University Press, pp. 367-370.

Seddon, D., 2001. The Contradictions of Rural Transformation in Nepal : Reply to Macfarlane's article "Sliding down hill". *EBHR*, 20-21, 117-122.

Seddon, D., Adhikari, J. & Gurung, G., 2002. Foreign labor migration and the remittance economy of Nepal. *Critical Asian Studies*, 34(1), 19-40.

Seddon, D., Blaikie, P., & Cameron, J., 1979. *Peasants and Workers in Nepal*. England: Aris & Phillips.

Senior, H.W.R., 1977. *A Vocabulary of the Limbu Language of Eastern Nepal*, Kathmandu: Ratna Pustak Bhandar.

Shafer, R., 1954. *Ethnography of Ancient India*, O. Harrassowitz.

Shah, N., & Menon, I. 1999. Chain Migration through the Social Network: Experience of Labour Migrants in Kuwait. *International Migration* 37(2): 361-382.

Sharma, J.R., 2007. *Mobility, Pathology and Livelihoods: An Ethnography of Forms of Human Mobility in/from Nepal*. PhD. University of Edinburgh.

Shivji, I.G. 1973. *The Silent Class Struggle*. Dar es Salaam: Tanzania Publishing House.

Shneiderman, S. & Turin, M., 2006. Seeking the Tribe: Ethnopolitics in Darjeeling and Sikkim. *Himal Southasian*, 18(5), 54-58.

Sloane, P., 1999. *Islam, Modernity and Entrepreneurship Among the Malays*, Basingstoke: Macmillan.

Slusser, M.S., 1982. *Nepal Mandala: A Cultural Study of the Kathmandu Valley*, Princeton: Princeton University Press.

Smith, G.A., 1979. The Use of Class Analysis in Social Anthropology. In D. H. Turner & G. A. Smith, eds. *Challenging Anthropology: A Critical Introduction to Social and Cultural Anthropology*. Toronto: McGraw-Hill Ryerson.

Smith, R.T., 1984. Anthropology and the Concept of Social Class. *Annual Review of Anthropology*, 13(1), 467-494.

Sprigg, R., 1959. Phonological Formulae for the Verbs in Limbu as a Contribution to the Tibeto-Burman Comparison. In C. Bazell, J.C. Catford, M.A.K. Halliday, R.H. Robins, ed. *In Memory of J.R. Firth*. London: Longmans, pp. 431-453.

Srinivas, M.N., 1956. A Note on Sanskritization and Westernization. *The Far Eastern Quarterly*, 15(4), 481-496.

Srinivas, M.N., 1952. *Religion and Society Among the Coorgs of South India*, Oxford: Clarendon Press.

Srinivas, M.N., 1968. Mobility in the Caste System. In M. Singer & B. S. Cohen, eds. *Structure and Change in Indian Society*. Chicago: Aldine Publishing Company, pp. 189-200.

Stark, O., 1991. *The Migration of Labor*, Oxford: Blackwell.

Stark, O. & Bloom, D.E., 1985. The New Economics of Labor Migration. *The American Economic Review*, 75(2), 173-178.

Steuart, J., 1770. *An Inquiry into the Principles of Political Oeconomy*, Dublin: Printed for James Williams and Richard Moncrieffe.

Stevens, S.F. 1993. *Claiming the High Ground: Sherpas, Subsistence, and Environmental Change in the Highest Himalaya.* Berkeley: University of California Press.

Stiller, L.F., 1973. *The Rise of the House of Gorkha : A Study in the Unification of Nepal, 1768-1816* 1st ed., New Delhi: Manjusri Publishing House.

Stoler, A.L., 1985. *Capitalism and Confrontation in Sumatra's Plantation Belt, 1870-1979*, New Haven: Yale University Press.

Stone, L., & Campbell, J. 1984. The Use and Misuse of Surveys in International Development: An Experiment From Nepal. *Human Organization* 43(1): 27-37.

Subba, C., 1995. *The Culture and Religion of Limbus* 1st ed., Kathmandu: K. B. Subba.

Subba, J.R., 1984. *Agriculture in the Hills of Sikkim*, Gangtok: Sikkim Science Society.

Subba, T.B., 1999. *Politics of Culture: A Study of Three Kirata Communities In,* Chennai: Orient Longman.

Taylor, E.J., 1999. The New Economics of Labour Migration and the Role of Remittances in the Migration Process. *International Migration*, 37(1), 63-88.

Thapa, B., 2003. *Status of large cardamom farming in Tellok VDC, Taplejung district.* M.A. Thesis. Tribhuvan University.

Thapa, S., & Chhetry, D. 1997. Inequality of Landholding in Nepal: some policy issues. *Contributions to Nepalese Studies* 24(2): 133-145.

Thieme, S., 2006. *Social Networks and Migration: Far West Nepalese Labour,* Münster: LIT.

Thieme, S., & Müller-Böker, U. 2009. Social networks and migration: Women's livelihoods between Far West Nepal and Delhi. *European Bulletin of Himalayan Research* 35-36: 107-121.

Timsima, J., 1986. Some Experiences and Achievements of Cropping Systems Research in Nepal. In C. Butler & M. Tomecek, eds.

Selected Proceedings of Kansas State University's 1986 Farming System Research Symposium. Kansas: Kansas State University, pp. 420-465.

Todaro, M.P., 1976. *Internal Migration in Developing Countries: A Review of Theory, Evidence, Methodology, and Research Priorities,* Geneva: International Labour Office.

Toffin, G. ed., 1981. *L'Homme et la Maison en Himalaya: Écologie du Népal,* Paris: Éditions du C.N.R.S.

TRPAP, 2005. Tourism Resource Mapping Profile: Taplejung district. Ministry of Culture, Tourism & Aviation; United Nations Development Programme.

Tumbahang, G.B., 2007. *A Descriptive Grammar of Chhatthare Limbu.* PhD. Tribhuvan University.

Tumbahang, G.B., 1986. *Noun Phrase Structure in Limbu.* M.A. Thesis. Tribhuvan University.

Turner, R.L., 1931. *A Comparative and Etymological Dictionary of the Nepali Language,* London: K. Paul, Trench, Trubner.

UNDP, 2009. *Human Development Report 2009 - Economic and inequality - Gini index.* Available at: http://bit.ly/HDR2009 [Accessed January 15, 2010]

Upreti, B.P., 1975. *Analysis of Change in Limbu-Brahmin Interrelationships in Limbuwan, Nepal.* PhD. University of Wisconsin.

USDS, 2009. *Trafficking in Persons Report 2009 - India,* United States Department of State. Available at: http://bit.ly/r0mEAY [Accessed January 15, 2010]

Vansittart, E., 1906(1890). *Gurkhas: Handbook for the Indian Army,* Calcutta: Government of India.

Varadarasan, S. & Biswas, A.K., 2002. Large Cardamom (Amomum subulatum Roxb.). In P. Ravindran & K. Madhusoodanan, eds. *Cardamom: The Genus Elettaria.* Taylor and Francis, London.

Venier, P. 2002. Migration of Keralites to the Persian Gulf: Increasing Ascendancy of International Labour Migration over a Developing Country. In A. Montanari (ed.) *Human Mobility in a Borderless World?,* 347-362. Rome: Union Géographique Internationale / Societa Geographica Italiana.

Vinding, M., 1984. Making a Living in the Nepal Himalayas: The Case of the Thakalis of Mustang District. *Contribution to Nepalese Studies*, 12(1), 51-104.

Wallerstein, I.M., 1974. *The Modern World-System*, New York: Academic Press.

Wax, R.H., 1971. *Doing Fieldwork: Warnings and Advice*, Chicago: University of Chicago Press.

Webb, S. & Webb, B., 1910. *The State and the Doctor*, London: Longmans, Green.

Weber, M., 1978. *Economy and Society: An Outline of Interpretive Sociology*, Berkeley: University of California Press.

Weidert, A. & Subba, B., 1985. *Concise Limbu Grammar and Dictionary*, Amsterdam: Lobster Publications.

Whelpton, J., 2005. *A History of Nepal*, Cambridge: Cambridge University Press.

Williams, G. 1976. Taking the Part of Peasants: Rural Development in Nigeria and Tanzania. In P. Gutkind & E. Wallerstein (eds) *The Political Economy of Contemporary Africa*, London: Sage Publications.

Wolf, E.R., 1982. *Europe and the People Without History*, London: University of California Press.

Wolf, E.R., 1997 (1982). *Europe and the People Without History: With a New Preface*, Berkeley: University of California Press.

Wolf, E.R., 1999 (1969). *Peasant Wars of the Twentieth Century*, Norman, Oklahoma: University of Oklahoma Press.

World Bank, 2005. *Nepal Development Policy Review: Restarting growth and povery reduction*, World Bank.

Wright, E.O., 2005. The shadow of exploitation in Weber's class analysis. In C. Camic, P. S. Gorski, & D. M. Trubek, eds. *Max Weber's Economy and Society: A critical companion*. Stanford, California: Stanford University Press.

Wright, E.O. & Perrone, L., 1977. Marxist Class Categories and Income Inequality. *American Sociological Review*, 42(1), 32-55.

Zachariah, K., Prakash, B., & Rajan, S. 2004. Indian Workers in UAE: Employment, Wages, and Working Conditions. *Economic and Political Weekly* May 29: 2227-2234.

Zivetz, L., 1992. *Private Enterprise and the State in Modern Nepal*, Madras: Oxford University Press.

Zomer, R.J. & Menke, J., 1993. Site Index and Biomass Productivity Estimates for Himalayan Alder-Large Cardamon Plantations: A Model Agroforestry System of the Eastern Middle Hills of Nepal. *Mountain Research and Development*, 13, 235-235.

Index